6th Joint SIGHUM Workshop on Computational Linguistics for Cultural Heritage, Social Sciences, Humanities and Literature (LaTeCH-CLfL 2022)

Held at COLING 2022

Gyeongju, South Korea
12-17 October 2022

ISBN: 978-1-7138-6152-2

Printed from e-media with permission by:

Curran Associates, Inc.
57 Morehouse Lane
Red Hook, NY 12571

Some format issues inherent in the e-media version may also appear in this print version.

Printed with permission by Curran Associates, Inc. (2023)

For permission requests, please contact the Association for Computational Linguistics at the address below.

Association for Computational Linguistics
209 N. Eighth Street
Stroudsburg, Pennsylvania 18360

Phone: 1-570-476-8006
Fax: 1-570-476-0860

acl@aclweb.org

Additional copies of this publication are available from:

Curran Associates, Inc.
57 Morehouse Lane
Red Hook, NY 12571 USA
Phone: 845-758-0400
Fax: 845-758-2633
Email: curran@proceedings.com
Web: www.proceedings.com

COLING

International Conference on Computational Linguistics

Proceedings of the Conference and Workshops

COLING

Volume 29 (2022), No. 3

The 6th Joint SIGHUM Workshop on Computational Linguistics for Cultural Heritage, Social Sciences, Humanities and Literature (LaTeCH-CLfL 2022)

The 29th International Conference on Computational Linguistics

October 12-17, 2022
Gyeongju, Republic of Korea

A word from the organizers

Here we go again. This is our sixth joint workshop; also, sixteenth LaTeCH and eleventh CLfL meeting. We have a fine program for you, with something for everyone in the community. We will not single out any paper: they are all worth a good look. There are repeat visitors (welcome back) and new contributors (hello). And Jacob Eisenstein, who has been on the program committee the past five years, is our invited speaker.

No preface to LaTeCH-CLfL can be complete without a huge thank-you to our wonderful program committee. And thanks to all those who submitted their papers.

Stefania, Anna, Nils, Stan

PS. Our workshop's Web site at
`https://sighum.wordpress.com/events/latech-clfl-2022/`
shows all the details. In particular, there is more about the guest speaker and his talk.

Program committee

Melanie Andresen, Hamburg University, Germany
JinYeong Bak, Sungkyunkwan University, Suwon, South Korea
Yuri Bizzoni, Aarhus University, Denmark
Anne-Sophie Bories, Universität Basel, Switzerland
Paul Buitelaar, National University of Ireland, Galway, Ireland
Miriam Butt, University of Konstanz, Germany
Thierry Declerck, Deutsche Forschungszentrum für Künstliche Intelligenz, Germany
Stefanie Dipper, Ruhr-Universität, Bochum, Germany
Jacob Eisenstein, Georgia Institute of Technology, United States
Anna Feldman, Montclair State University, United States
Mark Finlayson, Florida International University, United States
Antske Fokkens, Vrije Universiteit Amsterdam, The Netherlands
Heather Froehlich, Pennsylvania State University, United States
Francesca Frontini, National Research Council, Italy
Udo Hahn, JULIE Lab, Jena, Germany
Mika Hämäläinen, University of Helsinki, Finland
Serge Heiden, École normale supérieure de Lyon, France
Labiba Jahan, Florida International University, United States
Fotis Jannidis, Würzburg University, Germany
Mike Kestemont, University of Antwerp, Belgium
Dimitrios Kokkinakis, University of Gothenburg, Sweden
Stasinos Konstantopoulos, National Centre of Scientific Research "Demokritos", Greece
Markus Krug, Würzburg University, Germany
John Lee, City University of Hong Kong, Hong Kong
Chaya Liebeskind, Jerusalem College of Technology, Israel
Tom Lippincott, Johns Hopkins University, United States
Barbara McGillivray, The Alan Turing Institute, United Kingdom
David Mimno, Cornell University, United States
Syrielle Montariol, Jozef Stefan Institute, Slovenia
Vivi Nastase, University of Stuttgart, Germany
Borja Navarro Colorado, University of Alicante, Spain
Claes Neuefeind, University of Cologne, Germany
Kristoffer Laigaard Nielbo, Aarhus University, Denmark
Pierre Nugues, Lund University, Sweden
Petya Osenova, Sofia University and IICT-BAS, Bulgaria
Janis Pagel, University of Cologne, Germany
Andrew Piper, McGill University, Canada
Petr Plecháč, Institute of Czech Literature of the CAS, Czechia
Thierry Poibeau, CNRS Paris and Lattice, France
Jelena Prokic, Leiden University Centre for Digital Humanities, The Netherlands
Georg Rehm, DFKI, Germany
Martin Reynaert, Tilburg University, Radboud University Nijmegen, The Netherlands
Pablo Ruiz Fabo, Université de Strasbourg, France
Marijn Schraagen, Utrecht University, The Netherlands
Matthew Sims, University of California, Berkeley, United States
Pia Sommerauer, Vrije Universiteit Amsterdam, The Netherlands
Elke Teich, Saarland University, Germany
Laure Thompson, University of Massachusetts Amherst, United States
Ulrich Tiedau, University College London, United Kingdom

Ted Underwood, University of Illinois, Urbana-Champaign, United States
Menno van Zaanen, South African Centre for Digital Language Resources, Potchefstroom, South Africa
Albin Zehe, University of Würzburg, Germany
Heike Zinsmeister, University of Hamburg, Germany

Organizers

Stefania Degaetano-Ortlieb
Department of Language Science and Technology, Saarland University

Anna Kazantseva
National Research Council Canada

Nils Reiter
Department of Digital Humanities, University of Cologne

Stan Szpakowicz
School of Electrical Engineering and Computer Science, University of Ottawa

Table of Contents

Conference Program

Talks

Regular talks I

Automatized Detection and Annotation for Calls to Action in Latin-American Social Media Postings
Wassiliki Siskou, Clara Giralt Mirón, Sarah Molina-Raith and Miriam Butt

The Distribution of Deontic Modals in Jane Austen's Mature Novels
Lauren Levine

Towards a contextualised spatial-diachronic history of literature: mapping emotional representations of the city and the country in Polish fiction from 1864 to 1939
Agnieszka Karlińska, Cezary Rosiński, Jan Wieczorek, Patryk Hubar, Jan Kocoń, Marek Kubis, Stanisław Woźniak, Arkadiusz Margraf and Wiktor Walentynowicz

Regular talks II

Every picture tells a story: Image-grounded controllable stylistic story generation
Holy Lovenia, Bryan Wilie, Romain Barraud, Samuel Cahyawijaya, Willy Chung and Pascale Fung

Computational Detection of Narrativity: A Comparison Using Textual Features and Reader Response
Max Steg, Karlo H. R. Slot and Federico Pianzola

Measuring Presence of Women and Men as Information Sources in News
Muitze Zulaika, Xabier Saralegi and Iñaki San Vicente

Invited talk

Detecting Intellectual Influence from Dynamic Word Embeddings: Applications to Historical Newspapers and Contemporary Research Articles
Jacob Eisenstein

Posters

Evaluation of Word Embeddings for the Social Sciences

Ricardo Schiffers
RWTH Aachen
Aachen, Germany
rschiffers@posteo.de

Dagmar Kern and **Daniel Hienert**
GESIS - Leibniz Institute for the Social Sciences
Cologne, Germany
firstname.lastname@gesis.org

Abstract

Word embeddings are an essential instrument in many NLP tasks. Most available resources are trained on general language from Web corpora or Wikipedia dumps. However, word embeddings for domain-specific language are rare, in particular for the social science domain. Therefore, in this work, we describe the creation and evaluation of word embedding models based on 37,604 open-access social science research papers. In the evaluation, we compare domain-specific and general language models for (i) language coverage, (ii) diversity, and (iii) semantic relationships. We found that the created domain-specific model, even with a relatively small vocabulary size, covers a large part of social science concepts, their neighborhoods are diverse in comparison to more general models Across all relation types, we found a more extensive coverage of semantic relationships.

1 Introduction

Word embedding models learn word representations from large sets of text so that similar words have a similar representation. Models can be used to find semantically related words, for example for applications such as natural language understanding. Technically, word embeddings are distributed representations of words in a vector space (Bengio et al., 2003) so that related words are nearby in the space and can be found with distance measures such as the cosine similarity (Mikolov et al., 2013).

In general, word embedding models are trained on large and general language text collections, e.g., on Web corpora or on Wikipedia dumps. However, there are some initiatives to create and evaluate word embeddings for specific domains on a smaller scale, for example, for computer science (Roy et al., 2017; Ferrari et al., 2017), finance (Theil et al., 2018), patents (Risch and Krestel, 2019), oil & gas industry (Nooralahzadeh et al., 2018; da Silva Magalhães Gomes et al., 2021), and especially in the biomedical domain (Jiang et al., 2015; Chiu et al., 2016; Zhao et al., 2018; Chen et al., 2018; Moradi et al., 2020).

Word embeddings capture "precise syntactic and semantic word relationships" (Mikolov et al., 2013). However, general and domain-specific models can differ much in terms of included specialized vocabulary and semantic relationships (Nooralahzadeh et al., 2018; Chen et al., 2018; da Silva Magalhães Gomes et al., 2021). Intrinsic evaluation methods are used to test models for these relationships (Schnabel et al., 2015; Gladkova and Drozd, 2016). In this work, we focus on creating and evaluating word embeddings for the social science domain and comparing them to general language models.

Word embeddings are used in the social sciences domain for a number of NLP tasks. Matsui and Ferrara (2022) provide an overview of word embeddings techniques and applications in the social sciences based on a literature review. Word embeddings are used, for example, for the extraction of trends of biases or culture from data (Caliskan et al., 2017), using vectors to define working variables that embody the concept or research questions (Toubia et al., 2021), or use reference words and their semantic neighborhoods to analyze gender terms and its relation to specific occupations (Garg et al., 2018). Other applications are the processing of scientific documents, for example the extraction of acknowledged entities from full texts (Smirnova and Mayr, 2022). For the retrieval of specialized information, word embeddings can be used for query expansion (Roy et al., 2022). All these applications depend on meaningful word embeddings. The more precise the specialized language is available in the vector space and the better related terms are arranged in the vector space, the better the applications work.

Proceedings of the 6th LaTeCH-CLfL Workshop, pages 1–6
October 16, 2022.

2 Generation of Social Science Word Embeddings

2.1 Corpora and Pre-processing

The Social Science Open Access Repository (SSOAR)[1] is a document server that makes scientific articles from the social sciences freely available. At the time of this work, it contained 58,883 documents from which 37,604 were directly machine-readable. The rest was included via links and was not directly accessible for us. Most of the texts are written in German, followed by English-language ones. The publication years were mainly in the 2000s (*min*=1923, *max*=2020, *M*=2006, *SD*=9.36).

Extracting raw text from PDF files has proven to be an error-prone process, but is, on the other side, a crucial part for the creation of word embeddings. A pre-evaluation with standard python parsers showed massive problems, e.g., with word separation. We evaluated five different PDF parsers (PyPDF2, PyPDF4, PDFMiner, PDFBox, Tika) with a random sample of 238 documents taken from different publication years and with documents producing a lot of errors. PDFBox[2] showed the best results. Since it has been meanwhile integrated in Apache Tika,[3] we chose this library for further processing.

From the extracted raw texts, we built language-specific corpus files by applying a number of cleaning steps. All texts were cleaned from the cover pages, which are included in every SSOAR document. All hyphens and line breaks were removed, camel cases were separated using regular expressions. We used a line-based identification of the language based on word embeddings for language identification,[4] which helps to maximise content for a specific language. Subsequently, numbers in numeric form are converted to word numbers, multiple spaces are merged, and all characters are written in lower case. We use sentence-wise deduplication based on a hash value and sort out duplicate sentences. Finally, all texts were tokenized. As a result, we got two corpus files for the German and English languages. Table 1 gives an overview of the count of tokens, vocabulary size, number of raw data files, and the file sizes.

[1]https://www.gesis.org/ssoar/home

[2]https://github.com/apache/pdfbox

[3]https://github.com/apache/tika

[4]https://fasttext.cc/docs/en/language-identification.html

	ssoar.de.txt	**ssoar.en.txt**
Tokens	152,341,432	92,123,735
Vocabulary	1,678,657	367,574
Files	25,227	23,045
MB	1,076.31	540.49

Table 1: German and English corpus data files from n=37,604 SSOAR documents.

2.2 Training of Word Embeddings

We rely on the fastText model (Bojanowski et al., 2017) to train word embeddings. It uses a character-based model based on the word-based skipgram model (Mikolov et al., 2013). The representation of a word is the sum of its n-grams with a default size between three and six characters. German-language word embeddings benefit from using such a model due to the frequent occurrence of compounds which can be captured with longer character sequences (Bojanowski et al. 2017).

We used the fastText Python module for implementation. During the training, word embeddings with different dimensions (100, 150, 200, 300, 500) were created since the dimensionality of the models is a crucial parameter for the evaluation applied here. We used default values for the other hyperparameters: For the number of iterations of the data set, we apply five epochs, a learning rate of 0.05, five negative examples and a context window of five by using the skip-gram model. The resulting word embeddings are open-source and can be downloaded.[5]

2.3 Reference Knowledge Resources

In this evaluation, we aim to understand the impact of domain-specific language on the availability of specialized terms and semantic relations in the models. We use the thesaurus for the social sciences (TheSoz, Zapilko et al. 2013) as a reference knowledge resource. It contains 36,320 keywords with 5,986 descriptors, including the relations *broader*, *narrower*, *related*, *altLabel*, and 30,334 non-descriptors that are either used synonymously or represent more general terms related to a descriptor. Figure 1 shows the descriptor *social inequality* with its related concepts.[6]

Additionally, as reference models and as a baseline, we use the German word embeddings models *wiki.de*[7] offered by FastText and the fasttext model

[5]https://zenodo.org/record/5645048

[6]http://lod.gesis.org/thesoz/concept_10038124

[7]https://fasttext.cc/docs/en/pretrained-vectors.html

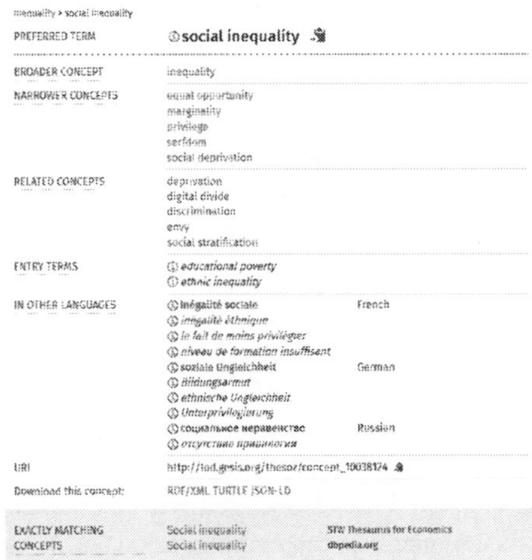

Figure 1: The descriptor *social inequality* in its environment of broader, narrower, and related terms

deepset.de[8] from Deepset. Both are trained on the German Wikipedia with the skip-gram-model and with 300 dimensions. Remaining with the example of "social inequality", this concept has its own Wikipedia page[9]. Links to other concepts result from the full text, the links in the text or the Wikipedia category system.

3 Evaluation

In what follows, we evaluate word embeddings trained on social science language versus those trained on general language. We want to understand the effects on domain-specific language coverage, diversity, and semantic relationships. The evaluation is performed with the German models, since a larger part of the source texts is written in German. These models are called *ssoar.de* in the remainder of this paper.

3.1 Coverage

To evaluate the coverage of the models' language with respect to the social science domain, keywords x_i from the TheSoz are iteratively compared with words in the vocabularies V (see Nooralahzadeh et al. 2018 for a similar method). Ratio string similarity from the Levenshtein Python C extension module[10] was used for the calculation of the word's similarity. We applied different thresholds $s = 0.9$, $s = 0.95$ and $s = 1$ to find identical but also very

[8] https://deepset.ai/german-word-embeddings

[9] https://de.wikipedia.org/wiki/Soziale_Ungleichheit

[10] https://github.com/ztane/python-Levenshtein

	ssoar.de	wiki.de	deepset.de
Vocab size	403,452	2,275,233	1,319,232
s=0.9	87.95	**92.22**	63.31
s=0.95	84.51	**90.08**	60.54
s=1.0	82.63	**88.80**	59.36

Table 2: Coverage of TheSoz keywords in the vocabulary of different models (n=36,320 keywords)

similar terms. In the case of compound descriptors, the result is only valid if all terms of a TheSoz entry are included in the vocabulary of the model. Since all ssoar.de models with different dimenions are based on the same text corpus, the vocabulary is identical, and we use the smallest model with $dimension = 100$. We used formula (1) to compute the coverage c for all $n = 36,320$ keywords.

$$c = \frac{\sum_{i=1}^{n} x_i \in V}{n} \quad (1)$$

Table 2 shows the results. The model wiki.de shows a coverage in 88%-92%, ssoar.de in 82%-88% and deepset.de only in 59%-63%. Thus, wiki.de shows the best results, but also has a vocabulary size five times larger. The other way around, deepset is three times larger in vocabulary size but shows worse results. This suggests that similarly good results for covering domain-specific language can be obtained with a small model trained on specialized texts compared to larger general language models.

3.2 Diversity

To determine the diversity d of a model relative to other models, we compare the neighbors related to a TheSoz keyword. The procedure for determining diversity is described in Formula 2. For this purpose, the nearest neighbors of the keywords x_i of two models (A and B) are compared. If the intersection between the neighbors A_{x_i} and B_{x_i} corresponds to the empty set, the diversity between the compared models increases with a return value $1 = true$ and $0 = false$. Here, the number of neighbors returned by the models is limited by the *top-k* entries. To obtain the relative diversity, the result is then divided by the number of keywords n to be tested. This ensures comparability between the different results.

$$d = \frac{\sum_{i=1}^{n} A_{x_i} \cap B_{x_i} = \emptyset}{n} \quad (2)$$

top-k	Model	ssoar.100	ssoar.150	ssoar.200	ssoar.300	ssoar.500	wiki	deepset
10	ssoar.100	-	0.23	0.19	0.47	1.19	21.59	**44.30**
	ssoar.150	0.23	-	0.10	0.17	0.44	19.52	42.52
	ssoar.200	0.19	0.10	-	0.08	0.17	18.81	42.29
	ssoar.300	0.47	0.17	0.08	-	0.07	17.94	41.84
	ssoar.500	1.19	0.44	0.17	0.07	-	17.56	41.63
	wiki	21.59	19.52	18.81	17.94	17.56	-	25.81
	deepset	**44.30**	42.52	42.29	41.84	41.63	25.81	-
50	ssoar.100	-	0.05	0.05	0.05	0.06	8.12	**20.20**
	ssoar.150	0.05	-	0.05	0.05	0.06	7.16	19.07
	ssoar.200	0.05	0.05	-	0.05	0.05	6.71	18.85
	ssoar.300	0.05	0.05	0.05	-	0.05	6.31	18.53
	ssoar.500	0.06	0.06	0.05	0.05	-	6.06	18.28
	wiki	8.12	7.16	6.71	6.31	6.06	-	5.86
	deepset	**20.20**	19.07	18.85	18.53	18.28	5.86	-
200	ssoar.100	-	0.05	0.04	0.05	0.05	3.82	**7.70**
	ssoar.150	0.05	-	0.05	0.05	0.05	3.40	7.50
	ssoar.200	0.04	0.05	-	0.05	0.04	3.06	7.31
	ssoar.300	0.05	0.05	0.05	-	0.05	2.92	7.06
	ssoar.500	0.05	0.05	0.04	0.05	-	2.79	7.00
	wiki	3.82	3.40	3.06	2.92	2.79	-	1.20
	deepset	**7.70**	7.50	7.31	7.06	7.00	1.20	-

Table 3: Diversity between models (n=36,320 TheSoz keywords)

Table 3 shows the results of the evaluation method described for all models, including the reference models and for the *top-k* $10, 50, 200$ neighbors. When looking at the results, it is noticeable that the diversity between the ssoar models and the reference model deepset.de consistently shows the greatest differences. When compared with the wiki.de model, the diversity to the ssoar.de model is still high but shows roughly only half of the values before. For the smallest *top-k* ($k = 10$), the diversity between the two reference models is even higher (25.81) than it is when comparing the ssoar.de models with the wiki.de model (21.59). As expected, the diversity decreases with increasing *top-k* entries.

In addition, it can be seen that the use of fewer dimensions in the training of the ssoar.de models has a positive effect on diversity. The ssoar.de model with the dimensionality 100 (ssoar.100) has the greatest diversity across all *top-k*.

3.3 Relations

To measure relational coverage r for the social science domain, we used an evaluation method inspired by the intrinsic evaluation of comparing semantic relations of established knowledge resources (Nooralahzadeh et al., 2018; Chen et al., 2018; da Silva Magalhães Gomes et al., 2021). A data set of TheSoz was used to determine the coverage of the relations. Related concepts were assigned to the descriptors using different relations: the relation *broader* describes superordinate concepts to the descriptor (Hypernyms). With *narrower* terms, concepts subordinate to the descriptor are distinguished (Hyponyms), and *related* refers to related terms. The relation *altLabel* describes concepts that can be used alternatively to the descriptor. These relations are based on the standard Simple Knowledge Organization System (SKOS, cf. Zapilko et al. 2013).

Equation 3 shows the basis for calculating the relational coverage of a model. The test is whether the concept $k(x_i)$ associated with the descriptor x_i is contained in the neighborhood set N_{x_i} with the return value $1 = true$ and $0 = false$. The number of neighbors returned by the models is limited to *top-k*. Finally, dividing the sum of found concepts and the total set of used descriptors n yields the domain-specific coverage of the model. The described procedure is performed per available relation type.

$$r = \frac{\sum_{i=1}^{n} k(x_i) \in N_{x_i}}{n} \tag{3}$$

For the evaluation, concepts consisting of multiple words were not considered since the neighborhood query returns only single words. In addition, only descriptors that are annotated in German language were applied. Accordingly, a total of $14,998$ out of $35,473$ descriptor-concept pairs were used, which in turn were subdivided by type of relations. The coverage of the relations was determined with neighborhoods for different *top-k* entries.

The results in Table 4 show that the ssoar.de models perform better than the models used for comparison across all *top-k*. Only for the *broader* relation with *top-k* $= 10$, the deepset.de model performs better than the ssoar.de models. The comparison with the reference models indicates a real specialization with respect to the social science domain. Deepset.de achieves better results for *broader* relations for *top-k* $= 10$, but the superiority fades away at larger neighborhoods. The results are better than those of the reference models above a *top-k* of 50 across all relation types.

Comparing the ssoar.de models to each other, it is noticeable that word embeddings trained on smaller dimensions perform better at smaller *top-k* than models with more dimensions. For larger neighborhoods, more dimensions tend to be pre-

top-k	Model	bro	nar	rel	alt
10	ssoar.100	8.54	**6.06**	**10.28**	**13.27**
	ssoar.150	9.20	5.67	9.91	12.59
	ssoar.200	9.39	5.49	9.40	12.47
	ssoar.300	9.20	4.78	9.30	11.68
	ssoar.500	8.81	4.34	8.08	10.34
	wiki.de	5.77	3.39	8.05	9.87
	deepset.de	**13.33**	5.17	9.91	8.12
50	ssoar.100	25.03	**21.00**	25.94	27.12
	ssoar.150	26.02	20.46	26.61	27.63
	ssoar.200	27.11	20.76	**26.89**	27.81
	ssoar.300	27.96	20.31	25.43	**28.08**
	ssoar.500	**28.73**	19.16	22.79	26.53
	wiki.de	19.13	14.02	21.34	23.89
	deepset.de	23.57	15.27	19.14	15.02
200	ssoar.100	43.36	40.04	42.34	42.6
	ssoar.150	45.81	41.46	44.17	44.66
	ssoar.200	47.73	41.64	44.57	45.11
	ssoar.300	49.06	**41.67**	**44.88**	45.96
	ssoar.500	**49.72**	41.25	43.25	**46.16**
	wiki.de	36.84	34.01	36.79	40.65
	deepset.de	33.01	24.89	29.49	21.93

Table 4: Relational coverage of all models (n=14,998 descriptor-concept pairs)

ferred. Nooralahzadeh et al. (2018); Chiu et al. (2016) report generally better performance for increasing dimensions, but we found that it also depends on the number of *top-k*.

4 Conclusion

In this work, we built domain-specific word embeddings for the social sciences and compared them to general language models. First, we checked for coverage of specialized language keywords. Wiki.de performed best with 92%, but ssoar.de followed closely with 88% with only one-fifth of vocabulary size. We then analysed the diversity of models to each other by comparing selected neighbourhoods: domain-specific and general-language models showed the highest diversities. However, diversity decreases with a larger number of returned neighbors. Concerning relational coverage, ssoar.de models performed best in all settings, except for the broader relation with $top\text{-}k = 10$. In summary, the word embeddings produced in this work showed much better results than the general language models when compared to established knowledge resources such as a thesaurus. Domain-specific word embeddings can improve the semantic relatedness metric and applications build upon. This is in line with related works (e.g., Nooralahzadeh et al. 2018; Chen et al. 2018; da Silva Magalhães Gomes et al. 2021) showing for other domains that domain-specific models can better capture semantic relations - even with a small corpus size (e.g., Zhao et al. 2018).

The experiments showed that the underlying texts and their language have a significant impact on the resulting word embeddings. This is even more true for the applications that are based on them. (1) *Coverage* of social science concepts is very different depending on the word embedding model. For example, applications that want to define and extend a working variable depend directly on the concepts contained in the model. (2) The models can be very *diverse* in terms of their semantic neighbors. Applications based on them, for example, query expansion or reference words and their neighborhoods, lead to different results depending on the model. (3) For *relational coverage*, the domain-specific model contains more relations in the sense of a domain thesaurus. This may be important, for example, to keep the precision of search results high in query term expansion or to keep working variables precise in expansion. In summary, the performance of applications is directly dependent on the alignment of word embeddings, their underlying language and their domain.

In future work, we want to compare the effects of specialized language with other embedding models such as Word2Vec, GloVe, or contextual embeddings such as BERT.

References

Yoshua Bengio, Réjean Ducharme, Pascal Vincent, and Christian Janvin. 2003. A neural probabilistic language model. *J. Mach. Learn. Res.*, 3:1137–1155.

Piotr Bojanowski, Edouard Grave, Armand Joulin, and Tomas Mikolov. 2017. Enriching word vectors with subword information. *Transactions of the Association for Computational Linguistics*, 5:135–146.

Aylin Caliskan, Joanna J Bryson, and Arvind Narayanan. 2017. Semantics derived automatically from language corpora contain human-like biases. *Science*, 356(6334):183–186.

Zhiwei Chen, Zhe He, Xiuwen Liu, and Jiang Bian. 2018. Evaluating semantic relations in neural word embeddings with biomedical and general domain knowledge bases. *BMC Medical Informatics Decis. Mak.*, 18(S-2):53–68.

Billy Chiu, Gamal K. O. Crichton, Anna Korhonen, and Sampo Pyysalo. 2016. How to train good word embeddings for biomedical NLP. In *Proceedings of the 15th Workshop on Biomedical Natural Language Processing, BioNLP@ACL 2016, Berlin, Germany,*

August 12, 2016, pages 166–174. Association for Computational Linguistics.

Diogo da Silva Magalhães Gomes, Fábio Corrêa Cordeiro, Bernardo Scapini Consoli, Nikolas Lacerda Santos, Viviane Pereira Moreira, Renata Vieira, Silvia Moraes, and Alexandre Gonçalves Evsukoff. 2021. Portuguese word embeddings for the oil and gas industry: Development and evaluation. *Comput. Ind.*, 124:103347.

Alessio Ferrari, Beatrice Donati, and Stefania Gnesi. 2017. Detecting domain-specific ambiguities: An NLP approach based on wikipedia crawling and word embeddings. In *IEEE 25th International Requirements Engineering Conference Workshops, RE 2017 Workshops, Lisbon, Portugal, September 4-8, 2017*, pages 393–399. IEEE Computer Society.

Nikhil Garg, Londa Schiebinger, Dan Jurafsky, and James Zou. 2018. Word embeddings quantify 100 years of gender and ethnic stereotypes. *Proceedings of the National Academy of Sciences*, 115(16):E3635–E3644.

Anna Gladkova and Aleksandr Drozd. 2016. Intrinsic evaluations of word embeddings: What can we do better? In *Proceedings of the 1st Workshop on Evaluating Vector-Space Representations for NLP, RepEval@ACL 2016, Berlin, Germany, August 2016*, pages 36–42. Association for Computational Linguistics.

Zhenchao Jiang, Lishuang Li, Degen Huang, and Liuke Jin. 2015. Training word embeddings for deep learning in biomedical text mining tasks. In *2015 IEEE International Conference on Bioinformatics and Biomedicine, BIBM 2015, Washington, DC, USA, November 9-12, 2015*, pages 625–628. IEEE Computer Society.

Akira Matsui and Emilio Ferrara. 2022. Word embedding for social sciences: An interdisciplinary survey.

Tomas Mikolov, Ilya Sutskever, Kai Chen, Greg Corrado, and Jeffrey Dean. 2013. Distributed representations of words and phrases and their compositionality. In *Proceedings of the 26th International Conference on Neural Information Processing Systems - Volume 2*, NIPS'13, page 3111–3119, Red Hook, NY, USA. Curran Associates Inc.

Milad Moradi, Maedeh Dashti, and Matthias Samwald. 2020. Summarization of biomedical articles using domain-specific word embeddings and graph ranking. *J. Biomed. Informatics*, 107:103452.

Farhad Nooralahzadeh, Lilja Øvrelid, and Jan Tore Lønning. 2018. Evaluation of domain-specific word embeddings using knowledge resources. In *Proceedings of the Eleventh International Conference on Language Resources and Evaluation (LREC-2018)*, Miyazaki, Japan. European Languages Resources Association (ELRA).

Julian Risch and Ralf Krestel. 2019. Domain-specific word embeddings for patent classification. *Data Technol. Appl.*, 53(1):108–122.

Arpita Roy, Youngja Park, and Shimei Pan. 2017. Learning domain-specific word embeddings from sparse cybersecurity texts. *CoRR*, abs/1709.07470.

Dwaipayan Roy, Mandar Mitra, Philipp Mayr, and Amritap Chowdhury. 2022. Local or global? a comparative study on applications of embedding models for information retrieval. In *5th Joint International Conference on Data Science Management of Data (9th ACM IKDD CODS and 27th COMAD)*, CODS-COMAD 2022, page 115–119, New York, NY, USA. Association for Computing Machinery.

Tobias Schnabel, Igor Labutov, David M. Mimno, and Thorsten Joachims. 2015. Evaluation methods for unsupervised word embeddings. In *Proceedings of the 2015 Conference on Empirical Methods in Natural Language Processing, EMNLP 2015, Lisbon, Portugal, September 17-21, 2015*, pages 298–307. The Association for Computational Linguistics.

Nina Smirnova and Philipp Mayr. 2022. Evaluation of embedding models for automatic extraction and classification of acknowledged entities in scientific documents. In *Proceedings of the EEKE workshop at JCDL*.

Christoph Kilian Theil, Sanja Stajner, and Heiner Stuckenschmidt. 2018. Word embeddings-based uncertainty detection in financial disclosures. In *Proceedings of the First Workshop on Economics and Natural Language Processing, ECONLP@ACL 2018, Melbourne, Australia, July 20, 2018*, pages 32–37. Association for Computational Linguistics.

Olivier Toubia, Jonah Berger, and Jehoshua Eliashberg. 2021. How quantifying the shape of stories predicts their success. *Proceedings of the National Academy of Sciences*, 118(26):e2011695118.

Benjamin Zapilko, Johann Schaible, Philipp Mayr, and Brigitte Mathiak. 2013. TheSoz: A SKOS representation of the thesaurus for the social sciences. *Semantic Web journal (SWJ)*, 4(3):257–263.

Mengnan Zhao, Aaron J. Masino, and Christopher C. Yang. 2018. A framework for developing and evaluating word embeddings of drug-named entity. In *Proceedings of the BioNLP 2018 workshop, Melbourne, Australia, July 19, 2018*, pages 156–160. Association for Computational Linguistics.

Developing a tool for fair and reproducible use of paid crowdsourcing in the digital humanities

Tuomo Hiippala and **Helmiina Hotti** and **Rosa Suviranta**
Department of Languages, University of Helsinki
Helsinki, Finland
{tuomo.hiippala, helmiina.hotti, rosa.suviranta}@helsinki.fi

Abstract

This system demonstration paper describes ongoing work on a tool for fair and reproducible use of paid crowdsourcing in the digital humanities. Paid crowdsourcing is widely used in natural language processing and computer vision, but has been rarely applied in the digital humanities due to ethical concerns. We discuss concerns associated with paid crowdsourcing and describe how we seek to mitigate them in designing the tool and crowdsourcing pipelines. We demonstrate how the tool may be used to create annotations for diagrams, a complex mode of expression whose description requires human input.

1 Introduction

Crowdsourcing is regularly used to create data for training and evaluating natural language processing and computer vision algorithms (Kovashka et al., 2016; Poesio et al., 2017). These fields often rely on paid crowdsourcing, which means that the work is distributed through online platforms and the performers are paid for their work. In the digital humanities, however, crowdsourcing is often associated with use of volunteers who are motivated by personal interests and altruism (Dunn and Hedges, 2013; Daugavietis, 2021). Conversely, paid crowdsourcing is viewed as ethically problematic (Terras, 2015) due to sweatshop wages (Fort et al., 2011) and other exploitative practices, such as invisible labour (Kummerfeld, 2021; Toxtli et al., 2021).

In this article, we present ongoing work on a tool for fair and reproducible use of paid crowdsourcing in the digital humanities. We argue that paid crowdsourcing offers a viable alternative to fields that fall under the umbrella of digital humanities, but are unlikely to attract a volunteer workforce. However, using paid crowdsourcing warrants attention to ethics. We demonstrate how ethical concerns may be addressed by incorporating mechanisms that discourage exploitative practices into the design of the tool and crowdsourcing pipelines.

2 Ethical issues related to crowdsourcing

As a portmanteau of *crowd* and *outsourcing*, the term crowdsourcing inherently evokes ideas of exploiting cheap labour in the global economy (Schmidt, 2013, p. 531). Paid crowdsourcing typically involves *requesters*, who post *tasks* on an online *platform*, which then distributes the tasks to *workers*. The platform thus acts as a mediator between the requesters and workers, and charges a commission from the requester. In natural language processing, crowdsourcing has become an established way of creating corpora due to the availability of a large pool of workers, short turnaround time and perceived cost efficiency (Fort et al., 2011).

Digital humanities have been cautious of paid crowdsourcing due to ethical issues related to low wages and workers' rights (Terras, 2015). Similar concerns have also been voiced in the field of natural language processing (Fort et al., 2011), which are increasingly supported by empirical evidence. Hara et al. (2018) show that only 4% of the workers on Amazon Mechanical Turk earn more than the federal minimum wage in the United States ($7.25 per hour). The average wage paid by the requesters amounts to $11.58 per hour, but requesters who pay less than the minimal wage outnumber those who pay fair wages (Hara et al., 2018, p. 7).

In addition to fair pay, recent research has highlighted issues arising from qualification labour, which refers to low- or non-paid work that workers must perform to qualify for tasks that pay more (Kummerfeld, 2021). Qualification labour emerges as a result of an information asymmetry between the requesters and workers. The requesters want to recruit high-performing workers by paying more, but higher wages also attract spammers who do not take the work seriously. Because the requesters cannot assess the quality of work in advance, they

Proceedings of the 6th LaTeCH-CLfL Workshop, pages 7–12
October 16, 2022.

are inclined to pay less, which drives away high-performing workers (Fort et al., 2011, p. 418). Making tasks only available to highly-qualified workers mitigates this problem, but to qualify for these tasks, the workers must perform approximately two months worth of non- or low-paying work (Kummerfeld, 2021).

Other forms of invisible labour on crowdsourcing platforms include the time spent searching for tasks, interacting with requesters and managing payments. Toxtli et al. (2021, p. 319) estimate that the median time spent on invisible labour accounts for 33% of active working time on crowdsourcing platforms. Because the workers are not compensated for this effort, invisible labour drives down their hourly wage. Additional forms of invisible labour include working on tasks that are rejected or expire, that is, the worker cannot complete the tasks within the timeframe set by the requester.

3 Crowdsourcing in digital humanities

Given the issues described above, it is not surprising that crowdsourcing in the digital humanities has mainly relied on volunteers who are motivated by personal interests and altruism (Dunn and Hedges, 2013; Daugavietis, 2021). Successful examples of volunteer-based crowdsourcing include platforms such as Zooniverse[1] and the *Transcribe Bentham* project (Causer et al., 2018), which have been able to attract a large body of motivated volunteers. This form of crowdsourcing in the digital humanities can also be conceptualised as a form of citizen science and peer production (Van Hyning, 2019).

However, some fields of study in the humanities may not be able to attract a sufficiently large body of volunteers. One such example is the emerging discipline of multimodality research, which studies how human communication relies on intentional combinations of expressive resources (see e.g. Bateman et al., 2017; Wildfeuer et al., 2020). As an emerging discipline, multimodality research is not widely known among the public at large, and its objects of study – everyday communicative situations and artefacts – are arguably less likely to attract the kind of attention needed for recruiting volunteers.

Multimodality research is currently undergoing a turn towards empirical research, which has been accompanied by calls for creating larger corpora to support this effort (Parodi, 2010; Thomas, 2014). Current multimodal corpora remain small, because creating multiple layers of cross-referenced annotations needed to capture multimodal phenomena requires time and resources (Bateman, 2014). Hiippala et al. (2021) have recently argued that the size of multimodal corpora can be increased by combining crowdsourced and expert annotations.

As researchers working in the field of multimodality research, our motivation to develop a tool for fair and reliable use of paid crowdsourcing arises from the prospect of building large multimodal corpora with multiple layers of rich annotation. At the same time, we acknowledge the ethical dimensions of using paid crowdsourcing and seek to address them in the design and use of the tool.

4 System design

4.1 Guiding principles for tool design and use

To mitigate the issues described in Section 2, we identify the following desiderata for developing and using the tool. First of all, the tool encourages the requesters to pay a fair wage to the workers (Fort et al., 2011; Hara et al., 2018). To do so, the tool asks requesters to estimate the time spent on a single task, which is used to calculate a task price that ensures that the workers are paid at least $12 per hour. We also encourage including explicit payment information in the instructions to reduce invisible labour related to wages (Toxtli et al., 2021).

To reduce invisible labour resulting from rejected or expired tasks, we emphasise the need for clear instructions and sufficient time to perform the tasks. Because crowdsourcing platforms attract a global workforce (Pavlick et al., 2014), we recommend the use of multimodal instructions that combine written language and visualisations to support workers who speak English as a foreign language. We also encourage the requesters to be transparent about their identity (Adda et al., 2013) and the purposes of their research to enable the workers make moral judgements about their willingness to participate (Schmidt, 2013). To reduce invisible labour from rejected work, we propose paying for work that contains human errors – e.g. a missing bounding box in an image segmentation task – and re-submitting these images for corrections.

To avoid hidden qualification work, we encourage using a combination of pedagogically-motivated training and paid examinations to train a workforce on the platform instead of using high-performing workers only (Kummerfeld, 2021). Pedagogically-motivated training refers to training

[1] https://zooniverse.org

tasks that teach the workers to perform the task. If the worker makes an error, they are provided with the correct answer and an explanation. The workers are later shown a similar task to assess their learning. Workers who pass the training are allowed to take a paid examination, which measures their performance. Those who pass the examination can then access to the actual tasks.

Implementing these desiderata into the tool design requires a modular structure, which allows constructing complex pipelines in a flexible manner, while simultaneously configuring the properties of individual tasks and their associated instructions and training data.

4.2 Technical description and architecture

The tool is written in Python 3.9 and designed for the Toloka[2] crowdsourcing platform, which has a well-documented and extensive API. Toloka also maintains a Python library for accessing the API, which we use for interacting with the platform.[3] The source code for the tool, which may be installed via the Python Package Index (PyPI), is available at: `https://github.com/thiippal/abulafia`

The architecture of the tool is based on three types of objects: tasks, actions and task sequences. Tasks allow creating individual crowdsourcing tasks and configuring payments, input/output data, quality control mechanisms and user interface. Actions, in turn, are used to manipulate the input/output data. These actions may include, for example, aggregating responses from multiple workers. Our tool implements the aggregation algorithms available in the Crowd-kit library for Python (Ustalov et al., 2021). To support reproducibility, both tasks and actions are configured using separate files that use the YAML markup language. The YAML configuration files are used for instantiating Python objects, which may be combined into task sequences to define and execute complex crowdsourcing pipelines.

5 System demonstration

In this section, we demonstrate how our tool can be used to crowdsource descriptions for a complex mode of communication, namely diagrams. Diagrams combine diverse expressive resources, such as natural language, photographs, illustrations, drawings, lines and arrows into a common discourse organisation (Hiippala and Bateman, 2022). Computational processing of diagrams is challenging, because their constituent parts are not fixed, but determined dynamically by the communicative goals set for the diagram (Hiippala et al., 2021). To exemplify, Figure 1 shows a diagram that uses written language and lines to pick out parts of an illustration, but we cannot know how the illustration should be decomposed without first considering the diagram as a whole, as the written labels determine how the depicted object should be decomposed into its constituent parts.

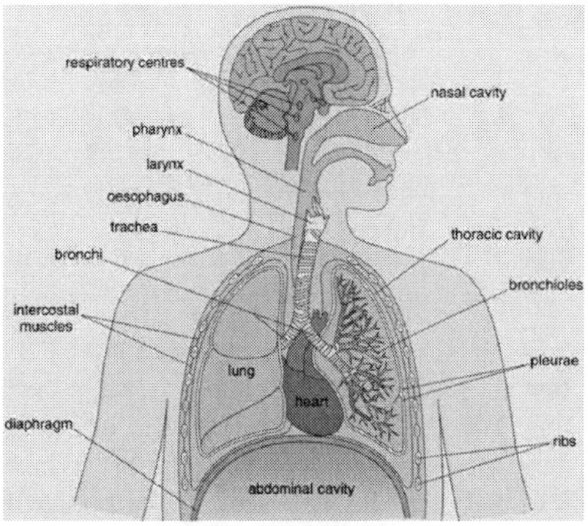

Figure 1: A primary school science diagram

To demonstrate how our tool may be used to decompose diagrams into analytical units, we define a pipeline with four steps. The pipeline aims to identify written labels and the parts they describe (see Figure 2). Each step consists of multiple tasks and actions. We first establish whether the diagram contains text (1), before asking the workers to outline all instances of written text (2). Next, we ask the workers to determine whether text elements refer to other parts of the diagram (3). Finally, we request the workers to outline the part(s) of the diagram referred to by the text (4).

Essentially, steps 1 and 3 consist of binary classification tasks (yes/no) in which agreement between the three workers is evaluated computationally. Steps 2 and 4, in turn, combine human verification with computational evaluation of agreement on the final decision between three workers (accept/reject).

As Figure 2 shows, each step combines a training with a paid examination, which is used to recruit the workforce needed for completing the step. Workers

[2] https://toloka.ai

[3] https://github.com/Toloka/toloka-kit

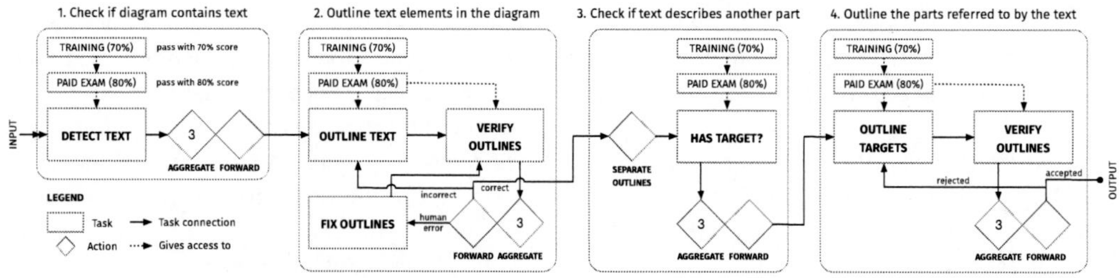

Figure 2: A crowdsourcing pipeline with four steps. See the legend in the lower left-hand corner for details.

Step	Task	Assignments	Total cost	% Re-annotated	Workers	Time
1	Detect text	300	$3.90	–	11	13 min
2	Outline text	103	$23.04	6.80%	32	38 min
2	Verify outlines	312	$44.46	–	42	34 min
2	Fix outlines	1	$0.38	–	1	2 min
3	Has target?	2980	$100.98	–	11	1 h 40 min
4	Outline target	1004	$255.90	14.94%	9	7 h 28 min
4	Verify outlines	3747	$184.07	–	64	4 h 26 min
	Total	8290	$612.73	1.86%	170	15 h 2 min

Table 1: Tasks, assignments, total cost, percentage of re-annotated assignments, number of workers and time spent

who pass the examination are also granted a skill that allows them to access similar tasks in the future. In each step, the AGGREGATE actions use the Dawid-Skene algorithm implemented in the Crowdkit library (Ustalov et al., 2021) to determine the most likely answer based on three responses from the workers. The FORWARD actions, in turn, determine where each assignment should be sent based on the result. Individual assignments are forwarded immediately upon completion.

We used 100 diagrams from the AI2D-RST corpus (Hiippala et al., 2021) as input to the pipeline. The pipeline and its configuration files can be found at: `https://github.com/thiippal/latech-clfl-2022`. We aimed to train at least 10 workers to perform each of steps 1–2 and 50 workers for each of steps 3–4 using paid examinations. The workers could take a paid examination if they passed the training with a 70% score. A score of 80% in the paid examination would grant access to the actual tasks. The total cost for paid examinations amounted to $183.71. This amount is excluded from the expenses in Table 1, which provides details on each task in the pipeline. The cost and time needed for training the workers depended largely on task type. Finally, we estimated the time needed to complete each assignment, and set the wage to $12 per hour.

6 Results and discussion

Based on the results of step 1, 96 out of 100 diagrams contained text elements. These 96 diagrams contained a total of 996 text elements, which were outlined and verified in step 2. 733 of these elements were classified as referring to another part of the diagram in step 3. Their targets were also outlined and verified, which yielded 784 annotations for non-textual elements in step 4.

Table 1 shows how crowdsourcing costs and time increase as the tasks become more demanding and the level of detail in the annotation increases. Whereas the tasks in steps 1–2 are fairly simple and describe entire diagrams, task complexity increases considerably for steps 3–4, because they target specific parts of the diagrams and require reasoning about their content and structure. This also increases the number of tasks needed for evaluating agreement between the workers, which is necessary for ensuring annotation quality.

Figure 3 shows example outputs from step 4. Whereas annotations for the diagram on the left are complete, annotations for the diagram on the right show considerable variation. In the right-hand diagram, stages 3, 5 and 6 feature rectangular bounding boxes which indicate that the numbers below refer to the text and illustration above. Zooming in on other stages shows that their outlines are drawn

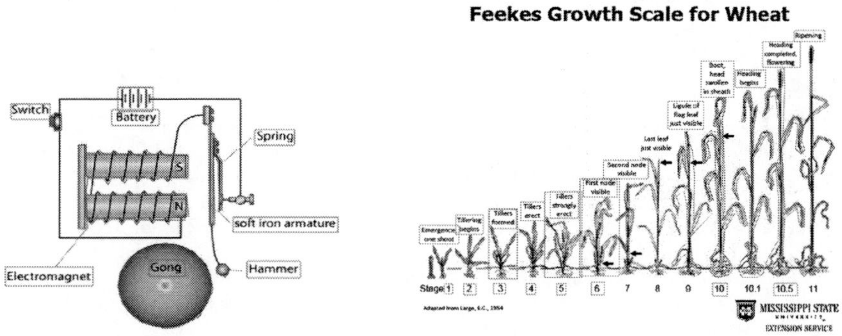

Figure 3: Two diagrams with crowdsourced annotations from step 4 of the pipeline. The diagrams have been converted into grayscale to highlight the annotations. The red bounding boxes indicate textual elements, whereas the blue boxes are used for the elements that the texts refer to. Note that bounding boxes for all text elements identified in step 2 are not visualised for the diagram on the right.

twice, as the workers have associated both written labels (above) and numbers (below) with the illustration. This shows how multiple workers who work on the same diagram make different inferences about the task and the diagram itself.

Furthermore, the annotations for stage 8 are missing altogether. This results from a false decision in step 3 of the crowdsourcing pipeline. Because three workers agreed that these written elements do not describe other elements in the diagram, they were not forwarded to step 4. These missing annotations could be created by adding a final verification step to the pipeline, which asks the workers to evaluate the completeness of the annotations.

Overall, the results suggest that paid crowdsourcing holds much potential for the digital humanities. As Table 1 showed, crowdsourced workers can create a large number of annotations in a relative short time. However, one must also account for the time needed for designing the pipeline, training materials and paid examinations, which are needed for ensuring quality results. In short, developing crowdsourcing pipelines is an iterative process of trial and error.

Our results may also be used to estimate the cost of creating similar annotations for all 1000 diagrams in the AI2D-RST corpus (Hiippala et al., 2021). Note, however, that the descriptions created above are partial, as they only target elements that consist of written text and the parts that they describe. Decomposing entire diagrams into analytical units by targeting other expressive resources such as arrows and lines would increase the costs considerably. In short, paid crowdsourcing is not cheap if used in an ethically responsible manner, but can be used to produce descriptions needed for building multimodal corpora.

Finally, researchers are responsible for applying paid crowdsourcing in a fair and ethical manner, which emphasises the need for transparency in relation to how crowdsourcing is used in academic research. However, not all issues outlined in Section 2 may be addressed by the requesters, as the platforms are ultimately responsible for designing the algorithms that distribute work and constrain the actions that workers and requesters can take. These are concerns that the research community should address together, as paid crowdsourcing has become a part of the research infrastructure in data-driven fields and beyond (cf. Fort et al., 2011).

7 Conclusion

In this article, we introduced a new tool for fair and reproducible use of paid crowdsourcing in the digital humanities. We showed how ethical issues associated with paid crowdsourcing can be mitigated by emphasising them in (1) tool development and (2) crowdsourcing pipeline design. We also demonstrated how the tool can be used to crowdsource descriptions of complex multimodal data. We conclude that paid crowdsourcing can be applied productively in the digital humanities, but its use warrants attention to ethical concerns at all stages of the process.

Acknowledgements

The development of the tool was supported by a $500 data grant from Toloka and by the Helsinki

Institute of Social Sciences and Humanities.

References

Gilles Adda, Joseph J. Mariani, Laurent Besacier, and Hadrien Gelas. 2013. Economic and ethical background of crowdsourcing for speech. In Maxine Eskenazi, Gina-Anne Levow, Helen Meng, Gabriel Parent, and David Suendermann, editors, *Crowdsourcing for Speech Processing: Applications to Data Collection, Transcription and Assessment*, pages 303–334. Wiley.

John A. Bateman. 2014. Using multimodal corpora for empirical research. In Carey Jewitt, editor, *The Routledge Handbook of Multimodal Analysis*, second edition, pages 238–252. Routledge, London and New York.

John A. Bateman, Janina Wildfeuer, and Tuomo Hiippala. 2017. *Multimodality: Foundations, Research and Analysis – A Problem-Oriented Introduction*. De Gruyter Mouton, Berlin.

Tim Causer, Kris Grint, Anna-Maria Sichani, and Melissa Terras. 2018. 'Making such bargain': Transcribe Bentham and the quality and cost-effectiveness of crowdsourced transcription. *Digital Scholarship in the Humanities*, 33(3):467–487.

Jānis Daugavietis. 2021. Motivation to engage in crowdsourcing: Towards the synthetic psychological–sociological model. *Digital Scholarship in the Humanities*, 36(4):858–870.

Stuart Dunn and Mark Hedges. 2013. Crowd-sourcing as a component of humanities research infrastructures. *International Journal of Humanities and Arts Computing*, 7(1-2):147–169.

Karën Fort, Gilles Adda, and K. Bretonnel Cohen. 2011. Amazon Mechanical Turk: Gold mine or coal mine? *Computational Linguistics*, 37(2):413–420.

Kotaro Hara, Abigail Adams, Kristy Milland, Saiph Savage, Chris Callison-Burch, and Jeffrey P. Bigham. 2018. A data-driven analysis of workers' earnings on Amazon Mechanical Turk. In *Proceedings of the 2018 CHI Conference on Human Factors in Computing Systems*, New York, NY, USA. Association for Computing Machinery.

Tuomo Hiippala, Malihe Alikhani, Jonas Haverinen, Timo Kalliokoski, Evanfiya Logacheva, Serafina Orekhova, Aino Tuomainen, Matthew Stone, and John A. Bateman. 2021. AI2D-RST: A multimodal corpus of 1000 primary school science diagrams. *Language Resources and Evaluation*, 55(3):661–688.

Tuomo Hiippala and John A. Bateman. 2022. Introducing the diagrammatic semiotic mode. In *Diagrammatic Representation and Inference: 13th International Conference (Diagrams 2022)*, volume 13462 of *Lecture Notes in Computer Science*, Cham. Springer.

Adriana Kovashka, Olga Russakovsky, Li Fei-Fei, and Kristen Grauman. 2016. Crowdsourcing in computer vision. *Foundations and Trends in Computer Graphics and Vision*, 10(3):177–243.

Jonathan K. Kummerfeld. 2021. Quantifying and avoiding unfair qualification labour in crowdsourcing. In *Proceedings of the 59th Annual Meeting of the Association for Computational Linguistics and the 11th International Joint Conference on Natural Language Processing (Volume 2: Short Papers)*, pages 343–349, Online. Association for Computational Linguistics.

Giovanni Parodi. 2010. Research challenges for corpus cross-linguistics and multimodal texts. *Information Design Journal*, 18(1):69–73.

Ellie Pavlick, Matt Post, Ann Irvine, Dmitry Kachaev, and Chris Callison-Burch. 2014. The language demographics of Amazon Mechanical Turk. *Transactions of the Association for Computational Linguistics*, 2:79–92.

Massimo Poesio, Jon Chamberlain, and Udo Kruschwitz. 2017. Crowdsourcing. In Nancy Ide and James Pustejovsky, editors, *Handbook of Linguistic Annotation*, pages 277–295. Springer, Dordrecht.

Florian A. Schmidt. 2013. The good, the bad and the ugly: Why crowdsourcing needs ethics. In *Proceedings of the 2013 International Conference on Cloud and Green Computing*, pages 531–535.

Melissa Terras. 2015. Crowdsourcing in the digital humanities. In Susan Schreibman, Ray Siemens, and John Unsworth, editors, *A New Companion to Digital Humanities*, pages 420–438. Wiley, Oxford.

Martin Thomas. 2014. Evidence and circularity in multimodal discourse analysis. *Visual Communication*, 13(2):163–189.

Carlos Toxtli, Siddharth Suri, and Saiph Savage. 2021. Quantifying the invisible labor in crowd work. *Proceedings of the ACM on Human-Computer Interaction*, 5(319).

Dmitry Ustalov, Nikita Pavlichenko, Vladimir Losev, Iulian Giliazev, and Evgeny Tulin. 2021. A general-purpose crowdsourcing computational quality control toolkit for Python. In *The Ninth AAAI Conference on Human Computation and Crowdsourcing: Works-in-Progress and Demonstration Track*.

Victoria Van Hyning. 2019. Harnessing crowdsourcing for scholarly and GLAM purposes. *Literature Compass*, 16:e12507.

Janina Wildfeuer, Jana Pflaeging, John A. Bateman, Ognyan Seizov, and Chiao-I Tseng, editors. 2020. *Multimodality: Disciplinary Thoughts and the Challenge of Diversity*. De Gruyter, Berlin, Munich and Boston.

Archive TimeLine Summarization (ATLS): Conceptual Framework for Timeline Generation over Historical Document Collections

Nicolas Gutehrlé
Laboratoire CRIT,
University of Bourgogne
Franche-Comté, France
nicolas.gutehrle
@univ-fcomte.fr

Antoine Doucet
Laboratoire L3i,
University of La Rochelle,
France
antoine.doucet
@univ-lr.fr

Adam Jatowt
Dept. of Computer Science &
Digital Science Center,
University of Innsbruck, Austria
adam.jatowt
@uibk.ac.at

Abstract

Archive collections are nowadays mostly available through search engines interfaces, which allow a user to retrieve documents by issuing queries. The study of these collections may be, however, impaired by some aspects of search engines, such as the overwhelming number of documents returned or the lack of contextual knowledge provided. New methods that could work independently or in combination with search engines are then required to access these collections. In this position paper, we propose to extend *TimeLine Summarization* (TLS) methods on archive collections to assist in their studies. We provide an overview of existing TLS methods and we describe a conceptual framework for an *Archive TimeLine Summarization* (ATLS) system, which aims to generate informative, readable and interpretable timelines.

1 Introduction

1.1 Exploring archives

In the recent years, archives and libraries across the world have frequently conducted digitization campaigns of their collections. This first opened access to thousands of historical documents to a wider public, but also propelled the emergence of new research fields such as Digital Humanities and Digital History. These collections are usually accessible through search engines, which return documents relevant to a query specified by the user. Unfortunately, standard search engines are not fully suited to assist users in exploring historical collections such as news archives where temporal aspects of documents play a key role. Firstly, search engines return documents by their relevance to the query, typically without considering the chronological or causal relations between them, which may prevent the user from understanding the interrelations between events. Furthermore when exploring such documents, the user might lack the contextual knowledge to understand the events that are mentioned in them. This is especially true when exploring news archives coming from distant pasts or exploring longitudinal collections, i.e. which span over a long time frame such as decades or centuries. Search engines do not seem to consider the importance of an event mention for a given query, thus less important events might be returned by the system, especially for broad queries. Improved search engines are then required to study such collections.

1.2 Augmenting search engines with timelines

One promising method to improve the output of search engines operating over archival collection is *TimeLine Summarization* (TLS). TLS consists in summarizing multiple documents by generating a timeline where important events detected in the dataset are associated with a time unit such as a day. TLS is a subfield of the *Multi-Document Summarization* (MDS) task and has been studied extensively in the NLP community: for instance, Swan and Allan (2000) generate clusters of Named Entities and noun chunks that best describe major news topics covered in a subset of the TDT-2 dataset (Allan et al., 1998), which contains text transcripts of broadcast news spanning from January 1, 1998, to June 30, 1998, in English; Nguyen et al. (2014) generate timelines by detecting events that are the most relevant to a user query. They apply their methodology on a dataset of newswire texts in English covering the 2004-2011 period provided by the AFP French news agency; Duan et al. (2017) extend these methods to summarize the common history of similar entities such as Japanese Cities or French scientists. Examples of timelines generated by such methods are shown in Figure 1.

Hence, TLS could serve as a distant reading tool and as a first step in exploring a dataset by providing an overview of its key events. Moreover, TLS could be combined with search engines and used as an interface to search results returned by issuing queries over large datasets, as suggested in Swan and Allan (2000); Alonso et al. (2021). From there,

Proceedings of the 6th LaTeCH-CLfL Workshop, pages 13–23
October 16, 2022. ©2022 International Conference on Computational Linguistics

Date	Summary
2011-01-25	Thousands of protesters spilled into the streets of Egypt on Tuesday , an unprecedented display of anti-government rage inspired in part by the tumult in the nearby North African nation of Tunisia.
2011-01-26	Twitter says its site is being blocked in Egypt Egyptians took to the streets in what could be a sequel to the recent revolution in Tunisia witter , Facebook and YouTube were widely used in Tunisia 's uprising and in Iran last year -LRB-.
2011-01-28	With parts of his capital ablaze , Mubarak said he was asking his government to resign and would soon announce a new one , pledging to address the concerns of thousand of Egyptians protesting in Cairo 's streets . Amre Moussa , the Arab League 's secretary-general and a veteran Egyptian diplomat , joined protesters in Cairo 's Tahrir Square on Friday , state-run Nile TV reported .

From	To	Top headlines
5/2010	7/2011	Syrian officials launch tear gas against protesters Security forces shoot at protesters New York Times journalist with the Pulitzer died of an Asthma attack in Syria
8/2011	3/2012	Assad promises elections in February in Syria US withdraws ambassador from Syria for security reasons NATO says goodbye to Libya and the world turns to Syria
7/2012	12/2012	Meeting of senior officials in Geneva failed agreement to end violence in Syria Russia delivers three war helicopters to Syria Red Cross says Syria is in civil war
7/2016	11/2016	Maternity unit among hospitals bombed in Idlib air strikes Russian helicopter shot down in Syria. Turkish army enters Syria

Figure 1: Examples of generated timelines by Yu et al. (2021) (left) and Campos et al. (2018) (right), summarizing a set of documents about respectively Egyptian protests and the Syrian War. The left timeline outputs a summary on a day-to-day basis, whereas the right timeline lists events using uneven periods of time.

the user could zoom into the documents in order to proceed to close reading. Furthermore, these summaries would be presented in chronological order, thus preserving the link between events, and could also be contextualized by adding data from external knowledge bases as in Ceroni et al. (2014).

Search engines augmented with timelines would be especially useful in a Digital Humanities (DH) context such as for facilitating the study of historical datasets, as they would provide necessary context to understand past events and to structure the event landscape. They could also help the user understand the history of a particular entity such as a person or a location, or even a group of such entities through providing a bird's-eye view of the relevant data. A good example of such search engine augmented with TLS is the Conta-me Histórias (Tell me stories) platform[1], where the user can query news articles from the Portuguese web archive. The user-friendly interface allows a distant reading of the documents returned by the query through a timeline that summarizes them, but also allows close reading by preserving the link to the original documents. To the best of our knowledge, works on applying TLS methods to structure archives of historical documents, or more broadly in the Digital Humanities field, are quite scarce.

1.3 Challenges of applying TLS to archives

Unfortunately, several aspects of such archives make the application of TLS methods not straightforward: first, these datasets are often processed with Optical Character Recognition (OCR). Previous studies have shown that downstream tasks such as Named Entity Recognition (NER), Event Detection (ED) (Boros et al., 2022), Topic Modelling (TM) (Mutuvi et al., 2018) or Named Entity Linking (NEL) (Linhares Pontes et al., 2019) are impacted by the quality of the OCR output. To our knowledge, there is no study on the impact of OCR on TLS, but we can assume it will be similar. Furthermore, archive collections may also differ from contemporary data because of their temporal context: orthographic rules may differ, places might have changed names (Smith and Crane, 2001) or concepts may have acquired another meaning. Most existing annotated resources necessary for NLP components such as NER or ED are created on contemporary data. Historical documents archives are thus harder to process because of this lack of suitable annotated resources.

Most TLS methods generate timelines through statistical analysis of the input dataset. They also often require that the input corpus contains documents of a similar type and similar content. However, an archive collection may be heterogeneous and contain documents of different authors, genres, topics and periods. It may also be fragmentary and not as complete as a contemporary dataset. Finally, although the timelines generated by TLS systems are often easy to read, the process that created them is often not made explicit. If timelines must assist the study of historical datasets by highlighting important events, they must be interpretable and explain why these events are deemed important.

In this position paper, we propose to extend *TimeLine Summarization* (TLS) methods to assist in the studies of archive collections. We first present an overview of existing TLS methods. We then describe a conceptual framework for an *Archive TimeLine Summarization* (ATLS) system, which aims to generate informative, readable and interpretable timelines, before suggesting several methods to implement it.

This paper is organized as follows: in Section 2 we present an overview of existing TimeLine Summarization methods. In Section 3 and 4, we respectively describe our conceptual framework and discuss some of its potential applications. Finally,

[1] https://contamehistorias.pt/arquivopt

we present our conclusion in Section 5, alongside possibilities for future works.

2 Related Work

2.1 TimeLine Summarization

Most TLS methods generate timelines by applying the two following steps: the **Date Selection** step which identifies and ranks the key dates in the documents, and the **Date Summarization** step which generates a summary of an event occurring at a specific date by picking important sentences in the documents published on that date. To identify important dates in the dataset, Gholipour Ghalandari and Ifrim (2020) select the most frequent date mentions, Tran et al. (2015b) use a graph-ranking model and Kessler et al. (2012) combine a clustering model and a supervised classifier. For the second step, La Quatra et al. (2021) apply state-of-the-art methods for Text Summarization (TS) such as TextRank (Mihalcea and Tarau, 2004) whereas Martschat and Markert (2018) adapt methods from the Multi-Document Summarization (MDS) field. TLS has been generally extractive, i.e. the summary is created by copying textual elements (e.g., sentences or paragraphs) from the input data (Tran et al., 2015a). Other works are abstractive, i.e. the summary is a completely new text generated by the system (Steen and Markert, 2019).

TLS methods in general tend to be applied to summarize datasets describing large events, such as the Egyptian protests or the Syrian War (Tran et al., 2015b; Martschat and Markert, 2018). These methods require that the dataset covers a constrained period of time and is homogeneous, i.e. that the documents cover the same topic. Standard TLS methods are thus not suited to summarize heterogeneous or longitudinal datasets. Some works such as Nguyen et al. (2014); Kessler et al. (2012); Chieu and Lee (2004); Pasquali et al. (2019) can be described as *Query-based TimeLine Summarization* (QTLS), as they apply TLS on documents related to a user query such as documents returned by a search engine.

QTLS generally consists in the two following steps: *Event Detection* and *Event Ranking*. To detect events, Chieu and Lee (2004) select any sentence where the terms of the query appear, Nguyen et al. (2014) cluster by a common date every sentence returned by the query and Pasquali et al. (2019) detect peaks of date occurrences in the time span covered by the documents. Other works train a classifier to detect important events (Chasin, 2010) or rank events by their importance with a Learning-to-Rank model (Ge et al., 2015). However, these classifiers need training data, which are difficult to create since defining what is important is a subjective matter. This can lead to disappointing results as shown in Chasin (2010). To determine the importance of events, Nguyen et al. (2014) first score them according to their relevancy and saliency to the query, then rerank them to ensure a diverse timeline. Chieu and Lee (2004) rank the importance of a sentence according to their "interest" and "burstiness", then remove duplicate sentences to ensure diversity. Pasquali et al. (2019) use the keyword extractor YAKE! (Campos et al., 2018) to weight the terms in the event description. Duplicate event descriptions are detected with the Levenshtein similarity measure and removed. Those methods finally select the top most important events to generate the timeline.

In order to generalize the application of TLS, Yu et al. (2021) propose a Multiple TimeLine Summarization (MTLS) system, which generates a timeline for each story found in the dataset. To do so, it first detects events mentioned in the dataset and measures their saliency and consistency. An event linking step determines the link between these events in order to generate each timeline. Similarly, Duan et al. (2020) propose the *Comparative TimeLine Summarization* (CTLS) task, which generates a comparative timeline highlighting the contrast between two timestamped timeline documents (e.g. biographies, historical sections, ...) by computing local and global importance of events.

There are few datasets for the TLS task such as 17 Timelines (T17) (Tran et al., 2013), CRISIS (Tran et al., 2015a), ENTITIES (Gholipour Ghalandari and Ifrim, 2020), CovidTLS (La Quatra et al., 2021) or TLS-Covid19 (Pasquali et al., 2021) which are constructed from contemporary news articles. However, datasets are often lacking in most projects. It is then necessary to create a dataset from scratch as in Minard et al. (2015); Nguyen et al. (2014); Ge et al. (2015); Bedi et al. (2017) or extend existing ones as in Yu et al. (2021).

Due to this lack of datasets, evaluating TLS systems is a difficult task. The date selection step can be evaluated with the F1-measure (La Quatra et al., 2021; Gholipour Ghalandari and Ifrim, 2020) or with the Mean Average Precision (MAP) metric (Nguyen et al., 2014). The date summary is often evaluated with one of the ROUGE metrics (Lin,

2004) to compare a ground-truth timeline and a generated one (Nguyen et al., 2014; Duan et al., 2020; Yu et al., 2021; Gholipour Ghalandari and Ifrim, 2020). Methods relying on event detection such as Ge et al. (2015); Minard et al. (2015); Bedi et al. (2017) often evaluate their system in terms of Precision, Recall and F1-measure. However, most projects often lack datasets and must then resort to human evaluation as in Duan et al. (2017); Swan and Allan (2000); Tran et al. (2015a).

2.2 TLS Variants

We present below formal definitions of several existing TLS variants:

TLS: takes as input a standalone homogeneous dataset of timestamped documents $\mathcal{D} = \{d_1, d_2, ..., d_{|D|}\}$ and generates a timeline $T = \{p_1, p_2, ..., p_{|T|}\}$ of time-summary pairs $p_i = (t_i, s_i)$, where s_i summarizes important events happening at time t_i;

QTLS: outputs a timeline $T = \{p_1, p_2, ..., p_{|T|}\}$ as a sequence of time-summary pairs $p_i = (t_i, s_i)$ from a set of timestamped documents $\{d_1, d_2, ..., d_{|D|}\}$ based on a query $\mathcal{Q} = \{w_1, w_2, ..., w_k\}$ where w_i denotes a word belonging to the query;

MTLS: takes as input a dataset of timestamped documents $\mathcal{D} = \{d_1, d_2, ..., d_{|D|}\}$ that can be standalone or returned using a query $\mathcal{Q} = \{w_1, w_2, ..., w_k\}$, and outputs a set of timelines $\mathcal{T} = \{T_1, T_2, ..., T_m\}$ for each story or topic detected in $\mathcal{D}$, where each timeline T_i is a sequence of time-summary pairs $p_i = (t_i, s_i)$;

CTLS: takes as input two datasets of timestamped documents $\mathcal{D}_\mathcal{A} = \{d_1, d_2, ..., d_{|D_A|}\}$ and $\mathcal{D}_\mathcal{B} = \{d_1, d_2, ..., d_{|D_B|}\}$ and outputs two timelines $\mathcal{T}_\mathcal{A}$ and $\mathcal{T}_\mathcal{B}$ made of contrasting events detected in $\mathcal{D}_\mathcal{A}$ and $\mathcal{D}_\mathcal{B}$, each as a sequence of time-summary pairs $p_i = (t_i, s_i)$;

3 Framework

In this section, we present a conceptual framework for an *Archive TimeLine Summarization* (ATLS) which addresses the challenges raised by archive collections such as the sparsity of data, OCR problems, context shifts and linguistic changes over time in order to generate timelines based on these datasets. We first provide a definition of ATLS and describe the type of dataset expected before presenting the framework and discussing how to evaluate its output.

3.1 Overview

The framework consists of the two key steps: *Timeline Generation* and *Timeline Presentation*. The first step extracts textual elements describing an event and attributes them an importance score. The second one generates the timeline by filtering events and selecting their description.

The processing stages of the framework are shown in Figure 2. The first step has to run only once over the processed dataset, since it aims to detect the elements composing the timeline to be generated. In contrast, the second step can be run multiple times to update the timeline.

3.2 Problem Definition

We define ATLS as follows:

Input: A longitudinal dataset of timestamped documents $\mathcal{D} = \{d_1, d_2, ..., d_{|D|}\}$ taken from an archival collection, either standalone or returned by a query $\mathcal{Q} = \{w_1, w_2, ..., w_k\}$. The period of time covered by $\mathcal{D}$ is usually much longer than the one typically used in TLS.

Output: A timeline $\mathcal{T}$ generated from $\mathcal{D}$ as a sequence of time-summary pairs $p_i = (t_i, s_i)$, where s_i summarizes important events happening at time t_i.

We compare the key characteristics of TLS and ATLS in Tab. 1.

3.3 Expected Dataset

The framework takes as input a longitudinal dataset composed of timestamped documents, such as news articles from a historical newspaper collection. This dataset can be standalone or made of documents returned by a search engine for a given query $\mathcal{Q}$. The dataset could be in raw format or have been pre-processed. We would suggest at least the two following pre-processing steps: first, we recommend to clean the dataset if it has been processed with OCR, either manually or semi-automatically, since the OCR quality will impact further steps (Nguyen et al., 2021). Secondly, we recommend to detect temporal expressions, as they are a good indicator of event mentions. Temporal expressions are either explicit (e.g. February 17, 1995) or implicit (e.g. yesterday, next month). One can use tools such as HeidelTime (Strötgen and Gertz, 2010) or SUTime (Chang and Manning,

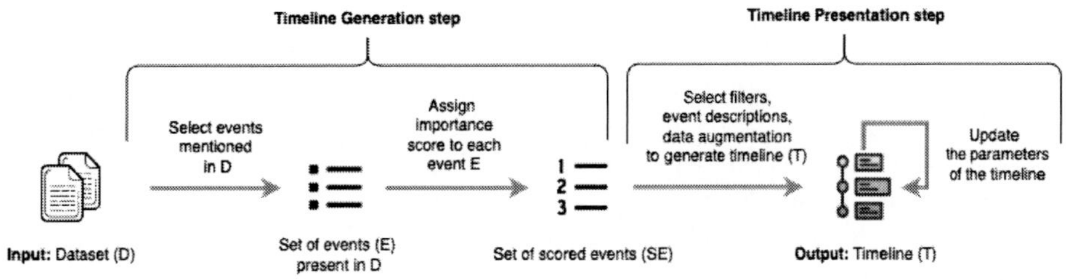

Figure 2: Conceptual pipeline for building the ATLS system

2012) to detect temporal expressions in text and resolve them to an absolute date format, simplifying their use in the TLS process. However, we must keep in mind that the detection of temporal expressions, especially implicit ones, is still a challenging task. Moreover, available tools such as these were mainly conceived for contemporary data, and thus may not work as properly on historical data.

The input dataset could be pre-processed further by applying NLP components such as Name Entity Recognition (NER), Topic Modelling (TM), Event Extraction (EE), Relation Extraction (RE), Keyword Extraction (KE), or Keyword Generation (KG). Such annotations could be used to index the dataset and allow the user to query documents about a specific Named Entity or topic, as in the impresso[2] or the NewsEye[3] platforms.

3.4 Timeline Generation

In this section, we present the first main step of the framework, which extracts mentions of events and attributes them an importance score.

3.4.1 Event Detection

Although events can be defined in many ways, a commonly accepted definition is "something that is *happening* or that is holding true in a given circumstance", as stated in the TimeML guidelines Saurí et al. (2006). Events can be detected in multiple ways: one could detect them through statistical analysis of the corpus. For instance, Chieu and Lee (2004) measure the occurrences of similar sentences associated with the same date, whereas Pasquali et al. (2019) measure the occurrences of articles in atomic time intervals to later aggregate them and determine the bursty time periods. These statistical methods are especially suited for homogeneous datasets, but may not work as well on heterogeneous or fragmentary datasets. One could also train a Learning-to-Rank model on summaries created by experts in order to detect important sentences as in (Tran et al., 2013). This would, however, require training data which tend to be scarce, even when for contemporary data.

Alternatively, one could use an Event Detection model to detect and annotate events in the dataset as in Chasin (2010). Event Detection is another task in the NLP community that has been extensively studied, and some previous works such as Nguyen et al. (2020) have already applied these methods in humanities contexts. However, we need to keep in mind that training such a model requires annotated resources that are often lacking, especially for historical data, and that the OCR quality of documents impacts the output of these models.

Finally, we could select as event any sentence containing at least a time expression, either explicit or implicit as in Duan et al. (2019); Nguyen et al. (2014). This selection could be made even finer by taking sentences that also contain a Named Entity as in Abujabal and Berberich (2015); Bedi et al. (2017). One can then apply algorithms such as Affinity Propagation (Frey and Dueck, 2007) or Chinese Whispers (Biemann, 2006) to gather sentences describing the same event as in Rusu et al. (2014); Yu et al. (2021); Steen and Markert (2019).

Regardless of the method used to detect them, events should all be associated with time. These could be the time expressions occurring with the event mentions, or the Document Creation Date (DCD) if no time expressions are present. Alternatively, approaches for estimating the focus time of text (Jatowt et al., 2015), in absence of any temporal expressions can be applied to associate event-related sentences with particular points of time.

3.4.2 Event Importance Estimation

As mentioned in Section 2, the importance of an event can be measured in a supervised or semi-supervised manner with a classifier (Chasin, 2010; Ge et al., 2015). This method, however, requires

[2]https://impresso-project.ch/app/
[3]https://www.newseye.eu/

training data that are difficult to obtain or produce. Furthermore, the process leading a classifier to a prediction is generally not explained. Since the goal of this framework is to assist in the study of longitudinal datasets, it is necessary that the process of generating a timeline is interpretable. Thus, we would suggest to measure the importance score in an unsupervised manner by extracting features from the dataset as in (Nguyen et al., 2014; Chieu and Lee, 2004; Campos et al., 2018). Some of the features that we think could help measure this importance score are listed below, with suggestions on how to compute them:

Redundancy: The more frequently an event is mentioned, the more important it should be. One can then simply count the occurrences of events, or as an alternative, assign them importance weights by calculating their TF-IDF scores over all the time units. However, as the data might be fragmentary in archive datasets, this feature should rather not be used alone;

Contemporary references: an event may be important at a given time if other events occurring around the same period of time refer to it. Thus, to evaluate this feature, we could count how often an event is referred to from the descriptions of other events in a given short period of time around that event;

Retrospective references: Similarly, an event is likely to be important if documents keep mentioning it some time after it occurred. To assess this kind of across-time reference to the event, one could count how often (and perhaps for how long) an event is mentioned by other events that occurred after a given period of time. Other solutions may rely on computing random walks over graphs composed of timestamped events and/or entities to measure the amount of signal propagation from the past towards "the recent times" (Jatowt et al., 2016);

Causality: an event is likely to be important if it is the cause of other events that occurred after it. To evaluate the causality of an event, one could use *date reference graphs* as in Tran et al. (2015b), which measure the frequency of references, the topical influence and temporal influence between two events to determine a causal link. It is also possible to use Causal Relation Extraction (CRE) methods as presented by Gao et al. for example. However, the CRE task is far from solved and may require much more dataset pre-processing;

Common sense: some events are clearly more important than other, e.g. the birth of a child or marrying a partner are usually more important events in a family history than repainting a house. To represent that kind of common sense knowledge and compute this feature, it may be necessary to create a dataset of events that are deemed important to train a 1-class classifier (1CC) as in Duan et al. (2019) or a Learning-to-Rank model as in Ge et al. (2015). Note that while important events can be collected from historical textbooks or history-related content, gathering unimportant events may be less easy and more problematic; hence the solution could be to rely on a 1CC task.

Using these features, a straightforward formula to calculate the importance of an event could be:

$$\alpha \cdot F1 + \beta \cdot F2 + \gamma \cdot F3 + \delta \cdot F4 + \epsilon \cdot F5$$

where $F1, F2, F3, F4, F5$ are the scaled values of the features described above and $\alpha, \beta, \gamma, \delta, \epsilon$ are hyper-parameters of which value is defined by the user or document archive custodians. Similarly to event detection, the user could be asked to select any of these features to compute this score.

Some periods may contain much more documents than others. For instance, fewer documents may be available during a war time because of censorship or paper restriction. This lack of documents may lead to events that are far more or far less mentioned than others, and bias frequency-based features such as *redundancy*, *contemporary* and *retrospective references*. Thus, these features should be normalized before being incorporated.

Furthermore, we suggest these features since they are easy to compute, but we also acknowledge that they may not be sufficient to measure the importance of an event from the perspective of an expert such as a historian. Because the formula to compute the importance score is modular, one could incorporate more features in collaboration with experts.

3.5 Timeline Presentation

In this section, we describe the second main step of the framework, which generates the timeline from events scored in the previous step. We present sets of filters to select which events should appear on the timeline and how they should be presented. We also describe an optional step of timeline augmentation using external data.

3.5.1 Event Filtering

A dataset may contain hundreds or thousands of mentioned events. It is necessary to select those that will be added to the timeline. To do so, we can use filters such as described below. The weight of these filters could be changed on the user interface, thus allowing users to instantly update the timeline.

Top N: top N most important events are retained;

Importance Threshold (IT): only events of which the importance score is superior to a pre-fixed threshold IT are taken. Individual thresholds for the features described in Section 3.4 that make up the importance score can also be set;

Topical Diversity Threshold ($TopDT$): removes redundant event mentions and ensures the timeline is topically diverse. Topical diversity can be simply measured using Maximal Marginal Relevance (MMR) (Goldstein-Stewart and Carbonell, 1998) or the n-gram blocking metric as in Liu (2019);

Temporal Diversity Threshold ($TempDT$) : ensures every time unit on the generated timeline is evenly represented by setting a minimum and maximum number of events that can appear at each time unit.

3.5.2 Event Description Selection

There are multiple ways to represent an event on a timeline. One could select a sentence that describes the event. If this sentence is too long, one could use sentence compression methods (Filippova and Strube, 2008) to only keep its most important part. As mentioned earlier, an event might be represented by a cluster of sentences. The user can thus select one sentence among this cluster or generate a cloud of terms of all sentences contained in it, as in Duan et al. (2019). One could also use headlines if the target documents are articles as in Tran et al. (2015a); Pasquali et al. (2019).

Finally, we could also use a Natural Language Generation (NLG) system as in Steen and Markert (2019), as these generated texts are often easier to understand than text extracted from the documents. However, abstractive methods such as these may suffer from inaccuracies or hallucinations, i.e. generate information that is not present in the original documents. Thus, abstractive methods might generate improper event descriptions and lose the connection with the original documents. On the other hand, a common drawback of purely extractive methods is that selected sentences may require some context or at least post-processing for users to be able to properly understand them (e.g. pronouns may need to be resolved or we need to add definitions or descriptions of some entities or events).

3.5.3 Timeline Augmentation

To properly understand them, some events may require contextual knowledge that is missing from the processed dataset. This can especially happen if the user is not a domain expert. Such contextual knowledge may be found in knowledge bases such as Wikidata or Wikipedia Year pages (see for example (Tran et al., 2015c)). Thus, timelines generated by an ATLS system could be augmented with contextual data provided by external knowledge bases as in (Ceroni et al., 2014). These augmented timelines could help in explaining a dataset by summarizing it and providing the user with the necessary knowledge to understand it. Unfortunately, most resources created by experts are not in a machine-readable format (Gutehrlé et al., 2021). Hence, this step may require more effort.

3.6 Timeline Evaluation

As mentioned earlier, the evaluation of a TLS system is a difficult task because of the lack of evaluation datasets and the inherent subjectivity of the task. In order to evaluate the output, we would suggest to manually assess the produced timelines, either by following some evaluation criteria as in Duan et al. (2017), or by comparing them with resources created by experts such as timelines derived from history books as in Bedi et al. (2017). One could also use this framework to bootstrap an evaluation dataset specific to the given corpus, towards an automatic evaluation.

4 Discussion

In this section, we describe two hypothetical use cases comparing the application of TLS and ATLS systems, and compare in Table 1 the types of datasets and timelines both methods can process. Finally, we discuss potential extensions of ATLS.

4.1 Use cases

In the first hypothetical use case, a user has curated a homogeneous dataset of timestamped documents from Web archives. This dataset is made of news articles related to a story spanning over a year. It has been pre-processed to remove HTML tags and

	TLS	ATLS
Covered period	Shorter	Longer
Input Data Size	Small / Medium	Large
Documents type	Timestamped documents (e.g. news articles)	
Document Format	Usually born digital	Often digitized
Data Integrity	Usually complete	Can be fragmentary
Presence of noise	Less likely	Depends on OCR quality
Semantic evolution	Less common	Possible (esp. over long time)
Need for query-based filtering	Optional (depends on data size and heterogeneity)	
Need for contextualization	Less likely	More likely (esp. over long time)
Need for interpretable output	Yes	

Table 1: Comparison of TLS and ATLS tasks

extract temporal expressions. To generate the timeline, the user applies the TLS method: important dates are first selected before generating a summary of events occurring at each date. The user can select the sentence mentioning the event, the headline of the article or apply abstractive methods to generate its description.

In the second hypothetical use case, a user has curated a heterogeneous corpus to study the economical life of a certain French region in the 20th century. This corpus is composed of periodicals, newspapers and magazines from different sources (parishes, libraries, etc.) published over a century and processed with OCR. This dataset has also been pre-processed: the documents have been first cleaned of OCR errors, then automatically annotated with Temporal Expression Extraction and Named Entity Recognition components. Furthermore, the dataset has been indexed so as to allow query-based searching. To generate the timeline, the user applies some of the ATLS approaches mentioned in this paper: events are first detected by clustering similar sentences that contain a temporal expression and a Named Entity. The importance of these events is then scored using the formula described in Section 3.4.2. The timeline is generated by setting high values to the topical and temporal diversity thresholds, and augmented with external data from Wikidata, so as to ensure a comprehensive and contextualized timeline. Similarly, the user can select from the user interface to use a cloud of terms or a sentence from the cluster to generate event descriptions.

4.2 Extensions of ATLS systems

Timelines are usually represented linearly, where each time unit is of the same size (usually a day or a year). However, the optimal granularity of temporal units might vary when generating a timeline over a long period of time. For example, when referring to a distant past, humans tend to often describe entire decades or years rather than discussing each day or month which is more common for the recent past. Furthermore, events mentioned in historical documents might not always be recorded with the same temporal precision (e.g., some events may have missing dates, the dates can be imprecise or difficult to be inferred). A possible solution would be to generate logarithmic timelines, where the granularity of the time unit changes over time, as suggested in Jatowt and Au Yeung (2011).

If the documents in the datasets are annotated with Named Entities, one could generate entity-based timelines. This could help understand the history of a specific entity such as a person or a location as in Duan et al. (2019). This idea could be extended by generating aggregate timelines for multiple entities at the same time. These timelines could be agglomerative or contrastive and respectively show the similarities and differences between the history of multiple entities of the same type (e.g., cities in the same region or country, scientists of the same area). Similar to Duan et al. (2020), such comparative timelines would allow to study the history of entities of the same or similar type, e.g. Berlin vs. Paris or even entities of different types, e.g. Paris and the writer Victor Hugo.

5 Conclusion

TimeLine Summarization can be a useful tool for getting an overview of historical collections as well as it can serve as a novel information access means to news article archives. In this position paper, we have presented an overview of existing TLS methods and described a conceptual framework for Archive TimeLine Summarization systems.

The implementation of the framework outlined in this paper will be the subject of our future work. We also intend to ask humanities scholars (historians, archivists, ...) to evaluate the quality of generated timelines and the effectiveness of our framework for the study of archive collections.

References

Abdalghani Abujabal and Klaus Berberich. 2015. Important events in the past, present, and future. pages 1315–1320.

James Allan, Ron Papka, and Victor Lavrenko. 1998. On-line new event detection and tracking. In *Proceedings of the 21st Annual International ACM SIGIR Conference on Research and Development in Information Retrieval*, SIGIR '98, page 37–45, New York, NY, USA. Association for Computing Machinery.

Omar Alonso, Stefano Marchesin, Marc Najork, and Gianmaria Silvello, editors. 2021. *Proceedings of the Second International Conference on Design of Experimental Search & Information REtrieval Systems, Padova, Italy, September 15-18, 2021*, volume 2950 of *CEUR Workshop Proceedings*. CEUR-WS.org.

Harsimran Bedi, Sangameshwar Patil, Swapnil Hingmire, and Girish Palshikar. 2017. Event timeline generation from history textbooks. In *Proceedings of the 4th Workshop on Natural Language Processing Techniques for Educational Applications (NLPTEA 2017)*, pages 69–77, Taipei, Taiwan. Asian Federation of Natural Language Processing.

Chris Biemann. 2006. Chinese whispers - an efficient graph clustering algorithm and its application to natural language processing problems. In *Proceedings of TextGraphs: the First Workshop on Graph Based Methods for Natural Language Processing*, pages 73–80, New York City. Association for Computational Linguistics.

Emanuela Boros, Nhu Khoa Nguyen, Gaël Lejeune, and Antoine Doucet. 2022. Assessing the impact of OCR noise on multilingual event detection over digitised documents. *International Journal on Digital Libraries*.

Ricardo Campos, Vítor Mangaravite, Arian Pasquali, Alípio Mário Jorge, Célia Nunes, and Adam Jatowt. 2018. Yake! collection-independent automatic keyword extractor. In *Advances in Information Retrieval*, pages 806–810, Cham. Springer International Publishing.

Andrea Ceroni, Nam Khanh Tran, Nattiya Kanhabua, and Claudia Niederée. 2014. Bridging temporal context gaps using time-aware re-contextualization. In *Proceedings of the 37th International ACM SIGIR Conference on Research & Development in Information Retrieval*, SIGIR '14, page 1127–1130, New York, NY, USA. Association for Computing Machinery.

Angel X. Chang and Christopher Manning. 2012. SUTime: A library for recognizing and normalizing time expressions. In *Proceedings of the Eighth International Conference on Language Resources and Evaluation (LREC'12)*, pages 3735–3740, Istanbul, Turkey. European Language Resources Association (ELRA).

Rachel Chasin. 2010. Event and temporal information extraction towards timelines of wikipedia articles.

Hai Leong Chieu and Yoong Keok Lee. 2004. Query based event extraction along a timeline. In *Proceedings of the 27th Annual International ACM SIGIR Conference on Research and Development in Information Retrieval*, SIGIR '04, page 425–432, New York, NY, USA. Association for Computing Machinery.

Yijun Duan, Adam Jatowt, and Katsumi Tanaka. 2017. Discovering typical histories of entities by multi-timeline summarization. In *Proceedings of the 28th ACM Conference on Hypertext and Social Media*, HT '17, page 105–114, New York, NY, USA. Association for Computing Machinery.

Yijun Duan, Adam Jatowt, and Katsumi Tanaka. 2019. History-driven entity categorization. In *Web and Big Data*, pages 349–364, Cham. Springer International Publishing.

Yijun Duan, Adam Jatowt, and Masatoshi Yoshikawa. 2020. Comparative timeline summarization via dynamic affinity-preserving random walk. In *ECAI*.

Katja Filippova and Michael Strube. 2008. Dependency tree based sentence compression. In *INLG*.

Brendan J. Frey and Delbert Dueck. 2007. Clustering by passing messages between data points. *Science*, 315(5814):972–976.

Lei Gao, Prafulla Kumar Choubey, and Ruihong Huang. Modeling document-level causal structures for event causal relation identification. *Proceedings of the 2019 Conference of the North American Chapter of the Association for Computational Linguistics: Human Language Technologies, Volume 1 (Long Papers)*.

Tao Ge, Wenzhe Pei, Heng Ji, Sujian Li, Baobao Chang, and Zhifang Sui. 2015. Bring you to the past: Automatic generation of topically relevant event chronicles. In *Proceedings of the 53rd Annual Meeting of the Association for Computational Linguistics and the 7th International Joint Conference on Natural Language Processing (Volume 1: Long Papers)*, pages 575–585, Beijing, China. Association for Computational Linguistics.

Demian Gholipour Ghalandari and Georgiana Ifrim. 2020. Examining the state-of-the-art in news timeline summarization. In *Proceedings of the 58th Annual Meeting of the Association for Computational Linguistics*, pages 1322–1334, Online. Association for Computational Linguistics.

Jade Goldstein-Stewart and Jaime G. Carbonell. 1998. Summarization: (1) using MMR for Diversity-Based Reranking and (2) Evaluating Summaries. In *TIPSTER*.

Nicolas Gutehrlé, Oleg Harlamov, Farimah Karimi, Haoyu Wei, Axel Jean-Caurant, and Lidia Pivovarova. 2021. SpaceWars: A Web Interface for Exploring the Spatio-temporal Dimensions of WWI Newspaper Reporting. *CEUR Workshop Proceedings*.

Adam Jatowt and Ching-man Au Yeung. 2011. Extracting collective expectations about the future from large text collections. In *Proceedings of the 20th ACM International Conference on Information and Knowledge Management*, CIKM '11, page 1259–1264, New York, NY, USA. Association for Computing Machinery.

Adam Jatowt, Daisuke Kawai, and Katsumi Tanaka. 2016. Predicting importance of historical persons using wikipedia. In *Proceedings of the 25th ACM International Conference on Information and Knowledge Management, CIKM 2016, Indianapolis, IN, USA, October 24-28, 2016*, pages 1909–1912. ACM.

Adam Jatowt, Ching-man Au Yeung, and Katsumi Tanaka. 2015. Generic method for detecting focus time of documents. *Inf. Process. Manag.*, 51(6):851–868.

Rémy Kessler, Xavier Tannier, Caroline Hagège, Véronique Moriceau, and André Bittar. 2012. Finding salient dates for building thematic timelines. In *ACL*.

Moreno La Quatra, Luca Cagliero, Elena Baralis, Alberto Messina, and Maurizio Montagnuolo. 2021. *Summarize Dates First: A Paradigm Shift in Timeline Summarization*, page 418–427. Association for Computing Machinery, New York, NY, USA.

Chin-Yew Lin. 2004. ROUGE: A package for automatic evaluation of summaries. In *Text Summarization Branches Out*, pages 74–81, Barcelona, Spain. Association for Computational Linguistics.

Elvys Linhares Pontes, Ahmed Hamdi, Nicolas Sidère, and Antoine Doucet. 2019. Impact of OCR Quality on Named Entity Linking. In *International Conference on Asia-Pacific Digital Libraries 2019*, Kuala Lumpur, Malaysia.

Yang Liu. 2019. Fine-tune BERT for extractive summarization.

Sebastian Martschat and Katja Markert. 2018. A temporally sensitive submodularity framework for timeline summarization. In *Proceedings of the 22nd Conference on Computational Natural Language Learning*, pages 230–240, Brussels, Belgium. Association for Computational Linguistics.

Rada Mihalcea and Paul Tarau. 2004. TextRank: Bringing order into text. In *Proceedings of the 2004 Conference on Empirical Methods in Natural Language Processing*, pages 404–411, Barcelona, Spain. Association for Computational Linguistics.

Anne-Lyse Minard, Manuela Speranza, Eneko Agirre, Itziar Aldabe, Marieke van Erp, Bernardo Magnini, German Rigau, and Rubén Urizar. 2015. SemEval-2015 task 4: TimeLine: Cross-document event ordering. In *Proceedings of the 9th International Workshop on Semantic Evaluation (SemEval 2015)*, pages 778–786, Denver, Colorado. Association for Computational Linguistics.

Stephen Mutuvi, Antoine Doucet, Moses Odeo, and Adam Jatowt. 2018. Evaluating the Impact of OCR Errors on Topic Modeling. In *Maturity and Innovation in Digital Libraries. 20th International Conference on Asia-Pacific Digital Libraries, ICADL 2018, Hamilton, New Zealand, November 19-22, 2018, Proceedings*, pages 3 – 14.

Kiem-Hieu Nguyen, Xavier Tannier, and Veronique Moriceau. 2014. Ranking multidocument event descriptions for building thematic timelines. In *Proceedings of COLING 2014, the 25th International Conference on Computational Linguistics: Technical Papers*, pages 1208–1217, Dublin, Ireland. Dublin City University and Association for Computational Linguistics.

Nhu Khoa Nguyen, Emanuela Boros, Gaël Lejeune, and Antoine Doucet. 2020. Impact analysis of document digitization on event extraction. In *Proceedings of the 4th Workshop on Natural Language for Artificial Intelligence (NL4AI 2020) co-located with the 19th International Conference of the Italian Association for Artificial Intelligence (AI*IA 2020), Anywhere, November 25th-27th, 2020*, volume 2735 of *CEUR Workshop Proceedings*, pages 17–28. CEUR-WS.org.

Thi Tuyet Hai Nguyen, Adam Jatowt, Mickaël Coustaty, and Antoine Doucet. 2021. Survey of Post-OCR processing approaches. *ACM Comput. Surv.*, 54(6):124:1–124:37.

Arian Pasquali, Ricardo Campos, Alexandre Ribeiro, Brenda Salenave Santana, Alípio Mário Jorge, and Adam Jatowt. 2021. Tls-covid19: A new annotated corpus for timeline summarization. In *ECIR*.

Arian Pasquali, Vítor Mangaravite, Ricardo Campos, Alípio Mário Jorge, and Adam Jatowt. 2019. Interactive system for automatically generating temporal narratives. In *Advances in Information Retrieval*, pages 251–255, Cham. Springer International Publishing.

Delia Rusu, James Hodson, and Anthony Kimball. 2014. Unsupervised techniques for extracting and clustering complex events in news. In *Proceedings of the Second Workshop on EVENTS: Definition, Detection, Coreference, and Representation*, pages 26–34, Baltimore, Maryland, USA. Association for Computational Linguistics.

Roser Saurí, Jessica Moszkowicz, Bob Knippen, Rob Gaizauskas, Andrea Setzer, and James Pustejovsky. 2006. Timeml annotation guidelines version 1.2.1.

David A. Smith and Gregory Crane. 2001. Disambiguating geographic names in a historical digital library. In *Proceedings of the 5th European Conference on Research and Advanced Technology for Digital Libraries*, ECDL '01, page 127–136, Berlin, Heidelberg. Springer-Verlag.

Julius Steen and Katja Markert. 2019. Abstractive timeline summarization. In *Proceedings of the 2nd Workshop on New Frontiers in Summarization*, pages 21–31, Hong Kong, China. Association for Computational Linguistics.

Jannik Strötgen and Michael Gertz. 2010. HeidelTime: High quality rule-based extraction and normalization of temporal expressions. In *Proceedings of the 5th International Workshop on Semantic Evaluation*, pages 321–324, Uppsala, Sweden. Association for Computational Linguistics.

Russell Swan and James Allan. 2000. Automatic generation of overview timelines. In *Proceedings of the 23rd Annual International ACM SIGIR Conference on Research and Development in Information Retrieval*, SIGIR '00, page 49–56, New York, NY, USA. Association for Computing Machinery.

Giang Tran, Mohammad Alrifai, and Eelco Herder. 2015a. Timeline summarization from relevant headlines. In *Advances in Information Retrieval*, pages 245–256, Cham. Springer International Publishing.

Giang Tran, Eelco Herder, and Katja Markert. 2015b. Joint graphical models for date selection in timeline summarization. In *Proceedings of the 53rd Annual Meeting of the Association for Computational Linguistics and the 7th International Joint Conference on Natural Language Processing (Volume 1: Long Papers)*, pages 1598–1607, Beijing, China. Association for Computational Linguistics.

Giang Binh Tran, Tuan Tran, Nam Khanh Tran, Mohammad Alrifai, and Nattiya Kanhabua. 2013. Leveraging learning to rank in an optimization framework for timeline summarization.

Nam Khanh Tran, Andrea Ceroni, Nattiya Kanhabua, and Claudia Niederée. 2015c. Back to the past: Supporting interpretations of forgotten stories by time-aware re-contextualization. In *Proceedings of the Eighth ACM International Conference on Web Search and Data Mining, WSDM 2015, Shanghai, China, February 2-6, 2015*, pages 339–348. ACM.

Yi Yu, Adam Jatowt, Antoine Doucet, Kazunari Sugiyama, and Masatoshi Yoshikawa. 2021. Multi-TimeLine summarization (MTLS): Improving timeline summarization by generating multiple summaries. In *Proceedings of the 59th Annual Meeting of the Association for Computational Linguistics and the 11th International Joint Conference on Natural Language Processing (Volume 1: Long Papers)*, pages 377–387, Online. Association for Computational Linguistics.

Prabhupadavani: A Code-mixed Speech Translation Data for 25 Languages

Jivnesh Sandhan[1], Ayush Daksh[2], Om Adideva Paranjay[3], Laxmidhar Behera[1,4] and Pawan Goyal[2]

[1]IIT Kanpur, [2]IIT Kharagpur, [3]University of Pennsylvania, [4]IIT Mandi

jivnesh@iitk.ac.in, pawang@cse.iitkgp.ac.in

Abstract

Nowadays, the interest in code-mixing has become ubiquitous in Natural Language Processing (NLP); however, not much attention has been given to address this phenomenon for Speech Translation (ST) task. This can be solely attributed to the lack of code-mixed ST task labelled data. Thus, we introduce Prabhupadavani, which is a multilingual code-mixed ST dataset for 25 languages. It is multi-domain, covers ten language families, containing 94 hours of speech by 130+ speakers, manually aligned with corresponding text in the target language. The Prabhupadavani is about Vedic culture and heritage from Indic literature, where code-switching in the case of quotation from literature is important in the context of humanities teaching. To the best of our knowledge, Prabhupadvani is the first multi-lingual code-mixed ST dataset available in the ST literature. This data also can be used for a code-mixed machine translation task. All the dataset can be accessed at: https://github.com/frozentoad9/CMST.

1 Introduction

Speech Translation (ST) is a task in which speech is simultaneously translated from source language to a different target language.[1] It aids to overcome the language barriers across different communities for various applications such as social media, education, tourism, medical etc. Earlier attempts to build a robust speech translation system mainly focused on a cascaded approach where two separate architectures for Automatic Speech Recognition (ASR) and Machine Translation (MT) are used in pipeline mode (Cho et al., 2013; Post et al., 2013; Tsvetkov et al., 2014; Ruiz et al., 2015; Sperber et al., 2017). However, these approaches mainly suffer from cascading effect of error propagation. Thus, attention shifted to end-to-end approaches (Bérard et al., 2018; Duong et al., 2016; Weiss et al., 2017; Bansal et al., 2017) due to their ability to obliviate error propagation and ease of maintaining a single architecture. However, these end-to-end approaches could not match the performance of cascaded systems due to the lack of sufficiently large data (Niehues et al., 2021). Notably, with the recent upsurge in ST datasets (Di Gangi et al., 2019; Zanon Boito* et al., 2020; Iranzo-Sánchez et al., 2020; Wang et al., 2020), this gap has been closed (Niehues et al., 2021; Ansari et al., 2020).

Nowadays, most users prefer to communicate using a mixture of two or many languages on platforms such as social media, online blogs, chatbots, etc. Thus, code-mixing has become ubiquitous in all kinds of Natural Language Processing (NLP) resources/tasks (Khanuja et al., 2020; Chakravarthi et al., 2020; Singh et al., 2018a,b; Dhar et al., 2018). However, the existing NLP tools may not be robust enough to address this phenomenon of code-mixing for various downstream NLP applications (Srivastava and Singh, 2021). Therefore, there has been a surge in creating code-mixed datasets: (1) to understand reasons for the failure of existing models, and (2) to empower existing models for overcoming this phenomenon. Nevertheless, it is challenging to find natural resources that essentially capture different aspects of code-mixing for creating datasets for a wide range of NLP tasks. Although there has been considerable research in generating copious data and novel architectures for the ST task, we find that not much attention has been given to address the code-mixing phenomenon on the ST task. Possibly, this can be justified due to the lack of a code-mixed ST dataset. To the best of our knowledge, no such sufficiently large, multi-lingual, naturally occurring, code-mixed dataset is available for the ST.

Thus, in this work, we introduce **Prabhupadavani**, a multi-lingual, multi-domain, speech translation dataset for 25 languages containing 94 hours of speech by 130 speakers. The Prabhupadavani is about Vedic culture and heritage from Indic litera-

[1]We refer to speech translation as a speech-to-text task.

Proceedings of the 6th LaTeCH-CLfL Workshop, pages 24–29
October 16, 2022. ©2022 International Conference on Computational Linguistics

ture, where code-switching in the case of quotation from literature is important in the context of humanities teaching. The multiple domains cover utterances from public lectures, conversations, debates, and interviews on various social issues. This is the first code-mixed data for speech translation to the best of our knowledge. It is code-mixed with English, Bengali and Sanskrit. From the typological point of view, the languages covered vary over ten language families. All the audios files have been manually aligned and translated. We believe that our work will ignite research in this direction to understand- (1) How to make existing systems robust for handling this phenomenon effectively? (2) Can multi-lingual training help to improve performance on code-mixed speech translation? (3) Will the gap between the cascade and end-to-end systems be closed? (4) Can we train a single model for all languages using parallel nature of the dataset?[2]

2 Related Work

Speech Translation: Recently, there have been increased efforts for creating large speech translation data sets for many languages. Nevertheless, the available datasets are limited to certain languages or only underpaid licenses for non-English languages. Most of the relatively larger datasets are English-centric (Di Gangi et al., 2019; Bérard et al., 2018), domain-specific (Zanon Boito* et al., 2020; Iranzo-Sánchez et al., 2020) or with limited speech hours (Zanon Boito* et al., 2020; Zhang et al., 2021). Recently, there has been upsurge in ST datasets in the literature (Di Gangi et al., 2019; Iranzo-Sánchez et al., 2020; Wang et al., 2020; Salesky et al., 2021). To the best of our knowledge, there is no such naturally occurring, sufficiently large and multi-lingual ST dataset that contains a code-switching phenomenon. We fill this gap by contributing a code-mixed speech translation dataset for 25 languages.

Code-mixing: Code-mixing is ubiquitous and well addressed on variety of downstream NLP tasks. However, majority of code-mixed datasets are synthetically generated (Gonen and Goldberg, 2018; Khanuja et al., 2020); therefore, they may not be able to capture the different aspects of code-mixing. The code-mixed datasets for an ASR task are either limited to only one/two languages or contain only a few hours of speech data (Nakayama et al., 2019; Lyu et al., 2015). Synthetic code-mixed datasets may not capture the different aspects of code-mixing. To the best of our knowledge, Prabhupadavani is the first code-mixed dataset available for 25 languages on speech translation task.

3 Data Description

Resource: Vanimedia's Multi-language Subtitle Project[3] has created 1,080 audio mini-clips of Śrīla Prabhupāda's lectures, conversations, debates, interviews and is now transcribing them in multiple languages.[4] 700+ translators participate in creating subtitles for all 1,080 mini-clips for 108+ languages. Currently, this work has been completed for 25 languages. To procure subtitles for each clip in multiple languages, translators are provided with mini-clips and English subtitles that are manually aligned with each utterance. They use a third-party software named Dotsub.com[5] and the task of translators is to provide translation for the corresponding utterance with the help of given transcription. On average, there are 3-4 translators for each language, and each clip takes more or less one hour for translation. Each translator has invested an average of 6 hours every day in translating these clips. Collectively, the time taken to translate 1,080 clips into 25 languages is over 45 weeks. Current release of the dataset contains 25 languages (including transcription) for which transcription/translations are available. For these languages, we have over 53K utterances of transcription and translations.

Preprocessing: In this section, we describe preprocessing steps followed to arrive at the final version of the data. First, we scrape transcription and their translations in 25 languages from Dotsub and extracted the corresponding Youtube links of all audio clips. We use Selenium[6] web crawler to automatize the process of downloading. We convert those videos into MP3 audio clips using a third-party application[7]. We chop the converted audio files based on the timestamps provided in the subtitle (.srt) files.[8] This process boils down to 53,000

[2]Prabhupadavani has parallel translations available in all the 25 languages for all the utterances.

[3]https://vanimedia.org/wiki/Multi-language_Subtitle_Project

[4]https://vanimedia.org/wiki/Table:_Clips_to_subtitle

[5]https://dotsub.com

[6]https://www.selenium.dev/

[7]https://ytmp3.cc/uu100cc/

[8]https://pypi.org/project/audioclipextractor/

Languages	# Types	# Tokens	Types per line	Tokens per line	Avg. token length
English	40,324	601,889	10.58	11.27	4.92
French (France)	50,510	645,651	11.38	12.09	5.08
German	50,748	584,575	10.44	10.95	5.57
Gujarati	41,959	584,989	10.37	10.95	4.46
Hindi	29,744	716,800	12.36	13.42	3.74
Hungarian	84,872	506,608	9.13	9.49	5.89
Indonesian	39,365	653,374	11.54	12.23	6.14
Italian	52,372	512,061	9.23	9.59	5.37
Latvian	70,040	477,106	8.69	8.93	5.72
Lithuanian	75,222	491,558	8.92	9.20	6.04
Nepali	52,630	570,268	10.03	10.68	4.88
Persian (Farsi)	51,722	598,096	10.61	11.20	4.10
Polish	71,662	494,263	8.99	9.25	5.86
Portuguese(Brazil)	50,087	608,432	10.80	11.39	5.12
Russian	72,162	490,908	8.96	9.19	5.79
Slovak	73,789	520,465	9.39	9.75	5.37
Slovenian	68,619	516,649	9.35	9.67	5.30
Spanish	49,806	608,868	10.75	11.40	5.07
Swedish	48,233	581,751	10.31	10.89	5.00
Tamil	84,183	460,678	8.37	8.63	7.65
Telugu	72,006	464,665	8.34	8.70	6.56
Turkish	78,957	453,521	8.27	8.49	6.35
Bulgarian	60,712	564,150	10.10	10.56	5.24
Croatian	73,075	531,326	9.58	9.95	5.28
Danish	50,170	587,253	10.40	11.00	4.98
Dutch	42,716	595,464	10.52	11.15	5.05

Table 1: Statistics of the **Prabhupadavani** dataset

Language	Tokens	Types	Percentage
English	500,136	6,312	83.6
Bengali	46,933	3,907	7.84
Sanskrit	51,246	7,202	8.56
Total	598,315	17,421	100

Table 2: Statistics of code-mixing in **Prabhupadavani**

utterances with their transcription and translation in 25 languages. Table 4 illustrates the example from Prabhupadavani. In order to obliviate time and efforts needed for data pre-processing, we provide train, dev and test set splits using stratified sampling. There are 51,000, 1,000 and 1,000 utterances in train, dev and test set, respectively. We consider the following dimensions for stratified sampling: (1) different speakers (2) proportion of intra-sentential and inter-sentential code-mixing.

Code-mixing: Prabhupadavani is code-mixed across three languages: English, Sanskrit, and Bengali. Table 2 reports the overall statistics of the code-mixing present in Prabhupadavani. If we consider the number of tokens in utterances, then it is mainly dominated by English (83.0%) tokens; however, it is not the case in terms of a number of types. This attributes to the contrasting nature of morphology (English vs Sanskrit/Bengali). Code-mixing is categorized into two classes- (1) inter-sentential: speaker chooses to switch the language after completion of utterance (2) intra-sentential: speaker switches the language within an utterance. Table 3 illustrates examples of code-mixing from Prabhupadavani. Table 5 shows the statistics of both these types of code-mixing. Mainly speaker explains Sanskrit verses to the English audience; therefore, transitions between the Sanskrit-English pair is more. However, sometimes speaker also use Bengali literature to illustrate the points. Thus, we observe Bengali-English code-switching. Notably, there is no code-switching between Bengali-Sanskrit because the audience is English speaking.

Language diversity: From typological point of view, Prabhupadavani covers 25 languages (including ASR) from 10 language families. They are listed as follows: (1) *Indo-European:-* (a) *Romance:* Italian, Portuguese, Spanish, French (b) *Germanic:* German, Swedish, Danish, Dutch, English (c) *Baltic:* Lithuanian, Latvian (d) *Slavic:* Croatian, Polish, Slovak, Russian, Slovenian, Bulgarian, (e) *Indo-Aryan:* Bengali, Hindi, Sanskrit, Nepali (f) *Indo-Iranian:* Persian (Farsi) (2) *Uralic:-* (a) *Finno-Ugric:* Hungarian (3) *Austronesian:-* (a) *Malayo-Polynesian:* Indonesian (4) *Dravidian:-* Tamil, Telugu. Prabhupadavani contains fusional languages: Indo-European, Uralic and Agglutinative languages: Austronesian (Indonesian), Dravid-

Language	Type	Examples
English-Sanskrit	Inter	Kṛṣṇa is assuring. ahaṁ tvāṁ sarva-pāpebhyo mokṣayiṣyāmi
	Intra	Sense gratification means udara-upastha-jihvā
Sanskrit-English	Inter	Īśāvāsyam idaṁ sarvam. Everything belongs to God
	Intra	andhā yathāndhair upanīyamānāḥ and people, leaders.
English-Bengali	Inter	Give up their. Asat-saṅga-tyāga ei vaiṣṇava ācāra
	Intra	Therefore Caitanya Mahāprabhu said guru-kṛṣṇa-kṛpāya
Bengali-English	Inter	Guru-kṛṣṇa-kṛpāya pāya bhakti-latā-bīja. Then our devotional service is perfect
	Intra	tāṅhāra nāhika doṣa means he is not faulty.

Table 3: Examples of code-mixing in **Prabhupadavani**. English, Sanskrit and Bengali are indicated by black, red and violet color, respectively.

	Language	Translations
Source	English	You can become Brahman. Brahma-bhūyāya kalpate
Target	Bulgarian	Можете да станете Брахман. Брахма бхуяя калпате.
	Hindi	तुम ब्रह्म बन सकते हो । ब्रह्मभूयाय कल्पते ।
	Russian	Вы можете стать "Брахманом". "Брахма-бхуйайа калпате".
	Tamil	நீ ப்ரம்மன் ஆகலாம். ப்ரம்ம-பூயாய-கல்பதே.
	Gujarati	તમે બ્રહ્મ બની શકો છો. બ્રહ્મ-ભૂયાય-કલ્પતે.

Table 4: Sample data point from **Prabhupadavani**. For a code-mixed utterance, we show its English transcription (source) and the corresponding translations for 5 languages.

	Inter-Sentential	Intra-Sentential
English-Sanskrit	2,356	2,338
Sanskrit-English	2366	851
English-Bengali	339	124
Bengali-English	339	0

Table 5: Code-Mixing type for our dataset

ian and Turkic (Turkish). In the former languages, grammatical markers bear several meanings and for the latter ones, they exhibit only one meaning at the same time. Except Hindi (Indo-Aryan), all the languages in our dataset use nominative-accusative marking. Hindi uses ergative-absolutive marking upto a limited extent. We can also categorize languages based on the number of grammatical genders. Some languages pose (1) three genders: German, Russian, Swedish, etc. (2) two genders: French, Spain, Hindi, etc. (3) no genders: English, Nepali, Persian, Turkish, etc. Based on a syntactic construct, we can categorize the languages present in Prabhupadavani- (1) SVO word order: English, Italian, French, Indonesian, etc. (2) SOV word order: Indo-Aryan, Dravidian and Turkic (3) flexible word order: Russian, Hungarian.

Thus, the diversified language coverage of **Prabhupadavani** along with its code-mixed nature makes it a suitable dataset to investigate various linguistic phenomena for the speech translation task, ASR and machine translation.

Applications of dataset: In this section, we throw some light on possible applications of Prabhupadavani: (1) The full dataset of Prabhupadavani contains 2,400 hours of speech. The current release of Prabhupadavani dataset can be utilized to facilitate automatic subtitling of the remaining part of data in the different languages. In this way, it will also be helpful to generate relatively larger dataset. (2) This dataset can provide a fertile soil to investigate on- How to make existing systems robust to code-mixing phenomenon? Will the gap between cascade and end-to-end to approaches be closed? Can multi-lingual training help to address code-mixing phenomenon? Can we train single ST system for all languages? How robust will be these models on another domain?

4 Conclusion and Discussion

In this work, we focused on a code-mixed speech translation dataset. Although code-mixing is a spoken language phenomenon, not much attention has been given to address this phenomenon due to the unavailability of such a dataset. Thus, we released Prabhupadavani, a high-quality multilingual multi-domain code-mixed ST dataset containing 94 hours of speech data, 130+ speakers, for 25 languages covering 10 language families. The dataset is code-mixed with three languages: English, Bengali, and Sanskrit. In order to reduce the efforts needed for pre-processing, we provide stratified data splits for the dataset. The same dataset can be utilized for the code-mixed machine translation task. We believe that these efforts will (1) set a fertile soil for investigating the applicability of existing solutions, (2) help to analyze the kind of errors existing systems are making, and (3) facilitate researchers to propose a novel solution to make existing systems robust for code-mixing. We plan to extend this dataset for 108+ languages.

In code-switching conversations, speakers prefer a specific communication in a specific language of choice. In that context, the interesting factor is often when the boundary between languages becomes fuzzy, as in cases where an English verb stem is used with Spanish morphology. In the case of Prabhupadavani, the audience does not necessarily speak Sanskrit or Bengali, and the code-switching is primarily quotation or explanation. That is interesting as a phenomenon, but it is not the same as dual bilingual code-switching. We believe future work may help to get deep insights into this phenomenon.

Ethics Statement: We do not foresee any ethical concerns with the work presented in this manuscript. We have taken the consent of the Vanipedia team and Bhaktivedanta Book Trust International to use translations and audio in our dataset.

Acknowledgements

We would like to thank the Vanipedia team (`https://vanipedia.org/`) of 700+ translators for establishing this multi-lingual database for us to develop. We thank the Bhaktivedanta Book Trust International for permitting us to use Prabhupadavani audio in our dataset. We are grateful to Manish Gupta, Microsoft, for helping us with insightful discussions. We would like to thank the anonymous reviewers for their constructive feedback towards improving this work. The TCS Fellowship supports the first author's work under Project TCS/EE/2011191P.

References

Ebrahim Ansari, Amittai Axelrod, Nguyen Bach, Ondřej Bojar, Roldano Cattoni, Fahim Dalvi, Nadir Durrani, Marcello Federico, Christian Federmann, Jiatao Gu, et al. 2020. Findings of the iwslt 2020 evaluation campaign. In *Proceedings of the 17th International Conference on Spoken Language Translation*, pages 1–34.

Sameer Bansal, Herman Kamper, Adam Lopez, and Sharon Goldwater. 2017. Towards speech-to-text translation without speech recognition. In *Proceedings of the 15th Conference of the European Chapter of the Association for Computational Linguistics: Volume 2, Short Papers*, pages 474–479, Valencia, Spain. Association for Computational Linguistics.

Alexandre Bérard, Laurent Besacier, Ali Can Kocabiyikoglu, and Olivier Pietquin. 2018. End-to-end automatic speech translation of audiobooks. In *2018 IEEE International Conference on Acoustics, Speech and Signal Processing (ICASSP)*, pages 6224–6228. IEEE.

Bharathi Raja Chakravarthi, Vigneshwaran Muralidaran, Ruba Priyadharshini, and John P McCrae. 2020. Corpus creation for sentiment analysis in code-mixed tamil-english text. *arXiv preprint arXiv:2006.00206*.

Eunah Cho, Christian Fügen, Teresa Herrmann, Kevin Kilgour, Mohammed Mediani, Christian Mohr, Jan Niehues, Kay Rottmann, Christian Saam, Sebastian Stüker, et al. 2013. A real-world system for simultaneous translation of german lectures. In *INTERSPEECH*, pages 3473–3477.

Mrinal Dhar, Vaibhav Kumar, and Manish Shrivastava. 2018. Enabling code-mixed translation: Parallel corpus creation and mt augmentation approach. In *Proceedings of the First Workshop on Linguistic Resources for Natural Language Processing*, pages 131–140.

Mattia A. Di Gangi, Roldano Cattoni, Luisa Bentivogli, Matteo Negri, and Marco Turchi. 2019. MuST-C: a Multilingual Speech Translation Corpus. In *Proceedings of the 2019 Conference of the North American Chapter of the Association for Computational Linguistics: Human Language Technologies, Volume 1 (Long and Short Papers)*, pages 2012–2017, Minneapolis, Minnesota. Association for Computational Linguistics.

Long Duong, Antonios Anastasopoulos, David Chiang, Steven Bird, and Trevor Cohn. 2016. An attentional model for speech translation without transcription. In *Proceedings of the 2016 Conference of the North American Chapter of the Association for Computational Linguistics: Human Language Technologies*, pages 949–959, San Diego, California. Association for Computational Linguistics.

Hila Gonen and Yoav Goldberg. 2018. Language modeling for code-switching: Evaluation, integration of monolingual data, and discriminative training. *arXiv preprint arXiv:1810.11895*.

J. Iranzo-Sánchez, J. A. Silvestre-Cerdà, J. Jorge, N. Roselló, A. Giménez, A. Sanchis, J. Civera, and A. Juan. 2020. Europarl-st: A multilingual corpus for speech translation of parliamentary debates. In *ICASSP 2020 - 2020 IEEE International Conference on Acoustics, Speech and Signal Processing (ICASSP)*, pages 8229–8233.

Simran Khanuja, Sandipan Dandapat, Sunayana Sitaram, and Monojit Choudhury. 2020. A new dataset for natural language inference from code-mixed conversations. *arXiv preprint arXiv:2004.05051*.

Dau-Cheng Lyu, Tien-Ping Tan, Eng-Siong Chng, and Haizhou Li. 2015. Mandarin–english code-switching speech corpus in south-east asia: Seame. *Language Resources and Evaluation*, 49(3):581–600.

Sahoko Nakayama, Takatomo Kano, Andros Tjandra, Sakriani Sakti, and Satoshi Nakamura. 2019. Recognition and translation of code-switching speech utterances. In *2019 22nd Conference of the Oriental COCOSDA International Committee for the Coordination and Standardisation of Speech Databases and Assessment Techniques (O-COCOSDA)*, pages 1–6.

Jan Niehues, Elizabeth Salesky, Marco Turchi, and Matteo Negri. 2021. Tutorial proposal: End-to-end speech translation. In *Proceedings of the 16th Conference of the European Chapter of the Association for Computational Linguistics: Tutorial Abstracts*, pages 10–13, online. Association for Computational Linguistics.

Matt Post, Gaurav Kumar, Adam Lopez, Damianos Karakos, Chris Callison-Burch, and Sanjeev Khudanpur. 2013. Improved speech-to-text translation with the fisher and callhome spanish–english speech translation corpus. In *Proc. IWSLT*.

Nicholas Ruiz, Qin Gao, Will Lewis, and Marcello Federico. 2015. Adapting machine translation models toward misrecognized speech with text-to-speech pronunciation rules and acoustic confusability. In *Interspeech*. ISCA-International Speech Communication Association.

Elizabeth Salesky, Matthew Wiesner, Jacob Bremerman, Roldano Cattoni, Matteo Negri, Marco Turchi, Douglas W. Oard, and Matt Post. 2021. Multilingual tedx corpus for speech recognition and translation. In *Proceedings of Interspeech*.

Kushagra Singh, Indira Sen, and Ponnurangam Kumaraguru. 2018a. A twitter corpus for hindi-english code mixed pos tagging. In *Proceedings of the Sixth International Workshop on Natural Language Processing for Social Media*, pages 12–17.

Vinay Singh, Deepanshu Vijay, Syed Sarfaraz Akhtar, and Manish Shrivastava. 2018b. Named entity recognition for hindi-english code-mixed social media text. In *Proceedings of the seventh named entities workshop*, pages 27–35.

Matthias Sperber, Jan Niehues, and Alex Waibel. 2017. Toward robust neural machine translation for noisy input sequences. In *International Workshop on Spoken Language Translation (IWSLT)*, page 18.

Vivek Srivastava and Mayank Singh. 2021. Challenges and considerations with code-mixed nlp for multilingual societies.

Yulia Tsvetkov, Florian Metze, and Chris Dyer. 2014. Augmenting translation models with simulated acoustic confusions for improved spoken language translation. In *Proceedings of the 14th Conference of the European Chapter of the Association for Computational Linguistics*, pages 616–625, Gothenburg, Sweden. Association for Computational Linguistics.

Changhan Wang, Juan Pino, Anne Wu, and Jiatao Gu. 2020. CoVoST: A diverse multilingual speech-to-text translation corpus. In *Proceedings of The 12th Language Resources and Evaluation Conference*, pages 4197–4203, Marseille, France. European Language Resources Association.

Ron J Weiss, Jan Chorowski, Navdeep Jaitly, Yonghui Wu, and Zhifeng Chen. 2017. Sequence-to-sequence models can directly translate foreign speech. *arXiv preprint arXiv:1703.08581*.

Marcely Zanon Boito*, William Havard*, Mahault Garnerin, Eric Le Ferrand, and Laurent Besacier. 2020. MaSS: A Large and Clean Multilingual Corpus of Sentence-aligned Spoken Utterances Extracted from the Bible. In *Proceedings of the 12th Language Resources and Evaluation Conference*, pages 6486–6493, Marseille, France. European Language Resources Association.

Ruiqing Zhang, Xiyang Wang, Chuanqiang Zhang, Zhongjun He, Hua Wu, Zhi Li, Haifeng Wang, Ying Chen, and Qinfei Li. 2021. Bstc: A large-scale chinese-english speech translation dataset. *arXiv preprint arXiv:2104.03575*.

Using Language Models to Improve Rule-based Linguistic Annotation of Modern Historical Japanese Corpora

Jerry Bonnell and **Mitsunori Ogihara**
University of Miami
Coral Gables FL 33124, USA
{j.bonnell,m.ogihara}@miami.edu

Abstract

Annotation of unlabeled textual corpora with linguistic metadata is a fundamental technology in many scholarly workflows in the digital humanities (DH). Pretrained natural language processing pipelines offer tokenization, tagging, and dependency parsing of raw text simultaneously using an annotation scheme like Universal Dependencies (UD). However, the accuracy of these UD tools remains unknown for historical texts and current methods lack mechanisms that enable helpful evaluations by domain experts. To address both points for the case of Modern Historical Japanese text, this paper proposes the use of unsupervised domain adaptation methods to develop a domain-adapted language model (LM) that can flag instances of inaccurate UD output from a pretrained LM and the use of these instances to form rules that, when applied, improves pretrained annotation accuracy. To test the efficacy of the proposed approach, the paper evaluates the domain-adapted LM against three baselines that are not adapted to the historical domain. The experiments conducted demonstrate that the domain-adapted LM improves UD annotation in the Modern Historical Japanese domain and that rules produced using this LM are best indicative of characteristics of the domain in terms of out-of-vocabulary rate and candidate normalized form discovery for "difficult" bigram terms.

1 Introduction

Annotating unlabeled corpora with linguistic metadata is a fundamental task in many scholarly workflows in the digital humanities (DH) (Aurnhammer et al., 2019; Kirschenbaum, 2007). These can benefit from the application of "off-the-shelf", or pretrained, natural language processing (NLP) pipelines that supply tokenization, tagging, and dependency parsing simultaneously using an annotation scheme like Universal Dependencies (UD) (Nivre et al., 2020). For these tools to warrant any integration, the annotations produced must be accurate for the target corpus under study and enable helpful evaluation by domain experts. Current efforts have prioritized the former as the accuracy of pretrained UD tools remains unknown for historical texts sampled from domains that are different from pretraining domains (Suissa et al., 2022).

In applications to historical text in East Asian languages like Chinese and Japanese that can be written without specifying word boundaries, substantial errors in word segmentation can result in degraded accuracy of resulting dependency parsings (Yasuoka, 2020). The insufficiency of the vocabulary used by pretrained UD tools can be a major source of errors in word segmentation. Consequently, a straightforward application is likely not possible without extensive manual revision by domain experts and the process can be prohibitive when corpus size is large (Shirai et al., 2020).

Recent work in NLP has addressed the accuracy of sequence labeling tasks (e.g., word segmentation, part of speech annotation, named entity recognition) for historical materials through unsupervised finetuning of pretrained contextualized word embeddings using transformer-based language models (LMs) (Han and Eisenstein, 2019; Manjavacas and Fonteyn, 2022). These finetuned LMs are capable of capturing useful high-level features about the domain without requiring any labels from the target corpus. The improvements are encouraging, yet, the usefulness of a transformer-based method for a domain expert remains unknown. The lack of supervision in these methods means that direct mechanisms for finetuning the LM other than through the training data used are beyond the control of a domain expert. Put another way, the explicit representations of domain knowledge that occur during manual revision of pretrained output is not possible with current NLP for adapting pretrained LMs to historical corpora.

In prior work, Bonnell and Ogihara (2022) pro-

Proceedings of the 6th LaTeCH-CLfL Workshop, pages 30–39
October 16, 2022. ©2022 International Conference on Computational Linguistics

posed a rule-based expert system for the case of Modern Historical Japanese corpora that generates accurate UD annotations using a set of handcrafted rules. The rules compose a two-parted workflow that (1) *normalizes* non-standard lexical variants to a more canonical form so that the normalized text can receive a more accurate parsing by a pretrained tool, and (2) an *assignment* step where the updated UD is then linked to word forms from the original text. Figure 1 shows an overview. The use of rules allows for immediate improvement in UD annotation for out-of-vocabulary terms by parsing dependencies using substituted terms that are present in the vocabulary, and then restoring the historical forms in the parsed sentence. Moreover, each rule forms a direct application of domain knowledge and supports human comprehension. However, because rule generation cannot proceed without manual review, the workflow can be a time intensive undertaking when the number of rules needed to achieve improved accuracy is not known.

This paper aims to enrich the rule-based expert system by incorporating it into a workflow that is usefully guided by a pretrained LM adapted to the domain of Modern Historical Japanese. The contributions of the proposed workflow are as follows:

- Use of domain adaptation methods to train a LM that can flag instances of incorrect UD output from a pretrained tool not adapted to the historical domain.
- Automatic generation of a rule set from flagged differences in UD output using a domain-adapted LM trained with the masked language modeling objective. The developed rule set can be directly used to enhance a rule-based system for linguistic UD annotation.
- The domain-adapted LM improves pretrained UD annotation in the historical domain and rules suggested using this LM are best indicative of unique characteristics of the domain when compared to baseline methods, in terms of out-of-vocabulary rate and candidate rule discovery for "difficult" bigram terms.

The proposed method offers improved UD accuracy for Modern Historical Japanese corpora while also enabling useful evaluations by a domain expert. This can serve as welcome news to DH scholars who would like to make more frequent use of transformer-based NLP methods in their scholarship.

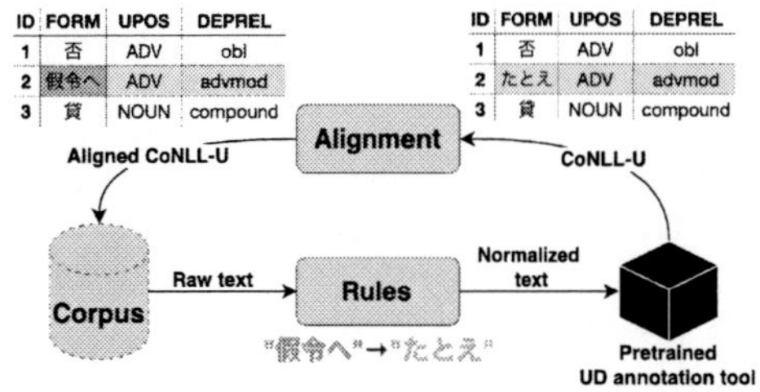

Figure 1: Overview of the rule-based expert system. In this example, the rule '假令へ'→ 'たとえ' is applied to the sentence '否假令へ貸倒れとならずとするも、'. After string replacement of the left-hand side with the right-hand side, the normalized sentence is submitted to a pretrained UD tool for annotation. The updated UD returned is then aligned with historical word forms (i.e., '假令へ') from the source text.

2 Related Work

Gururangan et al. (2020) has shown that continued pretraining of large pretrained language models using unlabeled data from the task domain yields improvements in task performance for both small and large corpus sizes. The literature is rich with proposals applying pretraining strategies in different domains (Gururangan et al., 2020; Desai et al., 2020). These methods have also been successfully applied in the case of historical texts (Manjavacas and Fonteyn, 2022; Han and Eisenstein, 2019).

Universal Dependencies (UD) is a community effort for cross-linguistic annotation of grammar (parts of speech, morphological information, and syntactic dependencies) (Nivre et al., 2020). Recent methods have been put forward for generating UD annotations using transformer-based language models, e.g., BERT and ELECTRA, as a backbone (Kondratyuk and Straka, 2019). These are also available for generating UD from Japanese text input. (Yasuoka, 2022; Matsuda et al., 2019). However, the transfer of adaptive BERT models when using these methods for the case of historical text – and specifically historical Japanese text – remains to be evaluated thoroughly.

The need for helpful evaluations of NLP-based tools is gaining traction in the DH community (McGillivray et al., 2020; Suissa et al., 2022). In the case of historical Japanese, Shirai et al. (2020) trains a combination of UDPipe and CRF++ for sequence labeling using training data made available through the labor-intensive corrections done by domain experts. To the best of our knowledge, this paper is the first to address the applicability of already pretrained tools through domain adaptation methods and the use of a pretrained neural architecture as a mechanism for enhancing an expert system that generates UD annotations for the case of Modern Historical Japanese corpora.

3 Method

3.1 Data and Model Selection

We adopt the Taiyo (太陽) magazine as a historical corpus of written Japanese published by Hakubunkan and maintained by the National Institute for Japanese Language and Linguistics (NINJAL) as part of its Corpus of Modern Japanese. Taiyo was the best-selling general interest magazine during the Meiji (明治) and Taisho (大正) periods (1895-1925) and contains 3400 documents written by 1000 different writers. The magazine saw significant changes in literary and colloquial writing during this period where both styles can coexist within the same article (Maekawa, 2006). Taiyo is made available without any linguistic metadata and, therefore, obtaining ground truth UD annotations for the corpus is not possible.[1]

For application of domain adaptation methods, we reference the Balanced Corpus of Contemporary Japanese (BCCWJ), a large corpus of contemporary written Japanese and Japan's first 100 million words balanced corpus (Maekawa et al., 2014).[2] UD-Japanese-BCCWJ r2.8 is a UD resource curated from BCCWJ and contains UD annotations from the core (edited) portion of BCCWJ (1980 documents; 57K sentences) (Asahara et al., 2018). To augment the labeled data available, we incorporate UD-Japanese-GSD, another UD Japanese resource from Google Universal Dependency Treebanks v2.0 (Asahara et al., 2018). Finally, for evaluation of our methods against the Modern Historical Japanese domain, we appeal to the UD-Japanese-Modern treebank, a small UD annotation corpus based on samples from the Meiroku Zasshi corpus in NINJAL's Corpus of Modern Japanese where Taiyo is also sourced from (822 labeled sentences) (Asahara et al., 2018).[3]

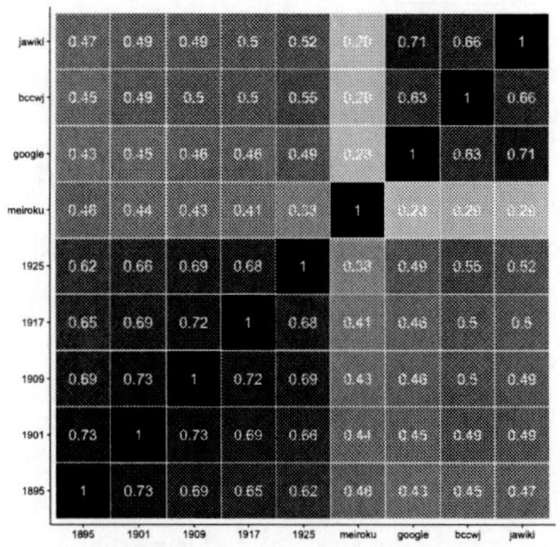

Figure 2: Heatmap matrix showing similarity between data sampled from target and pretraining domains. Similarity is defined as the percentage overlap in the top 10K words gathered from each sample. Texts are tokenized with MeCab initialized using UniDic for Modern Literary Japanese (Ogiso et al., 2013). '1895', '1901', '1917', and '1925' refer to publication year of texts sourced from Taiyo. The other samples compared with here: 'meiroku' (from Meiroku Zasshi), 'google' (from UD Japanese GSD), 'bccwj' (from UD Japanese BCCWJ), and 'jawiki' (from Japanese Wikipedia).

Pretrained models that generate Japanese UD annotations are selected based on the pretraining data used and if a significant difference in the vocabulary is observed between the pretraining domain and the Modern Historical Japanese domain.[4] This is also done in expectation of workflows in production where only a pretrained tool trained strictly on contemporary text is available. These models: (1) GiNZA (5.1.0), an ELECTRA-based model pretrained on large web crawl of Japanese text and UD Japanese BCCWJ r2.8 (Matsuda et al., 2019), and (2) esupar (1.1.5), a BERT-based model for UPOS prediction that also trains a BiLSTM with deep biaffine attention for dependency parsing (Yasuoka, 2022). esupar can be initialized using different models and we select KoichiYasuoka/bert-base-japanese-char-extended that is pretrained on Japanese Wikipedia. Figure 2 shows a heatmap quantifying vocabulary similarity in the selected domains by comparing overlap in the top 10K words from samples collected in each domain. Low similarity observed between Taiyo and pretraining do-

[1]Due to the presence of copyrighted text, the Taiyo corpus is not publicly available and obtaining the entire contents is possible only through DVD (CD-ROM) purchase through NINJAL.

[2]The OW, OB, OM, and OL registers have the longest coverage in the corpus, spanning 30 years from 1976-2005. DVD (CD-ROM) purchase is also required for access due to copyrighted articles.

[3]More specifically, the Meiroku Zasshin samples in the UD-Japanese-Modern resource are sourced from *CHJ Meiji / Taishō Era Series I: Magazines.*

[4]For the case of Japanese, several pretrained BERT models exist where the pretraining data used is similar to the historical domain where Taiyo is sourced form. However, for the purposes of the research questions forwarded here, we do not include said models here.

Corpus	UD Labels?	Domain Tuning	Task-specific Training	Rule Set Generation
Taiyo		✓		✓
UD-Japanese-BCCWJ	✓	✓	✓	
UD-Japanese-GSD	✓	✓	✓	
UD-Japanese-Modern	✓			

Table 1: Overview of the corpora used at each phase in the workflow.

mains offer credence to domain adaptation methods for this kind of data.

3.2 Workflow

We develop a domain-adapted LM that can predict accurate UD in the Modern Historical Japanese domain by employing pretraining methods that can enable transfer between disparate domains. We base our approach on the training steps proposed in Han and Eisenstein (2019) and treat Taiyo as a *target* corpus of unlabeled data, and UD-Japanese-BCCWJ and UD-Japanese-GSD as labeled *source* corpora. Then, following Yasuoka (2022), we train a combination of BERT and a BiLSTM-based neural biaffine network for UPOS and semantic dependency parsing prediction, respectively. The resulting domain-adapted LM is subsequently used for generating a rule set that brings improved pretrained UD annotation in the historical domain. Figure 3 presents an overview of the workflow and Table 1 shows the role of the corpora along each phase. Our code for realizing these steps are publicly available.[5]

3.2.1 Domain tuning

In this phase we fine-tune the BERT contextualized embeddings through continued pretraining on the dynamic masked language modeling (MLM) objective in the target domain. Ten random maskings are generated for each sample and, in each masking, 15% of the tokens are randomly masked as per Han and Eisenstein (2019). Three epochs are done over the masked data. We use all unlabeled training samples from the Taiyo corpus and add unlabeled samples from the training splits in UD-Japanese-BCCWJ and UD-Japanese-GSD. The maximum sequence length is set to 50 and we segment the text into chunks of this size; we find empirically that using smaller segments for this data helps drive down the training loss when compared to larger sequence lengths.

[5]`https://github.com/jerrybonnell/adapt-esupar`

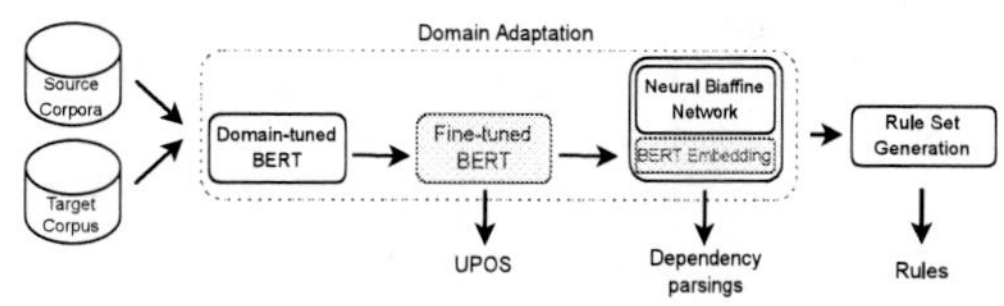

Figure 3: Component diagram showing different steps and outputs in the workflow.

3.2.2 Task-specific training

We develop two models for simultaneous prediction of UPOS and dependency parsings using the domain-tuned BERT. To learn the former we fine-tune the contextualized embeddings on the UPOS labeling objective using only labeled samples from the training splits in the source corpora; no labels from the target corpus are used during learning of the prediction model.

For learning the latter, the contextualized embeddings from the fine-tuned LM are then used as an embedding layer in a BiLSTM-based neural biaffine network for learning dependency parsings. The BiLSTM model is also trained using only labeled dependencies from the source corpora. An implicit assumption of this step is that the additional transfer of the fine-tuned contextualized embeddings to the BiLSTM-based model is useful for generating improved UD annotations in the target domain.

3.2.3 Generating a rule set using the domain-adapted LM

A domain-adapted LM that can produce accurate UD in the Modern Historical Japanese domain can be used to flag instances of inaccurate UD output generated by a pretrained LM. These flagged discrepancies provide critical regions where potential rules can be generated. Consistent with Bonnell and Ogihara (2022), we restrict our attention to differences only in the FORM field and define a rule as a mapping from a historical word form to a normalized usage such that, after rule application and submission of the normalized sentence to a pretrained system, the output FORM, UPOS, and DEPREL fields of the domain-adapted and pretrained LM become identical. Figure 4 provides an overview of this module.

We focus specifically on prediction of two-character bigrams consisting of at least one kanji character that are misclassified by a pretrained LM. Instances of this form are raised using sentences from the testing split of the Taiyo corpus. The mis-

Masked Contexts	**Masked Predictions**	**Rules**
世に立つ上に於ては何處までも**[MASK]**の點を避ける様に努めねばならぬと思ふ。	そ, こ, 此, 別, ...	之の → その*, 之の → この*, 之の → 此の, 之の → 別の, ...
世に立つ上に於ては何處までも之**[MASK]**點を避ける様に努めねばならぬと思ふ。	丶, 是, は, 二, ...	之の → 之丶*, 之の → 之是, 之の → 之は, 之の → 之二, ...

Table 2: Example flow showing candidate normalized form discovery for the flagged bigram '之の' in the context sentence '世に立つ上に於ては何處までも之の點を避ける様に努めねばならぬと思ふ。" where predicted UPOS and DEPREL for '之の' is "DET" and "det", respectively, according to ADAPT-ESUPAR. Normalized forms are candidates when, after substitution in the respective context sentences, pretrained annotation consistently aligns with the FORM, UPOS, and DEPREL fields given by ADAPT-ESUPAR for this term. Candidate normalized forms here are marked with asterisks.

classified bigram directly composes the left-hand side of the rule.

For discovery of candidate normalized forms (that then compose the right-hand side), we apply the domain-tuned BERT trained with a masked language modeling (MLM) head. We collect all contexts where the bigram appears in the Taiyo testing set and, with respect to each context, separately mask each of the two characters in the bigram and generate the top 15 predictions for the masked token.

The masked predictions are used to substitute the misclassified bigram term in its respective contexts, and are then submitted to a pretrained LM for UD annotation. Predicted terms are ranked best if, after substitution, UD supplied for the bigram in the parsed sentence consistently aligns with the domain-adapted LM annotation in terms of FORM, UPOS, and DEPREL fields. Table 2 demonstrates an example flow. The best ranked predicted terms compose a candidate normalized form list that can be further curated by a domain expert, and used to supplement and expand the rule set used to guide the rule-based expert system.

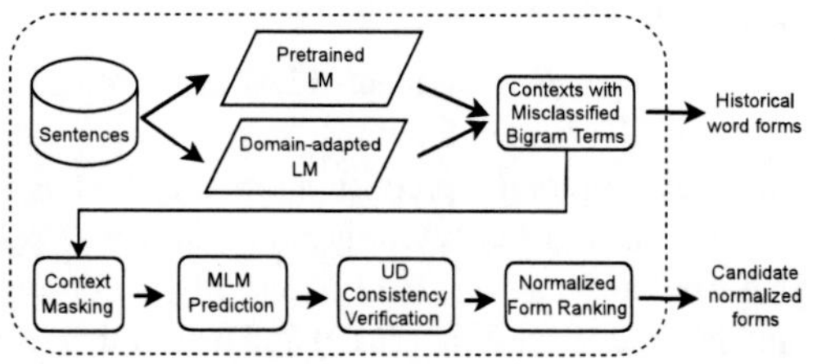

Figure 4: Flow diagram illustrating steps for rule generation using the domain-adapted LM. The goal of the module is to develop candidate normalized forms that can be used as substitutions for historical word forms. The mapping from a historical word form to some candidate normalized form composes one potential rule.

4 Evaluation

A prerequisite to using a domain-adapted LM to enrich the rule-based expert system is that it must first produce accurate UD in the target domain. Because Taiyo is unlabeled, we evaluate against ground truth labels from similar corpora in the target domain using the UD-Japanese-Modern treebank. Moreover, no canonical train-test split exists for Taiyo so we randomly partition the documents in a 75%/25% scheme (2121/707 documents) where the training set is used for domain tuning and the testing set for development of the rule set.

BERT and BiLSTM-based systems are implemented in PyTorch using the HuggingFace transformers (4.16.2) and esupar (1.1.5) libraries, respectively. Furthermore, we use the parallel shell tool for achieving speed-ups during UD annotation work (Tange, 2011). All experiments are performed on an NVIDIA Tesla P100 GPU.

4.1 Systems

We evaluate the following four systems:

- **ADAPT-ESUPAR.** This system fine-tunes the contextualized embeddings on unlabeled data from the source and target domains, and then applies task-specific training using source domain labeled data from UD-Japanese-BCCWJ and UD-Japanese-GSD.
- **FINETUNED-ESUPAR.** This baseline omits the domain tuning step and only applies task-specific training using labeled data from the source domain.
- **OMIT-ESUPAR.** This baseline *omits* any samples from the target domain. It applies domain tuning using only unlabeled data from the source domain, and task-specific training also using source domain labeled data.

- **SUB-ESUPAR.** This baseline *substitutes* all target domain samples used during domain tuning with an equal amount of unlabeled samples from the source domain collected from the non-core portion of BCCWJ. Task-specific training is then applied using source domain labeled data.

All above systems use the pretrained BERT model KoichiYasuoka/bert-base-japanese-char-extended as a starting point, the same base used for fine-tuning the default configuration used by esupar. For evaluation, we draw comparisons with the following two pre-trained UD annotation tools:

- **ESUPAR**. This pretrained tool is applied under the default setting (KoichiYasuoka/bert-base-japanese-upos), as described in Yasuoka (2022). The systems are compared against its output for flagging instances of inaccurate UD output and generating bigram rules.

- **GINZA**. This pretrained tool, as described in Matsuda et al. (2019), is used when evaluating performance on ground truth labels from the UD-Japanese-Modern treebank.

5 Results

The results we report in this section are designed to answer the questions: (1) does the use of domain adaptation bring an improvement in UD annotation for the Modern Historical Japanese domain, (2) when compared to baseline systems, do the flagged instances raised by ADAPT-ESUPAR suggest unique characteristics about the target corpus, and (3) does the application of ADAPT-ESUPAR bring the best discovery rate for potential rules in the target domain?

5.1 Improving UD annotation in the target domain

We evaluate each system against the UD-Japanese-Modern treebank using the UPOS, UAS, MLAS, LAS, and BLEX metrics defined in Zeman et al. (2018), and incorporate performance from GINZA into our results.[6] Table 3 reports F1 scores for each system.

[6]We do not report results from the baseline ESUPAR as the specification of its training data for task-specific training are not made clear and we are unable to confirm whether this treebank is used as part of any step during its training procedure.

Model	UPOS	UAS	MLAS	LAS	BLEX
ADAPT-ESUPAR	**74.04**	**71.63**	**32.76**	**51.89**	**42.95**
FINETUNED-ESUPAR	70.28	64.44	29.41	47.42	38.47
OMIT-ESUPAR	69.77	65.15	28.56	47.49	38.12
SUB-ESUPAR	68.87	63.97	28.62	47.39	38.17
GINZA	69.51	58.88	24.26	44.05	31.84

Table 3: F1 score performance on the UD-Japanese-Modern treebank. Best score on a metric is bolded.

ADAPT-ESUPAR brings the most improvement across all metrics when compared to GINZA, with a 4.53% improvement in UPOS prediction, 12.75% in UAS, 8.5% in MLAS, 7.84% in LAS, and 11.11% in BLEX. Moreover, ADAPT-ESUPAR also improves over the best performing baseline (FINETUNED-ESUPAR) with a 3.76% improvement in UPOS, 7.18% in UAS, 3.35% in MLAS, 4.47% in LAS, and 4.48% in BLEX.

We also find that smaller fine-tuned LMs can outperform larger generally-trained LMs on this treebank. We compare the systems tested against the generally trained UDify (Kondratyuk and Straka, 2019). All four systems improve on the BLEX benchmark (35.47%; 7.48% improvement from ADAPT-ESUPAR) and remain competitive across other metrics.

5.2 Flagged FORM differences in bigram prediction

We evaluate each system against ESUPAR by collecting instances where bigrams predicted by the system in the FORM field are split into denominations by ESUPAR, e.g., "夫れ" is parsed as "夫" and "れ". To quantify the importance of these discrepancies, we compare the degree of overlap in the flagged instances found for each system. Figure 5 shows the overlap in bigram parsing differences in the FORM field using a Venn diagram.

We observe heavy agreement in parsing differences among the four systems (33%). The similarity drops off considerably for any other pairing, however, there is notable agreement in the differences found by SUB-ESUPAR, FINETUNED-ESUPAR, and OMIT-ESUPAR (8%). Moreover, the diagram indicates regions that are unique to each system. SUB-ESUPAR has the largest share of these differences (9%), ADAPT-ESUPAR the second-largest (8%), and FINETUNED-ESUPAR the lowest (5%).

We explore these differences further by looking at the out-of-vocabulary (OOV) rate for bigram terms in the unique regions. We define an OOV

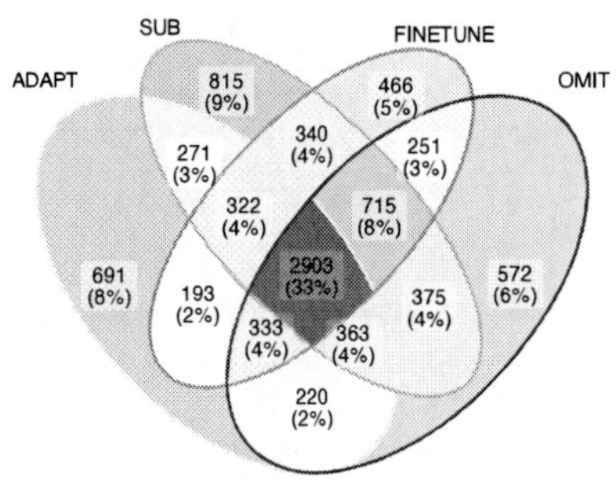

Figure 5: Venn diagram of differences in bigram parsing among the 4 tested systems. System names are abbreviated, e.g., "OMIT-ESUPAR" is shortened to "OMIT".

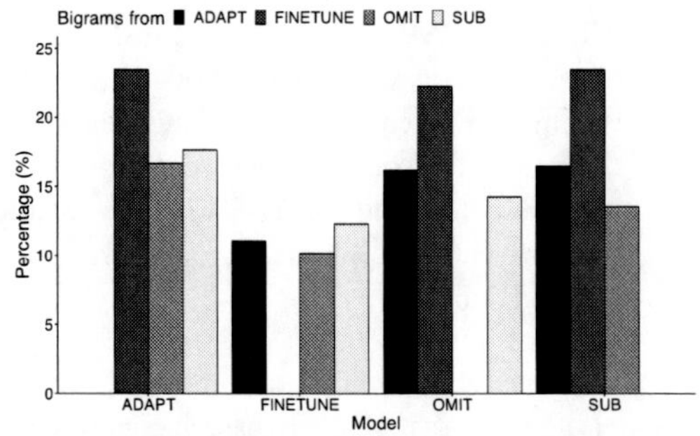

Figure 6: Bar plot showing candidate prediction success rate for "difficult" bigram terms. "Difficult" bigrams are defined as bigram terms identified by some system that do not contain any normalized forms that, according to ADAPT-ESUPAR, bring an improvement in UD annotation for that term when applied. X-axis shows the system being tested and Y-axis shows the percentage of difficult bigrams (with respect to another system) that have at least one candidate normalized form predicted by the tested system. System names are abbreviated.

term as any bigram that does not appear in the source domain training set: the concatenation of UD-Japanese-BCCWJ, UD-Japanese-GSD, and the samples collected from the non-core portion of BCCWJ. We find that for bigrams from these regions ADAPT-ESUPAR incurs the highest OOV rate (75.3%). For baseline systems, SUB-ESUPAR yields a 71.7% OOV rate, OMIT-ESUPAR 71.7%, and FINETUNED-ESUPAR 69.7%. Moreover, bigrams from the region consistent among all four systems incur the lowest OOV rate (67.8%).

5.3 Candidate normalized form discovery for difficult bigram terms

A prerequisite to rule generation is the discovery of candidate normalized forms that can serve as substitutions for bigram terms misclassified by ESUPAR. To determine whether ADAPT-ESUPAR offers the best potential for generating these candidates when compared to baseline systems, we focus specifically on bigram terms that are "difficult." Meaning, assuming that ADAPT-ESUPAR parsing is accurate, bigrams where a system is unable to produce any candidate normalized forms that, after substitution and submission to ESUPAR for annotation, align with the parsing given by ADAPT-ESUPAR for this term with respect to FORM, UPOS, and DEPREL fields. We test each of the other 3 systems on a given system's difficult bigram terms and collect the percentage of those that contain at least one candidate normalized form. In terms of the Venn diagram in Figure 5, we apply this procedure to bigrams from the consistent portion among the 4 systems. Figure 6 reports the results from this experiment.

In terms of bigrams found to be difficult, we observe systems are most successful when predicting bigrams from FINETUNED-ESUPAR (purple bars). ADAPT-ESUPAR and SUB-ESUPAR are both able to suggest candidates for 23.5% of its terms. Conversely, systems appear to have the most difficulty predicting terms from OMIT-ESUPAR (orange bars). ADAPT-ESUPAR can suggest candidates for 16.7% of its bigrams, FINETUNED-ESUPAR 10.2%, and SUB-ESUPAR 13.6%.

If performance is to be measured as a model's ability to maintain a high candidate suggestion rate while also minimizing the rate for other models to suggest candidates for its own bigrams, then ADAPT-ESUPAR exhibits strong results on this task. We find that, with respect to each model, ADAPT-ESUPAR either ties for or has the highest candidate prediction rate on the respective bigrams. Moreover, candidate prediction rate on bigrams from ADAPT-ESUPAR (black bars) is lower than the rate ADAPT-ESUPAR delivers on the bigrams from any other model. This observation does not hold for other setups.

6 Discussion

Use of domain adaptation methods. A crucial component of this research is determining whether the application of domain adaptation methods is required for discovery of candidate normalized forms that can be used for refinement of a rule-based expert system. While a large portion of the flagged differences in bigram parsing are consistent among the 4 systems tested here, we find these bigram terms incur the lowest OOV rate and, therefore, may not be best indicative of the lexical variants that are unique to the target domain. When putting this in context of rule generation, we also find that ADAPT-ESUPAR is the system that exhibits the best candidate discovery rate for difficult bigrams in this region.

It is important to highlight contributions made by our baselines. The domain tuned SUB-ESUPAR is able to flag more unique instances in bigram parsing than ADAPT-ESUPAR while only trading off a 3.6% reduction in the OOV rate incurred when compared to ADAPT-ESUPAR. It is only when domain tuning is excluded that deterioration in performance becomes apparent. FINETUNED-ESUPAR exhibits the lowest number of unique flagged instances and candidate discovery rate, and every other system finds most success when predicting its difficult bigram terms. These results are indicative of the effect of domain tuning and that any domain tuning, notwithstanding the use of target domain data in this step, is still able to bring improved performance on these tasks.

However, this result is strongly dependent on the source domain data used and the degree of overlap that exists between source and target domains. While the overlap in vocabularies between Taiyo and BCCWJ is relatively small ($\approx$50%), the overlap that does exist may present BERT an opportunity to learn useful representations about the target domain from the unlabeled source domain data. Nevertheless, the degree of difference in our results is maximized when unlabeled samples from the target domain are incorporated into domain tuning.

Enabling helpful evaluations by domain experts. The true test of the proposed workflow is the value it creates for the domain expert. The flagged instances direct attention to errors in pretrained output that may be most egregious and the suggested rules provide a mechanism for improving that output in a manner that supports both human comprehension and further manual revision. The workflow, then, offers a more principled strategy for manual labeling campaigns than by rote manual revision of pretrained output.

Indeed, the potential rules that can be suggested currently are limited by the single masked character predictions that are possible under the constraint of differences in two-character bigram tokenization. The number of flagged instances can be increased by relaxing the constraint to include predicted bigrams that should be split into denominations and formulations that involve more than two characters. In the case of the former, the current masking strategy has a direct extension.

LM refinement using the rule-based expert system. The current proposed workflow has made use of a rule-based expert system that is usefully guided by a domain-adapted LM. However, an intriguing implication of this work for the DH community is the possibility to apply the steps in the reverse: using the expert system as a means to inform the training of a pretrained LM. Because the output of the expert system is capable of bringing improved UD annotation in the target domain, its output can serve as a means for obtaining accurate labeled target domain data that can then be used for supervised task-specific training. This can serve as an additional means for obtaining improved UD annotation in the target domain while enabling the process to be driven by the domain expert.[7]

7 Conclusion

This paper demonstrates the use of domain adaptation methods for bringing improved UD annotation in the Modern Historical Japanese domain. It incorporates a domain-adapted LM into a workflow designed to enable evaluation by domain experts. Features salient to this workflow: the domain-adapted LM is deployed to flag instances of incorrect pretrained UD output and these are then used to form rules that, when applied, improve annotation accuracy in these contexts. The rules can be used to supplement and enrich a rule-based expert system.

Our experiments indicate that domain adaptation is a necessary step to enable flagging of incorrect UD output and generation of candidate normalized forms that can be used to build a rule set. However, we find that the choice of source domain data used for domain adaptation is significant, especially when there exists considerable similarity between data sampled from the source and target domains. To best maximize this transfer, the source data sampled should minimize similarity with the target domain. We are interested in exploiting associations between degree of dissimilarity in domains and

[7]We recognize that fine-tuning LMs on labeled data from the target domain can cause catastrophic forgetting in labeling accuracy in the source domain (Han and Eisenstein, 2019). Because the principal concern of this research is obtaining improvement exclusively in the target domain, we consider this side effect beyond the scope of this work.

margin of improvement brought by transfer learning in the context of historical texts. Future work will also do well to explore metrics other than vocabulary overlap for quantifying this similarity.

We hope to have the proposed workflow reviewed and evaluated by domain experts in the future, and that this work can help pave the path toward greater adoption of pretrained neural architectures into scholarly workflows in DH.

8 Acknowledgements

We would like to thank the Department of Computer Science at the University of Miami for providing computational resources necessary for running the experiments in this research. We would also like to thank the reviewers for their constructive comments and feedback.

References

Masayuki Asahara, Hiroshi Kanayama, Takaaki Tanaka, Yusuke Miyao, Sumire Uematsu, Shinsuke Mori, Yuji Matsumoto, Mai Omura, and Yugo Murawaki. 2018. Universal Dependencies version 2 for Japanese. In *Proceedings of the Eleventh International Conference on Language Resources and Evaluation (LREC 2018)*, Miyazaki, Japan. European Language Resources Association (ELRA).

Christoph Aurnhammer, Iris Cuppen, Inge van de Ven, and Menno van Zaanen. 2019. Manual annotation of unsupervised models: Close and distant reading of politics on reddit. *Digital Humanities Quarterly*, 13(3).

Jerry Bonnell and Mitsunori Ogihara. 2022. Rule-based adornment of modern historical japanese corpora using accurate universal dependencies. *Digital Humanities Quarterly*, 16(4).

Shrey Desai, Cornelia Caragea, and Junyi Jessy Li. 2020. Detecting perceived emotions in hurricane disasters. In *Proceedings of the 58th Annual Meeting of the Association for Computational Linguistics*, pages 5290–5305, Online. Association for Computational Linguistics.

Suchin Gururangan, Ana Marasović, Swabha Swayamdipta, Kyle Lo, Iz Beltagy, Doug Downey, and Noah A. Smith. 2020. Don't stop pretraining: Adapt language models to domains and tasks. In *Proceedings of the 58th Annual Meeting of the Association for Computational Linguistics*, pages 8342–8360, Online. Association for Computational Linguistics.

Xiaochuang Han and Jacob Eisenstein. 2019. Unsupervised domain adaptation of contextualized embeddings for sequence labeling. In *Proceedings of the 2019 Conference on Empirical Methods in Natural Language Processing and the 9th International Joint Conference on Natural Language Processing (EMNLP-IJCNLP)*, pages 4238–4248, Hong Kong, China. Association for Computational Linguistics.

Matthew Kirschenbaum. 2007. The remaking of reading: Data mining and the digital humanities. *The National Science Foundation Symposium on Next Generation of Data Mining and Cyber-Enabled Discovery for Innovation*, 134.

Dan Kondratyuk and Milan Straka. 2019. 75 languages, 1 model: Parsing Universal Dependencies universally. In *Proceedings of the 2019 Conference on Empirical Methods in Natural Language Processing and the 9th International Joint Conference on Natural Language Processing (EMNLP-IJCNLP)*, pages 2779–2795, Hong Kong, China. Association for Computational Linguistics.

Kikuo Maekawa. 2006. Kotonoha, the Corpus Development Project of the National Institute for Japanese Language. In *Proceedings of the 13th NIJL International Symposium: Language Corpora: Their Compilation and Application*, pages 55–62.

Kikuo Maekawa, Makoto Yamazaki, Toshinobu Ogiso, Takehiko Maruyama, Hideki Ogura, Wakako Kashino, Hanae Koiso, Masaya Yamaguchi, Makiro Tanaka, and Yasuharu Den. 2014. Balanced corpus of contemporary written Japanese. *Language Resources and Evaluation*, 48(2):345–371.

Enrique Manjavacas and Lauren Fonteyn. 2022. Adapting vs. Pre-training Language Models for Historical Languages. *Journal of Data Mining & Digital Humanities*, NLP4DH.

Hiroshi Matsuda, Mai Ohmura, and Masayuki Asahara. 2019. tan tani hinshi no youhou aimaisei kaiketsu to izon kankei raberingu no douji gakushyu (simultaneous learning of ambiguity resolution and dependency labeling). *gengo shori gakkai dai 25 kai nenji taikai (The 25th Annual Meeting of the Association for Natural Language Processing)*.

Barbara McGillivray, Thierry Poibeau, and Pablo Ruiz Fabo. 2020. Digital humanities and natural language processing: "je t'aime... moi non plus". *Digital Humanities Quarterly*, 14(2).

Joakim Nivre, Marie-Catherine de Marneffe, Filip Ginter, Jan Hajič, Christopher D. Manning, Sampo Pyysalo, Sebastian Schuster, Francis Tyers, and Daniel Zeman. 2020. Universal Dependencies v2: An evergrowing multilingual treebank collection. In *Proceedings of the 12th Language Resources and Evaluation Conference*, pages 4034–4043, Marseille, France. European Language Resources Association.

Toshinobu Ogiso, Mamoru Komachi, and Yuji Matsumoto. 2013. Morphological analysis of historical japanese text. *Journal of Natural Language Processing*, 20(5):727–748.

Ryosuke Shirai, Yukio Matsumura, Toshinobu Ogiso, and Mamoru Komachi. 2020. Machine Learning-based Sentence Boundary Detection for Modern Japanese Texts. *jouhoushori gakkai ronbunshi (Information Processing Society of Japan Journal)*, 61(2):152–161.

Omri Suissa, Avshalom Elmalech, and Maayan Zhitomirsky-Geffet. 2022. Text analysis using deep neural networks in digital humanities and information science. *Journal of the Association for Information Science and Technology*, 73(2):268–287.

O. Tange. 2011. Gnu parallel - the command-line power tool. *;login: The USENIX Magazine*, 36(1):42–47.

Koichi Yasuoka. 2020. keitaiso kaisekibu no tsukegae niyoru kindai nihongo (kyuu ji kyuu kamei) no kakari uke kaiseki (dependency analysis of modern japanese (old characters and old kana) by replacing the morphological analysis department). Technical Report 3, jouhoushori gakkai (Information Processing Society of Japan).

Koichi Yasuoka. 2022. Transformers to kokugokenchou tani niyoru nihongo kakari uke kaiseki moderu no seisaku (Production of Japanese dependency analysis model by Transformers and National Institute for Japanese Language and Linguistics). *IPSJ SIG Technical Report*, 2022-CH-128(7):1–8.

Daniel Zeman, Jan Hajič, Martin Popel, Martin Potthast, Milan Straka, Filip Ginter, Joakim Nivre, and Slav Petrov. 2018. CoNLL 2018 shared task: Multilingual parsing from raw text to Universal Dependencies. In *Proceedings of the CoNLL 2018 Shared Task: Multilingual Parsing from Raw Text to Universal Dependencies*, pages 1–21, Brussels, Belgium. Association for Computational Linguistics.

Every picture tells a story: Image-grounded controllable stylistic story generation

Holy Lovenia*, **Bryan Wilie***, **Romain Barraud***,
Samuel Cahyawijaya, **Willy Chung**, **Pascale Fung**
Center for Artificial Intelligence Research (CAiRE)
The Hong Kong University of Science and Technology
(hlovenia, bwilie, rmbarraud)@connect.ust.hk

Abstract

Generating a short story out of an image is arduous. Unlike image captioning, story generation from an image poses multiple challenges: preserving the story coherence, appropriately assessing the quality of the story, steering the generated story into a certain style, and addressing the scarcity of image-story pair reference datasets limiting supervision during training. In this work, we introduce Plug-and-Play Story Teller (PPST) and improve image-to-story generation by: 1) alleviating the data scarcity problem by incorporating large pre-trained models, namely CLIP and GPT-2, to facilitate a fluent image-to-text generation with minimal supervision, and 2) enabling a more style-relevant generation by incorporating stylistic adapters to control the story generation. We conduct image-to-story generation experiments with non-styled, romance-styled, and action-styled PPST approaches and compare our generated stories with those of previous work over three aspects, i.e., story coherence, image-story relevance, and style fitness, using both automatic and human evaluation. The results show that PPST improves story coherence and has better image-story relevance, but has yet to be adequately stylistic.

Seawake on the top of the top, swimming on the bottom of the ocean. Surfing the body of the waves, he continues to descend, but there are still waves in the waves that are rising above the ocean, making waves rise higher up the ocean body, increasing waves are rising perpendicularly along the

Figure 1: A story generated by action-styled PPST. Green denotes the words associated with the image. **Blue** denotes the words associated with the style.

1 Introduction

Enabling machine-generated stories based on visual cues opens up promising directions, and leads language models (LMs) to be viewed as an interface, allowing its involvement in artistic tasks such as advertisement creation and AI-generated movie scripting (McIntyre and Lapata, 2009; Ji et al., 2022; Xu et al., 2019; Hao et al., 2022).

In that direction, vision-language understanding and generation works succeed in leveraging image as well as text as cross-modal knowledge to solve various tasks (Kafle et al., 2019; Zhou et al., 2020; Yu et al., 2021). One fundamental task, image captioning, which involves the model to generate an informative textual caption according to a given image, opens up a venue for creativity to be explored. Humans can compose concise descriptions of pictures by focusing on what they find important. Mao et al. (2015); Xia et al. (2021); Mokady et al. (2021); Radford et al. (2021) lay a solid foundation on the current capability of machine learning models to relay cross-modal knowledge for the language models to do generation out of images. Beyond generating captions, creating stories–which utilize linguistics to compose and narrate an interrelated series of events (Li et al., 2018; Peng et al., 2018; Chandu et al., 2019)–according to a single input image offers even possibilities for creativity-based tasks (Wang et al., 2020b; Yang et al., 2019; Hsu et al., 2018).

From the recent advancement on the image-to-story task, it is evident that multiple challenges still remain to be properly solved. One of the main challenges is that model-generated stories tend to lose their coherence as their length increases. Further-

*The authors contributed equally to this work.

Proceedings of the 6th LaTeCH-CLfL Workshop, pages 40–52
October 16, 2022.

more, the generated text needs to go beyond the pure description of an image as captioning does. Data scarcity, in this context the lack of ready-to-use datasets of image associated with a short story, is also a challenge. Lastly, to the best of our knowledge, there is still limited control over generated stories aside from their relevance to the corresponding image, especially with regards to style (Alabdulkarim et al., 2021). Style has a role to convey a message or story through certain variations of diction and ways of delivery appropriate for a specific context (Ficler and Goldberg, 2017; Shen et al., 2017; Rishes et al., 2013).

In this work, we introduce Plug-and-Play Story Teller (PPST). We take a step towards generating a stylistic story from an image while alleviating the data scarcity issue by leveraging large pre-trained models such as CLIP (Radford et al., 2021) and GPT-2 (Radford et al., 2019), and to add the possibility to control the rendered style through plug-and-play adapters, explored in (Madotto et al., 2020) and (Radford et al., 2021). PPST yields improved natural and on-topic stories, and the resulting stylistic stories also have a strong image-story relevance. Our results highlight the performance of PPST, especially in story coherence and image-story relevance, improving the previous state-of-the-art performance. Lastly, we provide an analysis on the generated stories, including the occurring issues such as repetition and lack of common sense. We present an example of our generated stories using PPST in Figure 1.

2 Related work

2.1 Vision-language generation

In vision-language generation, we exploit both image and text as cross-modal knowledge to address various tasks. Taking on the fact that humans can prepare concise descriptions of pictures by focusing on what they find important, Mao et al. (2015) explore this direction by developing a multimodal recurrent neural network model (RNN) to generate novel image captions. Xia et al. (2021) build a method of cross-modal generative pre-training for text-to-image caption generators through multiple generation tasks. Huang et al. (2019) build an Attention on Attention (AoA) module, which extends conventional attention mechanisms to determine the relevance between attention results and queries. In the encoder, AoA helps to rectify model relationships among different objects in the image; in the decoder, AoA filters out irrelevant attention results and keeps only the useful ones.

Further, Pan et al. (2020) introduce a unified X-Linear attention block, that fully employs bilinear pooling to selectively capitalize on visual information or perform multimodal reasoning to leverage high order intra- and inter-modal interactions. Cornia et al. (2020) build a meshed transformer with memory architecture that improves both the image encoding and the language generation steps. It explores a multi-level representation of the relationships between image regions integrating learned a priori knowledge, and uses a mesh-like connectivity at decoding stage to exploit low- and high-level features. Mokady et al. (2021) show the effectivity of the encoding from a recent advancement on vision-language pre-training approach, CLIP (Radford et al., 2021) encoding as a prefix to the caption for image captioning.

2.2 Modeling on low-resource data

Modeling on low-resource data tends to lead to overfitting, which results in non-robust and overly-specific models. This problem is often solved by using augmentation methods. Different augmentation methods and toolkits for various data formats have been developed to better regularize models and increase robustness (Perez and Wang, 2017; Park et al., 2019; Dhole et al., 2021; Lovenia et al., 2022).

With the rise of large pre-trained models, astonishing progress has been made for handling low-resource data. Large pre-trained models, such as BERT (Devlin et al., 2019), GPT2 (Radford et al., 2019), and CLIP (Radford et al., 2021) have shown to be effective for handling multiple low-resource tasks (Wilie et al., 2020; Cahyawijaya et al., 2021; Winata et al., 2022, 2021). The labelled data for image-to-story task is also scarce, hence we extend these large pre-trained models to allow a more robust image-to-story generation.

2.3 Image-grounded story generation

In the image-grounded story generation task (Rameshkumar and Bailey, 2020; Wang et al., 2020a, 2018; Concepción et al., 2016; Ferraro et al., 2019; Mitchell et al., 2018; Min et al., 2021), the widely adopted pipeline includes: 1) extracting captions from an image, 2) encoding the caption, 3) altering the caption with pre-trained encoded stories, and 4) decoding the resulting story. Skip-thought vectors (Kiros et al., 2015)

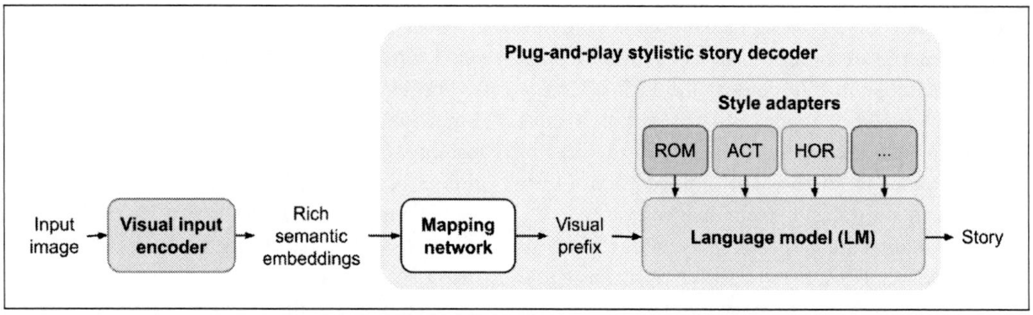

Figure 2: The inference pipeline of Plug-and-Play Story Teller (PPST) for controllable story generation based on a single image. Visual input encoder encodes the image into a rich semantic embedding, which is then projected into a fixed length visual prefix to be fed to the stylistic language model in order to generate a styled story.

and a sentence encoder-decoder have been used to build an image-to-story generator or to align books and movies (Zhu et al., 2015). Ba et al. (2016) design alternative pipelines by chaining a convolutional neural network (CNN) to extract feature and a recurrent neural network (RNN) with attention for story generation.

Other previous works have explored the use of a graph-based architecture (Wang et al., 2020b) for visual storytelling by modeling the two-level relationships on scene graphs. Yang et al. (2019) present a commonsense-driven generative model, which aims to introduce commonsense from an external knowledge base for visual storytelling. Hsu et al. (2018) propose an inter-sentence diverse beam search to produce expressive stories. One of the latest works in the field is Image2Story (Min et al., 2021), which will be further explained in §4.3.

2.4 Controllable text generation

One important aspect required in natural language generation is the control over the produced result. Recent approaches on style generation control have shown promising results. Dathathri et al. (2020) develop plug-and-play language models (PPLM), which combine a pre-trained LM with one or more simple attribute classifiers that guide text generation without any further training of the LM. Smith et al. (2020) adapt (Weston et al., 2018; Roller et al., 2021), and compare it with some of the previously mentioned approach on controlling the styles of generative models to match one among about 200 possible styles.

While Smith et al. (2020) mention that PPLM-style approach is cheaper at train time, Madotto et al. (2020) highlight its considerable computational overhead. Madotto et al. (2020) tackle this issue by developing a plug-and-play conversational model (PPCM) that uses residual adapters (Houlsby et al., 2019) and discards the need of further computation at decoding time and any fine-tuning of a large LM. At the same time, the generation result using PPCM is also more fluent and style-consistent. For this reason, we adapt PPCM to introduce style controllability into our method.

3 Plug-and-Play Story Teller (PPST)

We present the overview of our approach: Plug-and-Play Story Teller (PPST) during inference in Figure 2. To generate stories out of an image, PPST involves two main components: visual input encoder (Enc) and plug-and-play stylistic story decoder (Dec). We use two datasets: an image captioning dataset $\mathcal{D} = \{(v_i^{\mathcal{D}}, c_i^{\mathcal{D}})\}_{i=1}^{n}$, where $v^{\mathcal{D}}$ denotes image as the visual content and $c^{\mathcal{D}}$ denotes the caption with the textual description of the respective image, and a book passage collection $\mathcal{B} = \{(p_i^{\mathcal{B}}, g_i^{\mathcal{B}})\}_{i=1}^{n}$, where $p^{\mathcal{B}}$ denotes the passage chunk and $g^{\mathcal{B}}$ denotes its style (genre).

3.1 Visual input encoder

Initially, PPST needs to be able to grasp what the image depicts on a factual basis (e.g., objects, performed actions, and the implied associations) so it should have prior knowledge to develop the story on. For this purpose, we use CLIP (Radford et al., 2021), which learns and accumulates knowledge of visual concepts through a wide variety of image-sentence pairs. CLIP builds its comprehension of text-image alignment by pre-training an image encoder and a text decoder together, and employs a contrastive learning objective to maximize the cosine similarity for the correct image-sentence pairings. Leveraging the text-image alignment capability provided by CLIP, we utilize its image encoder as the visual input encoder (Enc) to produce rich semantic embeddings $\mathcal{R}^{\mathcal{E}} = \{r_i^{\mathcal{E}}\}_{i=1}^{n}$ from the images $\{v_i^{\mathcal{D}}\}_{i=1}^{n}$.

Mapping network Although Enc and Dec have been pre-trained using natural language supervision, both of them undergo the learning process separately, which leads to develop latent spaces that provide crucial knowledge but are independent from each other. Furthermore, Dec has yet to be familiar with the visual content offered by the representations generated by Enc ($\mathcal{R}^{\mathcal{E}}$). To align Dec with the latent space where $\mathcal{R}^{\mathcal{E}}$ is in, the straightforward way is to simply fine-tune Dec on $\mathcal{R}^{\mathcal{E}}$.

However, this method expands the number of parameters that Dec has and adds a notable amount of computation cost to the training process. Due to this reason, following (Mokady et al., 2021; Li and Liang, 2021), we introduce a mapping network Map to act as a bridge between the latent spaces of Enc and Dec. Using $\mathcal{R}^{\mathcal{E}}$ as its input, we train Map to produce a fixed length visual prefix $\mathcal{P}^{\mathcal{E}}$ adjusted to the latent space of Dec, so Dec can receive and understand visual information from the prefix $\mathcal{P}^{\mathcal{E}}$, making fine-tuning on $\mathcal{R}^{\mathcal{E}}$ more of an option rather than a necessity. The usage of Map in our pipeline is further explained in §3.2.

3.2 Plug-and-play stylistic story decoder

Borrowing the natural language ability that large pre-trained models possess, we utilize a pre-trained language model LM as a foundation for generating text in our story decoder Dec. Utilizing a pre-trained language model lets the generation leverage a large amount of unlabelled texts with a causal language modeling objective.

To equip our story decoder Dec with stylistic capabilities, we follow PPCM (Madotto et al., 2020) approach, by inserting residual adapters (Houlsby et al., 2019; Bapna and Firat, 2019) on top of each transformer layer of LM. The adapters act as style adapters $StyAdp = \{S_j\}_{j=1}^{m}$ which are responsible for guiding LM's text generation according to the style in use. Each adapter block S_j consists of a layer normalization (Ba et al., 2016) for efficient adaptation, followed by an auto-encoder (Hinton and Zemel, 1993) with a residual connection.

For each style from $j = 1$ to m, we first select a subset of $\mathcal{B}$ where $g_i^{\mathcal{B}}$ equals the j-th style, then

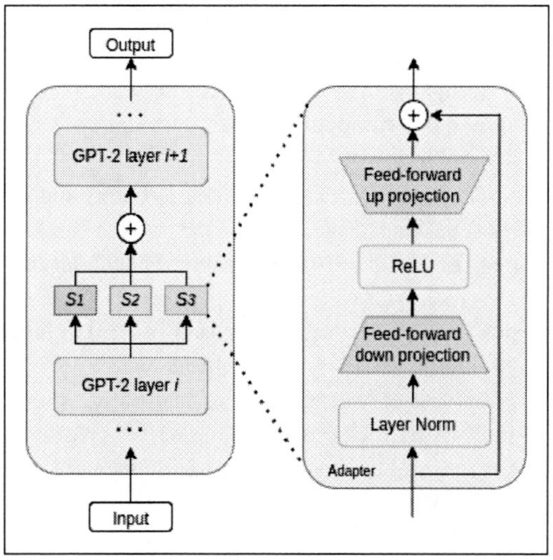

Figure 3: Architecture of our plug-and-play stylistic language model SLM using GPT-2 language model LM and style adapters $StyAdp$.

train S_j using frozen LM parameters and trainable S_j parameters on the passages in the subset $p^{\mathcal{B}_j}$. After training, the $StyAdp$ are then utilized to steer the output of the LM distribution at inference time without modifying the original weights. We refer to the LM with the trained $StyAdp$ as plug-and-play stylistic language model (SLM). The architecture of SLM is shown in Figure 3.

Without any modification, an LM is conditioned on a textual input to prompt text generation. To enable Dec to produce texts based on visual representations, we employ Map to translate $\mathcal{R}^{\mathcal{E}}$ to the input embedding space of SLM. During a forward pass, Map projects $\mathcal{R}^{\mathcal{E}}$ into fixed length visual prefixes $\mathcal{P}^{\mathcal{E}} = \{p_i^{\mathcal{E}}\}_{i=1}^{n}$ which is then fed to the Dec to perform text generation based on $\mathcal{P}^{\mathcal{E}}$. By using this pipeline, we train Map using D to allow Map to project meaningful semantic from $\mathcal{R}^{\mathcal{E}}$ into the input embedding space of LM. By combining Map and $StyAdp$, we enable SLM to ground its text generation based on a visual content under a weak supervision introduced by $\mathcal{D}$.

4 Experiment

4.1 Dataset

As described in §3, we utilize two types of datasets. The first dataset is related to images and captions. We use MS-COCO (Lin et al., 2014) as our image captioning dataset $\mathcal{D}$. MS-COCO is a large-scale 328K-image dataset commonly used for object detection, segmentation, and captioning. We use the image-caption pairs to obtain prefixes and text embeddings to train the mapping network (see §3). Due to our computing resource limitation, we utilize only 10% of MS-COCO total data.

The second dataset is related to books and genres. For the passage collection $\mathcal{B}$, we use BookCorpus (Zhu et al., 2015) to enable the adaptation of generated stories to a prompted genre. BookCorpus is a large dataset composed of 11,038 books adding up to nearly 985 millions words (1.3 millions unique words) used to train large models such as BERT (Devlin et al., 2019). We obtain the styles of the books by matching the book titles in BookCorpus with the genres in 2021 Smashwords (Bandy and Vincent, 2021) dataset. Smashwords is a dataset listing the e-books available on the Smashwords platform and recording their title, language, price, publication date, URL, and genre.

As a result, we classify the books in 16 genres: romance, fantasy, science fiction, new adult, young adult, thriller, mystery, vampires, horror, teen, adventure, literature, humor, historical, themes, and other. Finally, we split the book texts based on paragraphs, select the text chunks that consist of 30-60 words as passages, and discard the rest. The total number of passages in our dataset nears 7.7M.

4.2 Experiment setup

We use a pre-trained CLIP with Vision Transformer encoder to obtain text-image alignment representation as Enc. We note that different from the settings used in (Madotto et al., 2020), where they use open-domain generic dialogues to serve as a prefix to trigger the responses, here we use a visual prefix to trigger the generation in our experiments. Due to the difference in use case, and to enable tendency towards longer generation responses, we use a GPT-2 model instead of the proposed utilisation of DialoGPT (Zhang et al., 2020b) in (Madotto et al., 2020). In detail, as for the LM in §3.2, we utilize a pre-trained GPT-2 with 124M parameters, and employ the same model architecture and size as well for the adaptation of (Madotto et al., 2020).

We conduct the experiment using PPST with a non-stylistic setting (without style adapter), referred to as **Non-styled**, and with two stylistic settings, which are **Romance** and **Action**, since they are the styles represented by most amount of samples in the BookCorpus dataset. To filter out the samples that is strongly categorized as **Romance** and **Action**, we use the first three genres listed by BookCorpus entries to recognize those entries as **Romance** and **Action** entries.

For **Non-styled**, we utilize the same approach described in §3, but instead of using an LM guided by a style adapter, we use a regular pre-trained LM (no style adapter) LM directly fine-tuned on the book collection. We employ **Non-styled** as a comparison against the stylistic approaches in terms of a controllable story generation. For **Romance** and **Action**, fine-tuning of the GPT-2 with style adapters on the book collection data is done for a maximum of 10 epochs, with a learning rate of 1e-3, a batch size of 8, and a maximum sequence length of 512. During the training on image-sentence pairs, we only train the mapping network with a prefix size of 512, a prefix length of 10, and an activation function of `tanh`, and freeze the LM.

Our story generation employs beam search with a beam size of 5, a temperature of 0.8, and a top-k of 10. To avoid repetition, we apply a repetition penalty of 0.7 and limit any repetition of 3-gram phrases. To encourage the model to produce a longer story, we apply an exponentially decaying length penalty with a factor of 1.7 after 20 tokens and set a minimum generation length to be 750.

4.3 Baseline

We use **Image2Story** (Min et al., 2021) as our baseline. It combines an RNN and encoder-decoder structure to generate a short story out of an image. The model is built upon skip-thought encoders and structured in a 3-stage pipeline where: 1) a caption based on an input image and a skip-thought vector based on an image-caption dataset are created, 2) a skip-thought vector based on a story dataset is created, and 3) starting from the caption, the vector in 1) is subtracted and the vector in 2) is added so as to obtain a story fitted to the story dataset based on the input image.

4.4 Evaluation setup

PPST relies on visual semantics and information, so we need to ensure that they manage to extract sufficient knowledge from the input image. For this purpose, we use the original captions provided from the MS-COCO dataset as gold references representing the visual content conveyed by the input images for the text-to-text similarity metrics, and the images for the image-to-text similarity metric.

Model	ROUGE-L	ChrF++	MoverScore	BERTScore	BLEURT	BARTScore	CLIPScore
Image2Story	9.06	15.04	50.20	39.65	23.80	-4.00	59.95
PPST Non-styled	9.52	**16.81**	50.11	39.71	26.51	-4.05	61.99
PPST Romance	10.02	15.30	**51.94**	46.48	**36.70**	**-3.86**	69.02
PPST Action	**10.09**	15.28	**51.94**	**46.59**	36.69	**-3.86**	**69.21**

Table 1: Automatic evaluation results on the visual information retention in the generated stories. For image-to-text similarity, i.e., CLIPScore, we compare the generated stories directly with the corresponding images, while for text-to-text similarity metrics we use the original captions provided from the MS-COCO dataset.

Automatic evaluation We compute seven automatic evaluation metrics covering two n-gram-based text-to-text similarity metrics, i.e, ROUGE-L (Lin, 2004) and ChrF++ (Popović, 2017); four model-based text-to-text similarity metrics, i.e., MoverScore (Zhao et al., 2019), BERTScore (Zhang et al., 2020a), BLEURT (Sellam et al., 2020), and BARTScore (Yuan et al., 2021); and one image-to-text similarity metric, i.e. CLIPScore (Hessel et al., 2021). For the image-to-text similarity, we compare the text directly with the original image used for generating the story.

Human evaluation To further assess the quality of the generated stories from our system, we conduct a human evaluation in addition to computing the metrics previously mentioned. Each participant is given a questionnaire composed of 10 subsections. Each subsection has 1 image, randomly sampled from our dataset, followed by four stories respectively generated by 1) **Image2Story**, 2) our **Non-Styled** model, 3) our **Romance** model, and 4) our **Action** model. For all models, we ask if "the story makes sense" to assess story coherence, and if "there is a link between the image and the story" to assess image-story relevance. In addition, for our **Romance** and **Action** models, we ask a third question to know if "the story has the given style" to judge style fitness. The participants answer to the questions using a 5-point Likert scale with the choices: "A lot", "A little", "Neutral", "Not really", and "Not at all". The human evaluation is conducted on 13 participants.

5 Result and analysis

5.1 Image-to-story generation quality

As explained in §4.4, we utilize both automatic and human evaluation to measure the quality of the generated story of four models: 1) Min et al. (2021)'s **Image2Story**, 2) our **Non-styled**, 3) our **Romance**, and 4) our **Action**. Table 1 shows all the automatic evaluation metrics of the generated story. In general, all of our models outperform the baseline **Image2Story** in both n-gram-based text-to-text similarity, model-based text-to-text semantic similarity, and image-to-text semantic similarity metrics. More specifically, the **Romance** and **Action** models perform significantly better on semantic text-to-text and image-to-text similarity metrics by ~7% on the BERTScore, ~10% on the BLEURT, and ~8% on the CLIPScore. The **Non-styled** model performs not as good as the **Romance** and **Action** models but still yields a slightly better score compared to the **Image2Story** model in most metrics. This automatic evaluation result suggests that PPST, with and without the style adapter, can generate a better image-grounded story despite having no direct supervision for the image-to-story generation task itself.

The human evaluation result is shown in Figure 4. In terms of coherence, our evaluation result suggests that stories generated by **Non-styled** surpasses all other models, with an average rating of 3.12, followed by **Romance**, **Image2Story**, and **Action**). This suggests that pre-trained LM is sufficient to generate coherent stories without requiring tuning on the sentence-to-story generation task as incorporated in the prior work (Min et al., 2021), which shows PPST performs well despite the image-story data scarcity issue.

The relevance between the image and the story aligns with the automatic evaluation result. Our models, especially the stylistic **Romance** and **Action**, outperform the baseline **Image2Story** by a large margin, achieving a rating score 3.5 compared to only 2.77, which suggests a better text-image alignment compared to the prior work. For style fitness, we find that our **Action** model achieves an adequate style-story score of 2.78, while the **Romance** model, only obtain a romance style-story score of 1.91. We further explicate this phenomenon in §5.2.

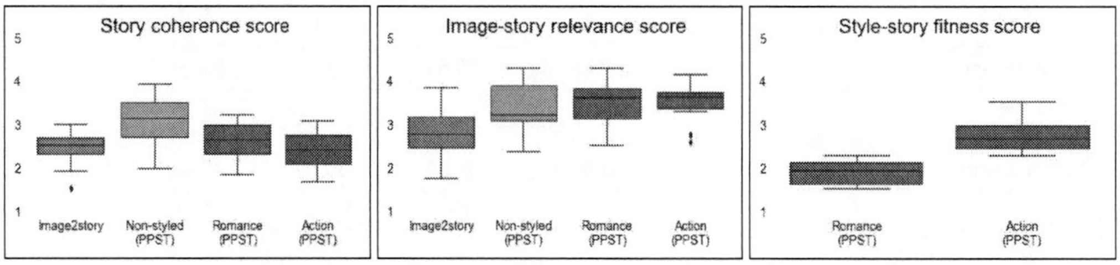

Figure 4: Human evaluations of the generated stories from all models in terms of story coherence **(left)**, image-story relevance **(middle)**, and style-story fitness **(right)**.

5.2 Analysis on the generated stories

Aside from the automatic and human evaluations, we manually inspect the stories to gather insights regarding the behaviors of our models. Table 2 provides 2 examples of our image-to-story generation. Similar to the majority of the book passages used in the training step, our generated stories are inclined to lean towards *describing* the visual aspects of the input image and slowly building the occurring events from there, which notably accounts for PPST's higher image-story relevance scores, rather than recounting a chain of events or actions in a straightforward manner as the baseline. We also find that while the surrounding contexts of our stories are relevant to the respective images, this relevance deteriorates as the stories grow longer.

Furthermore, we observe that our styled generation result can contain repetitions and tends to use a few words more often than the others. This aligns with the drawbacks of PPCM described by Madotto et al. (2020), which are mainly caused by the restricted use of vocabulary for generating attribute consistent responses. It is also mentioned that this abuse of restricted vocabulary harms fluency, because it cannot always fit within a given context. All these limitations negatively impact the coherence and fluency, therefore the overall quality of the generated stories. Finally, in spite of the proven capability of controlling the generation, the style-story score, on the right plot of Figure 4, shows that there is still potential for improvement. We leave this exploration for future work, specifically on realizing more generation control, in this case by improving the generated stories to be more related to the styles being adapted.

6 Discussions

Our works have moved image-grounded story generation forward by improving the generated story coherence and image-story relevance, and by adding a layer of style control on top of it. However, as explained in §5, the current progress still leaves room for improvement.

Story coherence Taking inspiration from recent works, a few strategies to refine story coherence can be implemented as the next step, for instance an unsupervised hierarchical story infilling (Ippolito et al., 2019), a semantic dependency skeleton generation to extract key information (Xu et al., 2018) or storyline (Yao et al., 2019), a deeper understanding of causal and temporal relations of events through commonsense knowledge (Mostafazadeh et al., 2016), the utilization of both sentence-level and discourse-level prefix information for decoding (Guan et al., 2020), and making use of a story dataset with rich and fine-grained annotations (Akoury et al., 2020).

Image-story relevance For the relevance, rather than simple embedding concatenation, other ways to incorporate visual information to textual (Liu et al., 2019) and deepen visual comprehension (Fang et al., 2015; Huang et al., 2016) can be further investigated.

Style control We also highlight the interesting directions in advancing the realization of control over stylistic story generation. Our exploration underlines the importance of improving generated stories to relate more to the styles being adapted. Improved and new approaches to control the generated stories with more specific, descriptive, even depicted by a short passage, styles will open up interesting venues on controllable text generations to assist artistic and creative tasks, whether these methods include a pre-trained model (Keskar et al., 2019; Gan et al., 2017; Hu et al., 2017) or not (Hu et al., 2022).

Image	Generated stories
	**Image2Story:** a a cat on a laptop top . Alice lay down , trying to decipher . She was a cat , too , so he did n't even know what to do . She resisted , yet she found herself wanting to keep her head on top of a computer . With every step she laid on top of a cat that had taken on as long as you could , I snapped my laptop shut . I lay on my computer , a reminder of a cat that had a job . **PPST Non-styled:** A cute cat reading a computer and a pad on a desk in a office. 'This is the best I've seen in a long while.' "I don't know how to say this, but I'm not going to let you do this to me. You're the one that's going to have to deal with me. I don **PPST Romance:** a cats pawing a tree is lying on a table. "I don't have a computer or computer monitor. I do have some photographs taken during the day. I am trying to find some time to spend together. I have been working on some photographs that show how long the cat has been sitting in the same room as the computer. Next to **PPST Action:** there is a cat on a table. and next to the table, a moving hand is used a hand. and the monitor is open. The cat is lying on the table with its legs folded up. The monitor is tilted slightly upward toward the table itself. The table itself is folded up slightly slightly from the table's edge to the floor surface.
	**Image2Story:** a a man is nothing . I was wrestling a picnic , he shouted . I had known he was going to throw his leg around my ankle , and Nate gave it to me . It s a kid , as a friend of mine . In the beginning , I realized I had been carrying her to the field and carrying him on a leash , making it all feel like a baseball game . I would practically twitch before he was responsible . **PPST Non-styled:** A human being that is having fun! It was the first time I've seen someone that I really like. I hope I'm doing the right thing. It wasn't long ago I was a stranger that someone I lost my virginity to."Well, I'm not sure, but I'm sure it's not the same. I **PPST Romance:** A person who is in the Frisbee field with two Frisbees in hand. In contrast to the frisbee riguring to catch a Frisbier. Behind them, however, there appears to be nothing unusual happening. Rather, it appears that there is little fuss that happens this year. However, nothing unusual has transpired this year **PPST Action:** A person who is in the Frisbee field with two frisbees. In the air they are holding them. Behind them stands a young man holding a frisb. They are holding Frisbees in their legs. Hands are placed over their necks to allow them to sit comfortably. They sit comfortably in their chairs to sit upright. They

Table 2: Samples of image-to-story generation result generated from **PPST Non-styled**, **PPST Romance**, and **PPST Action** against the baseline **Image2Story**.

7 Limitations

We discuss here about the limitations of our work, specifically concerning the chosen heuristic to align style and passages from BookCorpus, the limited amount of data in choice of style for the adapters, and possible biases.

As explained in section 4.1, we choose to split book texts based on paragraphs in order to retain a certain degree of logical fluency throughout each story samples, as a paragraph usually deals with a single theme or idea. While this helps keeping the passages relatively short, one limitation of this approach is that some passages might not fully reflect the style of narrative that it is classified as. For example, not every paragraph taken out of context from a romance book will exhibit its genre. There could be a sizable amount of passages that focus on world-building and laying the groundwork for the book's main plot to progress.

We decide to focus on romance and action because these styles are the most represented in the dataset used, as well as being more straightforward to capture in terms of style compared to other genres that rely on an underlying plot throughout the book such as historical or adventure. Generalizing PPST to these styles with a lower amount of resources might require further experiments.

Lastly, previous works have shown that captioning models can exhibit harmful biases, such as gender bias (Hendricks et al., 2018) and racial bias (Zhao et al., 2021). Since we pair those image captions data with written stories from a wide variety of books, those biases can be further amplified. Thus, such generative processes must be used with caution. While tackling unwanted biases in images or captions is a must, the bias exhibited in stories is sometimes justified by the context and the surrounding narrative. Not all stories should be completely neutral, and this balance should be considered carefully in future directions.

8 Conclusion

By leveraging text-image alignment representations to describe the visual content of a given image in words, we can use the resulting semantic embeddings as prior knowledge to generate a short story out of a given picture through a plug-and-play controllable language model approach. It also allows us to tackle the data scarcity issue in this task.

The results show that our Plug-and-Play Story Teller (PPST) generates more consistent and on-topic stories according to the visual information, as well as performing better in relevance and image-story relationship than the previous state-of-the-art. We also found that PPST without style adapters (**Non-styled**) generates more coherent stories, and PPST utilizing style adapters (**Romance** and **Action**) have a similar, if not a slightly better, image-story relationship than the other approaches.

References

Nader Akoury, Shufan Wang, Josh Whiting, Stephen Hood, Nanyun Peng, and Mohit Iyyer. 2020. Storium: A dataset and evaluation platform for machine-in-the-loop story generation. In *Proceedings of the 2020 Conference on Empirical Methods in Natural Language Processing (EMNLP)*, pages 6470–6484.

Amal Alabdulkarim, Siyan Li, and Xiangyu Peng. 2021. Automatic story generation: Challenges and attempts. *NAACL HLT 2021*, page 72.

Jimmy Lei Ba, Jamie Ryan Kiros, and Geoffrey E Hinton. 2016. Layer normalization. *arXiv preprint arXiv:1607.06450*.

Jack Bandy and Nicholas Vincent. 2021. Addressing "documentation debt" in machine learning research: A retrospective datasheet for bookcorpus. *arXiv preprint arXiv:2105.05241*.

Ankur Bapna and Orhan Firat. 2019. Simple, scalable adaptation for neural machine translation. In *Proceedings of the 2019 Conference on Empirical Methods in Natural Language Processing and the 9th International Joint Conference on Natural Language Processing (EMNLP-IJCNLP)*, pages 1538–1548.

Samuel Cahyawijaya, Genta Indra Winata, Bryan Wilie, Karissa Vincentio, Xiaohong Li, Adhiguna Kuncoro, Sebastian Ruder, Zhi Yuan Lim, Syafri Bahar, Masayu Khodra, Ayu Purwarianti, and Pascale Fung. 2021. IndoNLG: Benchmark and resources for evaluating Indonesian natural language generation. In *Proceedings of the 2021 Conference on Empirical Methods in Natural Language Processing*, pages 8875–8898, Online and Punta Cana, Dominican Republic. Association for Computational Linguistics.

Khyathi Chandu, Shrimai Prabhumoye, Ruslan Salakhutdinov, and Alan W Black. 2019. "my way of telling a story": Persona based grounded story generation. In *Proceedings of the Second Workshop on Storytelling*, pages 11–21.

Eugenio Concepción, Pablo Gervás, and Gonzalo Méndez. 2016. Mining knowledge in storytelling systems for narrative generation. In *Proceedings of the INLG 2016 Workshop on Computational Creativity in Natural Language Generation*, pages 41–50.

Marcella Cornia, Matteo Stefanini, Lorenzo Baraldi, and Rita Cucchiara. 2020. Meshed-memory transformer for image captioning. In *Proceedings of the IEEE/CVF conference on computer vision and pattern recognition*, pages 10578–10587.

Sumanth Dathathri, Andrea Madotto, Janice Lan, Jane Hung, Eric Frank, Piero Molino, Jason Yosinski, and Rosanne Liu. 2020. Plug and play language models: A simple approach to controlled text generation. In *International Conference on Learning Representations*.

Jacob Devlin, Ming-Wei Chang, Kenton Lee, and Kristina Toutanova. 2019. BERT: Pre-training of deep bidirectional transformers for language understanding. In *Proceedings of the 2019 Conference of the North American Chapter of the Association for Computational Linguistics: Human Language Technologies, Volume 1 (Long and Short Papers)*, pages 4171–4186, Minneapolis, Minnesota. Association for Computational Linguistics.

Kaustubh D. Dhole, Varun Gangal, Sebastian Gehrmann, Aadesh Gupta, Zhenhao Li, Saad Mahamood, Abinaya Mahendiran, Simon Mille, Ashish Srivastava, Samson Tan, Tongshuang Wu, Jascha Sohl-Dickstein, Jinho D. Choi, Eduard H. Hovy, Ondrej Dusek, Sebastian Ruder, Sajant Anand, Nagender Aneja, Rabin Banjade, Lisa Barthe, Hanna Behnke, Ian Berlot-Attwell, Connor Boyle, Caroline Brun, Marco Antonio Sobrevilla Cabezudo, Samuel Cahyawijaya, Emile Chapuis, Wanxiang Che, Mukund Choudhary, Christian Clauss, Pierre Colombo, Filip Cornell, Gautier Dagan, Mayukh

Das, Tanay Dixit, Thomas Dopierre, Paul-Alexis Dray, Suchitra Dubey, Tatiana Ekeinhor, Marco Di Giovanni, Rishabh Gupta, Rishabh Gupta, Louanes Hamla, Sang Han, Fabrice Harel-Canada, Antoine Honore, Ishan Jindal, Przemyslaw K. Joniak, Denis Kleyko, Venelin Kovatchev, and et al. 2021. Nl-augmenter: A framework for task-sensitive natural language augmentation. *CoRR*, abs/2112.02721.

Hao Fang, Saurabh Gupta, Forrest Iandola, Rupesh K Srivastava, Li Deng, Piotr Dollár, Jianfeng Gao, Xiaodong He, Margaret Mitchell, John C Platt, et al. 2015. From captions to visual concepts and back. In *Proceedings of the IEEE conference on computer vision and pattern recognition*, pages 1473–1482.

Francis Ferraro, Ting-Hao Huang, Stephanie Lukin, and Margaret Mitchell. 2019. Proceedings of the second workshop on storytelling. In *Proceedings of the Second Workshop on Storytelling*.

Jessica Ficler and Yoav Goldberg. 2017. Controlling linguistic style aspects in neural language generation. In *Proceedings of the Workshop on Stylistic Variation*, pages 94–104, Copenhagen, Denmark. Association for Computational Linguistics.

Chuang Gan, Zhe Gan, Xiaodong He, Jianfeng Gao, and Li Deng. 2017. Stylenet: Generating attractive visual captions with styles. In *Proceedings of the IEEE Conference on Computer Vision and Pattern Recognition*, pages 3137–3146.

Jian Guan, Fei Huang, Zhihao Zhao, Xiaoyan Zhu, and Minlie Huang. 2020. A knowledge-enhanced pretraining model for commonsense story generation. *Transactions of the Association for Computational Linguistics*, 8:93–108.

Yaru Hao, Haoyu Song, Li Dong, Shaohan Huang, Zewen Chi, Wenhui Wang, Shuming Ma, and Furu Wei. 2022. Language models are general-purpose interfaces. *arXiv preprint arXiv:2206.06336*.

Lisa Anne Hendricks, Kaylee Burns, Kate Saenko, Trevor Darrell, and Anna Rohrbach. 2018. Women also snowboard: Overcoming bias in captioning models. In *Proceedings of the European Conference on Computer Vision (ECCV)*, pages 771–787.

Jack Hessel, Ari Holtzman, Maxwell Forbes, Ronan Le Bras, and Yejin Choi. 2021. CLIPScore: a reference-free evaluation metric for image captioning. In *EMNLP*.

Geoffrey E Hinton and Richard Zemel. 1993. Autoencoders, minimum description length and helmholtz free energy. *Advances in neural information processing systems*, 6.

Neil Houlsby, Andrei Giurgiu, Stanislaw Jastrzebski, Bruna Morrone, Quentin De Laroussilhe, Andrea Gesmundo, Mona Attariyan, and Sylvain Gelly. 2019. Parameter-efficient transfer learning for nlp. In *International Conference on Machine Learning*, pages 2790–2799. PMLR.

Chao-Chun Hsu, Szu-Min Chen, Ming-Hsun Hsieh, and Lun-Wei Ku. 2018. Using inter-sentence diverse beam search to reduce redundancy in visual storytelling. In *First Workshop on Storytelling, NAACL 2018*.

Zhiqiang Hu, Roy Ka-Wei Lee, Charu C Aggarwal, and Aston Zhang. 2022. Text style transfer: A review and experimental evaluation. *ACM SIGKDD Explorations Newsletter*, 24(1):14–45.

Zhiting Hu, Zichao Yang, Xiaodan Liang, Ruslan Salakhutdinov, and Eric P Xing. 2017. Toward controlled generation of text. In *International conference on machine learning*, pages 1587–1596. PMLR.

Lun Huang, Wenmin Wang, Jie Chen, and Xiao-Yong Wei. 2019. Attention on attention for image captioning. In *Proceedings of the IEEE/CVF international conference on computer vision*, pages 4634–4643.

Ting-Hao Huang, Francis Ferraro, Nasrin Mostafazadeh, Ishan Misra, Aishwarya Agrawal, Jacob Devlin, Ross Girshick, Xiaodong He, Pushmeet Kohli, Dhruv Batra, et al. 2016. Visual storytelling. In *Proceedings of the 2016 Conference of the North American Chapter of the Association for Computational Linguistics: Human Language Technologies*, pages 1233–1239.

Daphne Ippolito, David Grangier, Chris Callison-Burch, and Douglas Eck. 2019. Unsupervised hierarchical story infilling. In *Proceedings of the First Workshop on Narrative Understanding*, pages 37–43, Minneapolis, Minnesota. Association for Computational Linguistics.

Ziwei Ji, Yan Xu, I Cheng, Samuel Cahyawijaya, Rita Frieske, Etsuko Ishii, Min Zeng, Andrea Madotto, Pascale Fung, et al. 2022. Vscript: Controllable script generation with audio-visual presentation. *arXiv preprint arXiv:2203.00314*.

Kushal Kafle, Robik Shrestha, and Christopher Kanan. 2019. Challenges and prospects in vision and language research. *Frontiers in Artificial Intelligence*, 2:28.

Nitish Shirish Keskar, Bryan McCann, Lav R Varshney, Caiming Xiong, and Richard Socher. 2019. Ctrl: A conditional transformer language model for controllable generation. *arXiv preprint arXiv:1909.05858*.

Ryan Kiros, Yukun Zhu, Russ R Salakhutdinov, Richard Zemel, Raquel Urtasun, Antonio Torralba, and Sanja Fidler. 2015. Skip-thought vectors. *Advances in neural information processing systems*, 28.

Xiang Lisa Li and Percy Liang. 2021. Prefix-tuning: Optimizing continuous prompts for generation. In *Proceedings of the 59th Annual Meeting of the Association for Computational Linguistics and the 11th International Joint Conference on Natural Language Processing (Volume 1: Long Papers)*, pages 4582–4597.

Zhongyang Li, Xiao Ding, and Ting Liu. 2018. Generating reasonable and diversified story ending using sequence to sequence model with adversarial training. In *Proceedings of the 27th International Conference on Computational Linguistics*, pages 1033–1043, Santa Fe, New Mexico, USA. Association for Computational Linguistics.

Chin-Yew Lin. 2004. ROUGE: A package for automatic evaluation of summaries. In *Text Summarization Branches Out*, pages 74–81, Barcelona, Spain. Association for Computational Linguistics.

Tsung-Yi Lin, Michael Maire, Serge Belongie, James Hays, Pietro Perona, Deva Ramanan, Piotr Dollár, and C Lawrence Zitnick. 2014. Microsoft coco: Common objects in context. In *European conference on computer vision*, pages 740–755. Springer.

Fenglin Liu, Yuanxin Liu, Xuancheng Ren, Xiaodong He, and Xu Sun. 2019. Aligning visual regions and textual concepts for semantic-grounded image representations. *Advances in Neural Information Processing Systems*, 32.

Holy Lovenia, Bryan Wilie, Willy Chung, Zeng Min, Samuel Cahyawijaya, Dan Su, and Pascale Fung. 2022. Clozer: Adaptable data augmentation for cloze-style reading comprehension. In *Proceedings of the 7th Workshop on Representation Learning for NLP*, pages 60–66, Dublin, Ireland. Association for Computational Linguistics.

Andrea Madotto, Etsuko Ishii, Zhaojiang Lin, Sumanth Dathathri, and Pascale Fung. 2020. Plug-and-play conversational models. In *Findings of the Association for Computational Linguistics: EMNLP 2020*, pages 2422–2433, Online. Association for Computational Linguistics.

Junhua Mao, Wei Xu, Yi Yang, Jiang Wang, Zhiheng Huang, and Alan Yuille. 2015. Deep Captioning with Multimodal Recurrent Neural Networks (m-RNN). *ICLR*.

Neil McIntyre and Mirella Lapata. 2009. Learning to tell tales: A data-driven approach to story generation. In *Proceedings of the Joint Conference of the 47th Annual Meeting of the ACL and the 4th International Joint Conference on Natural Language Processing of the AFNLP*, pages 217–225.

Kyunbok Min, Minh Dang, and Hyeonjoon Moon. 2021. Deep learning-based short story generation for an image using the encoder-decoder structure. *Digital Object Identifier 10.1109/ACCESS.2021.3104276*.

Margaret Mitchell, Ting-Hao Huang, Francis Ferraro, and Ishan Misra. 2018. Proceedings of the first workshop on storytelling. In *Proceedings of the First Workshop on Storytelling*.

Ron Mokady, Amir Hertz, and Amit H Bermano. 2021. Clipcap: Clip prefix for image captioning. *arXiv preprint arXiv:2111.09734*.

Nasrin Mostafazadeh, Alyson Grealish, Nathanael Chambers, James Allen, and Lucy Vanderwende. 2016. Caters: Causal and temporal relation scheme for semantic annotation of event structures. In *Proceedings of the Fourth Workshop on Events*, pages 51–61.

Yingwei Pan, Ting Yao, Yehao Li, and Tao Mei. 2020. X-linear attention networks for image captioning. In *Proceedings of the IEEE/CVF conference on computer vision and pattern recognition*, pages 10971–10980.

Daniel S. Park, William Chan, Yu Zhang, Chung-Cheng Chiu, Barret Zoph, Ekin Dogus Cubuk, and Quoc V. Le. 2019. Specaugment: A simple augmentation method for automatic speech recognition. In *INTERSPEECH*.

Nanyun Peng, Marjan Ghazvininejad, Jonathan May, and Kevin Knight. 2018. Towards controllable story generation. In *Proceedings of the First Workshop on Storytelling*, pages 43–49.

Luis Perez and Jason Wang. 2017. The effectiveness of data augmentation in image classification using deep learning. *arXiv preprint arXiv:1712.04621*.

Maja Popović. 2017. chrF++: words helping character n-grams. In *Proceedings of the Second Conference on Machine Translation*, pages 612–618, Copenhagen, Denmark. Association for Computational Linguistics.

Alec Radford, Jong Wook Kim, Chris Hallacy, Aditya Ramesh, Gabriel Goh, Sandhini Agarwal, Girish Sastry, Amanda Askell, Pamela Mishkin, Jack Clark, et al. 2021. Learning transferable visual models from natural language supervision. In *International Conference on Machine Learning*, pages 8748–8763. PMLR.

Alec Radford, Jeffrey Wu, Rewon Child, David Luan, Dario Amodei, Ilya Sutskever, et al. 2019. Language models are unsupervised multitask learners. *OpenAI blog*, 1(8):9.

Revanth Rameshkumar and Peter Bailey. 2020. Storytelling with dialogue: A critical role dungeons and dragons dataset. In *Proceedings of the 58th Annual Meeting of the Association for Computational Linguistics*, pages 5121–5134.

Elena Rishes, Stephanie M Lukin, David K Elson, and Marilyn A Walker. 2013. Generating different story tellings from semantic representations of narrative. In *International Conference on Interactive Digital Storytelling*, pages 192–204. Springer.

Stephen Roller, Emily Dinan, Naman Goyal, Da Ju, Mary Williamson, Yinhan Liu, Jing Xu, Myle Ott, Eric Michael Smith, Y-Lan Boureau, and Jason Weston. 2021. Recipes for building an open-domain chatbot. In *Proceedings of the 16th Conference of the European Chapter of the Association for Computational Linguistics: Main Volume*, pages 300–325, Online. Association for Computational Linguistics.

Thibault Sellam, Dipanjan Das, and Ankur Parikh. 2020. Bleurt: Learning robust metrics for text generation. In *Proceedings of the 58th Annual Meeting of the Association for Computational Linguistics*, pages 7881–7892.

Tianxiao Shen, Tao Lei, Regina Barzilay, and Tommi Jaakkola. 2017. Style transfer from non-parallel text by cross-alignment. *Advances in neural information processing systems*, 30.

Eric Michael Smith, Diana Gonzalez-Rico, Emily Dinan, and Y-Lan Boureau. 2020. Controlling style in generated dialogue. *arXiv preprint arXiv:2009.10855*.

Ruize Wang, Zhongyu Wei, Ying Cheng, Piji Li, Haijun Shan, Ji Zhang, Qi Zhang, and Xuan-Jing Huang. 2020a. Keep it consistent: Topic-aware storytelling from an image stream via iterative multi-agent communication. In *Proceedings of the 28th International Conference on Computational Linguistics*, pages 2250–2260.

Ruize Wang, Zhongyu Wei, Piji Li, Qi Zhang, and Xuanjing Huang. 2020b. Storytelling from an image stream using scene graphs. In *Proceedings of the AAAI Conference on Artificial Intelligence*, volume 34, pages 9185–9192.

Xin Wang, Wenhu Chen, Yuan-Fang Wang, and William Yang Wang. 2018. No metrics are perfect: Adversarial reward learning for visual storytelling. In *Proceedings of the 56th Annual Meeting of the Association for Computational Linguistics (Volume 1: Long Papers)*, pages 899–909.

Jason Weston, Emily Dinan, and Alexander Miller. 2018. Retrieve and refine: Improved sequence generation models for dialogue. In *Proceedings of the 2018 EMNLP Workshop SCAI: The 2nd International Workshop on Search-Oriented Conversational AI*, pages 87–92.

Bryan Wilie, Karissa Vincentio, Genta Indra Winata, Samuel Cahyawijaya, Xiaohong Li, Zhi Yuan Lim, Sidik Soleman, Rahmad Mahendra, Pascale Fung, Syafri Bahar, and Ayu Purwarianti. 2020. IndoNLU: Benchmark and resources for evaluating Indonesian natural language understanding. In *Proceedings of the 1st Conference of the Asia-Pacific Chapter of the Association for Computational Linguistics and the 10th International Joint Conference on Natural Language Processing*, pages 843–857, Suzhou, China. Association for Computational Linguistics.

Genta Indra Winata, Alham Fikri Aji, Samuel Cahyawijaya, Rahmad Mahendra, Fajri Koto, Ade Romadhony, Kemal Kurniawan, David Moeljadi, Radityo Eko Prasojo, Pascale Fung, Timothy Baldwin, Jey Han Lau, Rico Sennrich, and Sebastian Ruder. 2022. Nusax: Multilingual parallel sentiment dataset for 10 indonesian local languages.

Genta Indra Winata, Samuel Cahyawijaya, Zihan Liu, Zhaojiang Lin, Andrea Madotto, and Pascale Fung. 2021. Are multilingual models effective in code-switching? In *Proceedings of the Fifth Workshop on Computational Approaches to Linguistic Code-Switching*, pages 142–153, Online. Association for Computational Linguistics.

Qiaolin Xia, Haoyang Huang, Nan Duan, Dongdong Zhang, Lei Ji, Zhifang Sui, Edward Cui, Taroon Bharti, and Ming Zhou. 2021. Xgpt: Cross-modal generative pre-training for image captioning. In *CCF International Conference on Natural Language Processing and Chinese Computing*, pages 786–797. Springer.

Jingjing Xu, Xuancheng Ren, Yi Zhang, Qi Zeng, Xiaoyan Cai, and Xu Sun. 2018. A skeleton-based model for promoting coherence among sentences in narrative story generation. In *Proceedings of the 2018 Conference on Empirical Methods in Natural Language Processing*, pages 4306–4315, Brussels, Belgium. Association for Computational Linguistics.

Peng Xu, Chien-Sheng Wu, Andrea Madotto, and Pascale Fung. 2019. Clickbait? sensational headline generation with auto-tuned reinforcement learning. In *Proceedings of the 2019 Conference on Empirical Methods in Natural Language Processing and the 9th International Joint Conference on Natural Language Processing (EMNLP-IJCNLP)*, pages 3065–3075.

Pengcheng Yang, Fuli Luo, Peng Chen, Lei Li, Zhiyi Yin, Xiaodong He, and Xu Sun. 2019. Knowledgeable storyteller: A commonsense-driven generative model for visual storytelling. In *IJCAI*, volume 3, page 7.

Lili Yao, Nanyun Peng, Ralph Weischedel, Kevin Knight, Dongyan Zhao, and Rui Yan. 2019. Plan-and-write: Towards better automatic storytelling. In *Proceedings of the AAAI Conference on Artificial Intelligence*, volume 33, pages 7378–7385.

Tiezheng Yu, Wenliang Dai, Zihan Liu, and Pascale Fung. 2021. Vision guided generative pre-trained language models for multimodal abstractive summarization. In *Proceedings of the 2021 Conference on Empirical Methods in Natural Language Processing*, pages 3995–4007.

Weizhe Yuan, Graham Neubig, and Pengfei Liu. 2021. Bartscore: Evaluating generated text as text generation. In *Advances in Neural Information Processing Systems*, volume 34, pages 27263–27277. Curran Associates, Inc.

Tianyi Zhang, Varsha Kishore, Felix Wu, Kilian Q. Weinberger, and Yoav Artzi. 2020a. Bertscore: Evaluating text generation with bert. In *International Conference on Learning Representations*.

Yizhe Zhang, Siqi Sun, Michel Galley, Yen-Chun Chen, Chris Brockett, Xiang Gao, Jianfeng Gao, Jingjing Liu, and William B Dolan. 2020b. DIALOGPT:

Large-Scale Generative Pre-training for Conversational Response Generation. In *Proceedings of the 58th Annual Meeting of the Association for Computational Linguistics: System Demonstrations*, pages 270–278.

Dora Zhao, Angelina Wang, and Olga Russakovsky. 2021. Understanding and evaluating racial biases in image captioning. In *Proceedings of the IEEE/CVF International Conference on Computer Vision*, pages 14830–14840.

Wei Zhao, Maxime Peyrard, Fei Liu, Yang Gao, Christian M. Meyer, and Steffen Eger. 2019. Moverscore: Text generation evaluating with contextualized embeddings and earth mover distance. In *Proceedings of the 2019 Conference on Empirical Methods in Natural Language Processing*, Hong Kong, China. Association for Computational Linguistics.

Luowei Zhou, Hamid Palangi, Lei Zhang, Houdong Hu, Jason Corso, and Jianfeng Gao. 2020. Unified vision-language pre-training for image captioning and VQA. In *Proceedings of the AAAI Conference on Artificial Intelligence*, volume 34, pages 13041–13049.

Yukun Zhu, Ryan Kiros, Rich Zemel, Ruslan Salakhutdinov, Raquel Urtasun, Antonio Torralba, and Sanja Fidler. 2015. Aligning books and movies: Towards story-like visual explanations by watching movies and reading books. In *The IEEE International Conference on Computer Vision (ICCV)*.

To the Most Gracious Highness, from Your Humble Servant: Analysing Swedish 18th Century Petitions Using Text Classification

Ellinor Lindqvist[1] **Eva Pettersson**[1] **Joakim Nivre**[1,2]

[1]Uppsala University
Dept. of Linguistics and Philology
firstname.lastname@lingfil.uu.se

[2]RISE Research Institutes of Sweden
Dept. of Computer Science
joakim.nivre@ri.se

Abstract

Petitions are a rich historical source, yet they have been relatively little used in historical research. In this paper, we aim to analyse Swedish texts from around the 18th century, and petitions in particular, using automatic means of text classification. We also test how text pre-processing and different feature representations affect the result, and we examine feature importance for our main class of interest – petitions. Our experiments show that the statistical algorithms NB, RF, SVM, and kNN are indeed very able to classify different genres of historical text. Further, we find that normalisation has a positive impact on classification, and that content words are particularly informative for the traditional models. A fine-tuned BERT model, fed with normalised data, outperforms all other classification experiments with a macro average F1 score at 98.8. However, using less computationally expensive methods, including feature representation with word2vec, fastText embeddings or even TF-IDF values, with a SVM classifier also show good results for both unnormalised and normalised data. In the feature importance analysis, where we obtain the features most decisive for the classification models, we find highly relevant characteristics of the petitions, namely words expressing signs of someone inferior addressing someone superior.

1 Introduction

In many pre-modern and pre-democratic societies, ordinary people had the right to address those in power through written petitions in order to ask for help or confirmation of existing rights. Petitions usually addressed a social and economic superior, for example a court of law, a parliament, a landlord, or even the monarch (Houston, 2014). In other words – petitions allowed the powerless to speak to the powerful. Petitions are a rich historical source that could answer questions about the everyday life of ordinary people in the past. Even so, petitions have been relatively little used in historiography. For this reason, we are involved in an interdisciplinary research project at Uppsala University, funded by the Swedish Research Council, with the goal of enhancing accessibility to and knowledge of Swedish 18th century petitions, and using this source to answer questions about people's ways of supporting themselves and claiming rights in the past.[1] This project, titled "Speaking to One's Superiors: Petitions as cultural heritage and sources of knowledge", is coordinated by the Gender and Work (GaW) research project, conducted at the Department of History, Uppsala University. The GaW project studies how women and men sustained and provided for themselves in Sweden in the period from 1550 to 1800. As part of the project, thousands of historical sources have been gathered, classified and stored in a unique database that has been made accessible for researchers, students, and the general public (Fiebranz et al., 2011).

The computational linguistic part of the project aims to contribute to the field of digital philology and the development of automatised historical text analysis. In this paper, we explore computational approaches, more specifically text classification and feature importance, as means to study petitions and other historical documents. Firstly, we examine the possibility to distinguish petitions from other historical texts using different automatic classification methods. If possible, we also want to see what sort of features that characterise different genres of historical texts, and petitions in particular. Due to the noisy nature of historical data, as well as generally limited resources, we are also interested in studying how much is gained when using different variants of pre-processing methods, and how to best represent our data for a classification task. We show that the different text genres in our data set are certainly possible to classify, using both more state-of-the art and traditional methods. We also

[1]https://gaw.hist.uu.se/petitions/

Proceedings of the 6th LaTeCH-CLfL Workshop, pages 53–64
October 16, 2022.

find that our approach to feature importance analysis, where we obtain the features most decisive for some of the classification models, indeed finds highly relevant and interpretable characteristics of the petitions. As a third step, which we plan to proceed with in future work, we want to examine the possibility to distinguish different parts of the petitions. Research suggests that petitions follow a certain structure, based on a classical rhetorical division (Houston, 2014). It would be interesting to investigate how informative specific parts of the petitions are to a classification task, or where the most relevant features are placed. We hope that our work can facilitate the task of information extraction for historians and other scholars interested in studying petitions further.

2 Related Work

Text Classification (TC), the task of assigning text documents to one or more predefined categories, has traditionally been solved by using supervised learning algorithms such as Naive Bayes (NB) (McCallum et al., 1998), Random Forest (RF) (Xu et al., 2012), Support Vector Machines (SVM) (Joachims, 1998) and K-Nearest Neighbor (kNN) (Yang and Liu, 1999). TC could be implemented either topic-based, paying attention to *what* the text is about, or stylistic, being more concerned with *how* a text is written. While topic-based categorisation often uses models based on "bags of content words", style is somewhat more elusive and can include, but is not limited to, the use of function words and syntactic structures (Argamon et al., 2007). For historical texts, a common application for TC is automatic dating of documents (Niculae et al., 2014; Boldsen and Wahlberg, 2021).

As with most NLP applications, the raw data used for TC typically undergoes several steps of text pre-processing, though the best pre-processing strategy might differ depending on the data set and the TC algorithm at hand (HaCohen-Kerner et al., 2020). Fewer pre-processing steps and less need of annotation could be particularly advantageous for historical text, since its spelling variations, possible OCR-errors and limited resources of (annotated) data pose challenges for NLP tools. A common approach to tackle spelling variations is to view it as a translation task, where character-based statistical machine translation (SMT) (Pettersson et al., 2014a) and corresponding neural methods (NMT) (Tang et al., 2018) have proven to work well. Bollmann (2019) points out that while neural approaches have become popular for a variety of NLP tasks, there is no clear consensus about the state-of-the-art for the task of normalisation. To the best of our knowledge, no method yet has substantially outperformed a character SMT-based approach for historical Swedish.

An important question in TC is how to represent the documents of interest as input to the machine learning algorithms, where common techniques include bag-of-words (BOW) representation in the form of term frequencies or TF-IDF values, or distributed representations of words in the form of word embeddings (Kowsari et al., 2019), such as word2vec (Mikolov et al., 2013a,b) or fastText (Bojanowski et al., 2017). More recent, deep neural language models such as BERT (Devlin et al., 2019) produce contextualised word vectors that are sensitive to the context in which they appear. Such a pre-trained model is commonly fine-tuned to perform a specific task, such as text classification, simply by changing the final output layer. However, due to memory limitations, the maximum length for the input sequence is limited, which is problematic for long documents, although (Sun et al., 2019) have shown that state-of-the-art results can be obtained with 512 tokens, by concatenating text from the head and tail of a document. Another potential challenge when using large language models such as BERT, especially relevant for historical data, are observed instabilities when fine-tuning with small data sets (Zhang et al., 2020).

Instead of applying techniques to standardise variations in orthography, one could also develop tools that are trained on text more similar to the target data. Hengchen and Tahmasebi (2021) have released a collection of Swedish diachronic WE models trained on historical newspaper data. Their models include word2vec and fastText models, trained on 20-year time bins from 1740 to 1880, with two temporal alignment strategies: independently-trained models for post-hoc alignment, and incremental training.

As described in Section 1, the petition project seeks to use historical sources to study how ordinary people claimed their rights and what they did for a living. The latter has been approached by computational manners within the coordinating GaW project, using historical court records and church documents as a source, by implementing a verb-oriented approach to find text passages describing work activities (Pettersson et al., 2014b). This has also resulted in a web-based tool for automatic information extraction from historical text (Pettersson et al., 2). Though, to use petitions as a source of information has, to the best of our knowledge, not yet been approached by computational manners.

3 Data Collection

As part of our project, we make use of a transcribed collection of 18th century petitions submitted to the regional administration in Örebro, Sweden. In order to compare the petitions to other relevant historical documents, we select data from other genres based on the following criteria: (a) each genre should to be fairly easy to divide into smaller documents in an automatic or semi-automatic manner, (b) the selected genres, and each document within them, should be reasonably similar to the petitions in terms of size (number of tokens) and time period, and (c) the selected genres should vary in terms of similarity in content to the petitions (to the best of our knowledge), with the purpose of having some variety in challenge for the classification models. Given that transcribed historical documents are a limited resource, it is not possible to meet all criteria for every genre, though we strive to come as close as possible. Our selected genres, which will be referred to as classes from now on, can be viewed in Table 1, and is further described in the following sections. The text pre-processing procedures, including tokenisation, normalisation, lemmatisation and part-of-speech (POS) tagging, are described in Section 4.2.

3.1 Petitions

Through the project, a large volume of handwritten 18th century petitions has been scanned and made publicly accessible, and a smaller subset of the petitions have been manually transcribed by historians for refined analysis. We use this transcribed subset in our data set, which consists of petitions written in 1719 and 1782. Also, another set of petitions from another region in Sweden is used in our test set only, with the purpose of evaluating the generalisability of our classification models. This data set, which we from now on describe as "out-of-domain", is a small collection of manually transcribed petitions from Västmanland, Sweden.

3.2 Letters

The data subset of letters was collected from the Swedish Diachronic Corpus (Pettersson and Borin, 2022), available online.[2] This class contains texts written by several authors, digitised through OCR-scanning with manual post-correction. Included are the letters of military Jon Stålhammar, who wrote to his wife Sofia Drake, Pehr Wahlström's letters to a friend during a trip in the countryside, the letters of princess Anna Vasa, and a fictional letter conversation written by Karl August Tavaststjerna. Lastly, we have Sophie von Knorring's letters to her home, during a summer trip in 1846, which we use as an out-of-domain test set.

3.3 Laws

The digitised law documents are manual transcriptions provided by Fornsvenska textbanken,[3] also collected from the Swedish Diachronic Corpus. The first data subset, Sveriges Rikes Lag (Law of Swedish Kingdom) consists of two legislations: 'Giftermåls balk' (Marriged Legislation) and 'Missgiernings Balk' (Misdeed Legislation), both from 1734. The second part of the law subset is 'Regeringsformen' (The Instrument of Government) from 1809.

3.4 Parish Protocols

The Gender and Work (GaW) research project, conducted at the Department of History, Uppsala University, studies how women and men sustained and provided for themselves in Sweden in the period from 1550 to 1800 (Fiebranz et al., 2011). We use a smaller set of the GaW corpus, namely a subset of Stora Malm, which are OCR-scanned protocols of parish meetings between the years 1728 and 1812. We select protocols from the years 1728-1741 and 1784-1812 in order to better match the petition data set in terms of time period and numbers of documents. During these parish meetings, the parish's residents met to discuss common matters under the pastor's leadership. These meetings could also include some administration of justice. [4]

3.5 Court Records

We also collect a subset of manually transcribed court records from the GaW corpus. Courts in Sweden in older times dealt with a number of different

[2] https://cl.lingfil.uu.se/svediakorp/

[3] https://project2.sol.lu.se/fornsvenska

[4] https://gaw.hist.uu.se/vad-kan-jag-hitta-i-gaw/kallunderlag/stora-malm—sockenstamman/

Classes and Subsets	Period	# Docs	Train–Test	# Tokens$_{raw}$	# Tokens$_{norm}$
Petitions all	1719–1800	**119**	75/25	**34,286**	**34,302**
Petitions Örebro earlier	1719–1720	51	80/20	16,285	16,286
Petitions Örebro later	1782–1800	60	80/20	15,814	15,812
Petitions Västmanland	1758	8	0/100	2,187	2204
Letters all	1591–1893	**178**	**66/34**	**196,980**	**198,975**
Written by Anna Vasa	1591–1612	23	80/20	7,714	7.690
Written by Jon Stålhammar	1700–1708	84	80/20	49,562	51,142
Written by Pehr Wahlström	1800	17	80/20	29,538	29,536
Written by Karl August Tavaststjerna	1893	23	80/20	87,550	87,983
Written by Sophie von Knorring	1846	31	0/100	22,616	22,624
Laws all	1734–1809	**196**	80/20	**34,798**	**34,792**
Sveriges Rikes Lag	1734	76	80/20	22,709	22,703
Regeringsformen	1809	120	80/20	12,089	12,089
Parish protocols all	1728–1812	**131**	80/20	**158,585**	**160,415**
Stora Malm earlier	1728–1741	46	80/20	59,688	59,910
Stora Malm later	1784–1812	85	80/20	98,897	100,505
Court records all	1691–1771	**137**	72/28	**251,351**	**263,899**
Underåker	1691–1700	22	80/20	119,330	124,622
Åsbo	1707–1716	15	80/20	7,750	7,754
Linköping	1709–1710	86	80/20	79,869	86,794
Skellefteå	1771	14	0/100	44,402	44,729
All		**761**	**74/26**	**676,000**	**692,383**

Table 1: Overview of the data sets with information about period, number of documents, proportions of training and test data, and number of tokens: unnormalised (raw) vs. normalised.

types of cases. The court records therefore contain various types of text files, including court documents from criminal cases, accounts of and the settlement of civil disputes, as well as the handling of various administrative cases.[5] These court records are from different locations in Sweden; Underåker, Åsbo, Linköping and Skellefteå, where we use the documents from Skellefteå as our out-of-domain test set.

4 Method

4.1 Text Classification Models

We first make use of the traditional statistical algorithms NB, RF, SVM, and kNN through Scikit Learn's implementations (Pedregosa et al., 2011): MultinomialNB, RandomForestClassifier, LinearSVC, and KNeighborsClassifier. A grid-search is performed to find the optimal hyperparameter setting for each algorithm, where we run a 5-fold cross validation on a unnormalise version of our training data vectorized with TF-IDF (using a rather narrow combination of parameters to limit the search). We refer to this unnormalised data set as a raw version of our corpus. The selected hyper-parameter settings can be found in Appendix A. To further examine different manners to represent our data, we also fine-tune a pre-trained BERT model for a later experiment, described in Section 4.4.

We perform a multiclass classification with each algorithm. Even though a binary classification would be sufficient enough to explore whether the models can distinguish petitions from other historical texts, we find it interesting to also study how well other historical genres of texts are separable by automatic means.

4.2 Data Pre-Processing

Our TC experiments are run on several versions of our data set, using different amounts of pre-processing. As a baseline, we use a raw version of our data set. We experiment by adding the pre-processing steps of spelling normalisation, lemmatisation and selection of certain POS tags. The latter is done with the aim of capturing terms that are more informative. Our data set is normalised

[5] https://gaw.hist.uu.se/what-can-i-find-in-gaw/sources-in-gaw/dombocker-i-gaw/

using the SMT-based approach of Pettersson et al. (2014a), which is available as an online tool[6] (the normalised version of our data set, compared to the raw version, differs a bit in number of tokens since some non-alphanumeric characters are treated and separated differently). The annotation is done with Språkbanken's Sparv pipeline version 4.1.1 (Borin et al., 2016), including tokenisation, POS tagging using the Stanza tagger (Qi et al., 2020), trained on SUC3[7] with Talbanken_SBX_dev[8] as development set, and lemmatisation using the Saldo lexicon (Borin et al., 2013).

4.3 Topic-based vs Stylistic Classification

In order to see what types of features are the most informative to our models and how stable our predictions are, we perform both a variant of a topic-based approach and a more stylistic-like classification. A topic-based classification is covered by our approach to select only certain, more content-like POS tags, including nouns, proper nouns, adjectives, verbs, and adverbs. To perform a stylistic classification, we instead target the complement of those tags (though removing foreign words, delimiters, and cardinal and ordinal numbers) to use function words as stylometric features.

4.4 Data Representations

We also try different approaches to represent our historical texts. As a baseline, we vectorise the texts using term frequencies. First, we compare the use of term frequencies with TF-IDF scores. Second, we use a raw, unnormalised version of our data to try language models implemented for historical Swedish texts. Here, we make use of the Swedish pre-trained WEs by Hengchen and Tahmasebi (2021). We try both their Word2vec and fastText models,[9] using the incremental trained embeddings from 1740 up to the year of 1800 in order to best match our data. For these experiments, we follow the cleaning procedure described in Hengchen and Tahmasebi (2021) by lowercasing the text, removing all characters not belonging to the Swedish alphabet (including digits and punctuation marks), and removing tokens with the length of two characters or smaller. For simplicity, all out-of-vocabulary (OOV) words get a plain zero embedding. To obtain one vector for each text in our data set, we use the pre-trained word2vec and fastText to look up individual words, and average all word embeddings for each text.

As a third approach, we use language models implemented for modern Swedish texts in combination with a normalised version of our data. We work with a word2vec model[10] by Kutuzov et al. (2017), trained on the Swedish CoNLL17 corpus. We also make use of a Swedish fastText model[11] by Grave et al. (2018), trained on Wikipedia data. As before, all OOV words get a plain zero embedding, and we average the word vectors for each text to get one vector per document.

As a final text classification approach, we use a pre-trained Swedish BERT model created by KBLab (Malmsten et al., 2020), and fine-tune the model on the classification task with our (relatively small) data. We carry out the experiment in Google Colaboratory with one NVIDIA Tesla T4 GPU, and load the BERT model using HuggingFace's Transformers library (Wolf et al., 2019). Like Holmer and Jönsson (2020), we use the default PyTorch cross-entropy loss function utilised by HuggingFace's Transformers together with the hyperparameters learning rate=2e-5, and epochs=4, with an exception of the batch size, in which we use 16. The input sequence is limited to 512 tokens, so we include the 510 first tokens of each document, together with the required [CLS] and [SEP] tokens.

4.5 Feature Importance

In our second task, we aim to study the characteristics of our main class of interest - the petitions. Here, we will move in the other direction and use the method of text classification in order to extract the most important features for our class. We make use of the MultinomialNB classifier and the LinearSVC with the same settings and models that we use in Section 4.2. Through their implementation in SciKit Learn, the importance of each feature for each class is calculated and easily accessible. The feature importance scores that we use are calculated in different manners for the different classifiers. The MultinomialNB classifier uses the empirical log probability of features given a class, $P(x_i|y)$, to score the importance of each feature. The LinearSVC has the attribute coef_attribute, which assigns weights to the features for each class versus all other classes (coefficients in the primal prob-

[6]https://cl.lingfil.uu.se/histcorp/tools.html

[7]https://spraakbanken.gu.se/en/resources/suc3

[8]https://spraakbanken.gu.se/resurser/talbanken

[9]https://zenodo.org/record/4301658 (June, 2022)

[10]http://vectors.nlpl.eu/repository/ (July, 2022)

[11]https://github.com/facebookresearch/fastText/blob/master/docs/crawl-vectors.md (July, 2022)

lem). We are interested to see which features get high rankings consistently. Therefore, as a final step, we do exactly this by merging both of our ranked results. We select the top important features by examining which ones that often appear in the top ranked results throughout all approaches. We merge the rank of each feature in three steps: (1) extract the top 100 features for each approach to a sorted list, (2) calculate the average rank for each feature that appears in at least one of the sorted lists (features without a rank in a specific list will get a ranking score of 101 for that list), and (3) rank the features by their average score.

4.6 Evaluation Procedure

To evaluate the classification model performance for each class, we use precision, recall and F1 metrics. When looking at the overall performance for each classifier, including all classes, and each data representation, we use the metrics macro average F1-scores and accuracy. Macro average F1 metric computes a simple average of F1-score over classes, with equal weight to each class (Manning et al., 2008). We also perform an error analysis, where we look more closely at what types of errors the models produce. Furthermore, we evaluate how well our models are able to generalise by computing recall scores for the data sets not included in the training set (which we refer to as "out-of-domain", see Section 3). It is noteworthy that due to the limited amount of data points in these new data sets, it is difficult to draw any certain general conclusions for this type of experiment. Even so, we still include this experiment to get an indication of our models' generalisation capacity.

The result from the feature importance analysis is not quantitatively evaluated. Instead, the result is qualitatively interpreted and discussed.

5 Results and Discussion

5.1 Text Classification

The results of the text classification task for the different classes of our data set can be viewed in Table 2. As a baseline, we have here used a raw (unnormalised) version of our data set, vectorised with TF-IDF values. Though the result differs somewhat between the classes and the different TC models, we can see that all models are able to distinguish between these different classes quite well. Generally, the classes of letters, laws and petitions are easier for the models to differentiate, while parish protocols and law documents get lower scores. The differences between classes is further discussed in Section 5.1.2. Out of all the models, kNN has the overall lowest performance for this raw version of our data set, while the SVC model gets the strongest result.

Class	NB	RF	SVC	kNN
Petitions	94.7	93.8	**98.4**	76.4
Letters	**100.0**	94.8	99.2	96.7
Laws	**100.0**	92.0	**100.0**	97.5
Parish	75.4	**88.1**	82.5	76.9
Court	78.1	78.1	**83.6**	76.5
Macro avg F1	89.6	89.4	**92.7**	84.8
Accuracy all	91.3	90.3	**93.8**	87.2

Table 2: F1 scores, macro avg F1 scores and overall accuracy for raw (unnormalised) data, vectorised with TF-IDF values.

5.1.1 The Impact of Pre-Processing

To study the impact of different amounts of pre-processing, we compare the performance when feeding our classification models with different versions of our data: raw tokens, normalised tokens, normalised lemmas, and finally normalised content words (nouns, proper nouns, adjectives, verbs, and adverbs). The result in Table 3 shows that normalisation has a positive effect for the SVC and the kNN models, a modest positive impact for the NB model, while the RF model instead decreases in performance. By contrast, using normalised lemmas seems to harm the performance of all models. It may well be that errors in lemmatisation lead to these results (we did not evaluate the lemmatisation quality). The results indicate that content words are important features for all classifiers that essentially increase the models' performance, something we investigate further in Section 5.1.3. Even so, we can also conclude that the baseline results, in which we use all tokens, are quite high, and therefore imply that the classes have characteristics that sets them apart from each other. Finally, when comparing the classifiers, we see that even if kNN has the highest performance when using normalised content words, the SVC has the most consistently high results no matter the amount of pre-processing.

5.1.2 Error Analysis and Class Comparison

To study the differences between classes, we look at the recall, precision and F1-score for all classes when using one of the best performing models (the

Pre-processing	NB	RF	SVC	kNN
Raw tokens	89.6	89.4	92.7	84.8
Norm tokens	90.8	88.1	95.0	89.3
Norm lemmas	88.4	83.7	92.8	84.9
Norm content words	**91.4**	**93.7**	**96.5**	**97.0**

Table 3: Macro average F1-scores for the TC models when using different amounts of pre-processing. Normalisation is performed using an SMT-based approach described in Section 4.2.

Class	Prec	Rec	F1
Petitions	100.0	100.0	100.0
Letters	100.0	98.3	99.2
Laws	97.6	100.0	98.8
Parish	83.9	100.0	91.2
Court	100.0	87.2	93.2

Table 4: Precision, recall and F1-scores for all classes when using one of the best performing models (SVC and TF-IDF values of normalised content words)

consistently high performing SVC together with TF-IDF values of normalised content words). As can be seen in Table 4, the model makes few or no mistakes regarding petitions, letters and law documents. Parish protocols and court records are harder for the model to separate. As we can see in the precision and recall scores for these classes, the most common error for the model is to label parish protocols as court records. This is not surprising, since the parish meetings of this time period also could contain testimonies and administration of justice cases, which we write about in Section 3.4.

When it comes to the models' abilities to generalise to new data sets of petitions, law documents and court records, we use recall scores for the in-domain and out-of-domain data sets, presented in Table 5. As described in Section 3, the out-of-domain data are petitions and court records from other geographical areas, and letters written by other authors, than those seen in the training data.

We can see that the models generally are doing well for the class letters, while the results for petitions and especially court records vary considerably between the models. It is difficult to draw any safe conclusions due to very few data points in our new data sets, but the results suggest that letters of various authors have more features in common than petitions and court documents from different regions, at least for our chosen time periods.

TC	Petitions		Letters		Court	
model	ID	OOD	ID	OOD	ID	OOD
NB	100.0	62.5	100.0	100.0	100.0	21.4
RF	100.0	87.5	99.3	96.8	95.9	78.6
SVC	100.0	100.0	100.0	96.8	100.0	64.3
kNN	100.0	62.5	100.0	96.8	100.0	92.9

Table 5: Generalisability of the TC models: recall for petitions, letters and court records when using out-of-domain (OOD) and in-domain (ID) data.

Features	NB	RF	SVC	kNN
All words	88.4	83.7	92.8	84.9
Content words	**91.4**	**93.7**	**96.5**	**97.0**
Function words	68.4	76.6	83.3	69.5

Table 6: Macro average F1-scores for the TC models when using lemmas for the whole corpus, only content words, and only function words (all data normalised and lemmatised).

5.1.3 Topic-Based vs. Stylistic Classification

For this experiment, we use a normalised and lemmatised version of our data set, represented with TF-IDF values. We compare the results when using all lemmas in our data set, using only the lemmas of content words, and using only the lemmas of function words (see more in Section 4.3). As can be seen in Table 6, the best results are reached when using only content words as features. In contrast, the classification does not benefit from a stylistic approach, as using only function words harm the models.

5.1.4 The Effect of Different Data Representations

As a final experiment for our TC task, we test the performance of our models when using different types of data representation. Here, we use term frequencies as baseline, and compare it with the use of TF-IDF values, and Swedish pre-trained word2vec and fastText word embeddings. We run experiments on both a raw version and a normalised version of our data. For the raw version of our data, we use the word embedding models trained on historical Swedish texts, and for the normalised data, we use the corresponding pre-trained word embeddings trained on contemporary Swedish text (cf. Section 4.4). To reduce the comparisons, we here show the results for different data representation when using SVC, since this classifier provides the most consistently high results result. For the nor-

Using raw (unnormalised) data				
	Acc	Prec	Rec	F1
Term freq + SVC	89.2	89.4	89.9	87.9
TF-IDF + SVC	93.8	93.4	94.0	92.7
hist w2v + SVC	90.3	89.8	89.6	88.5
hist ft + SVC	94.9	93.6	94.5	93.9
Using normalised data				
Term freq + SVC	86.7	86.6	87.7	84.9
TF-IDF + SVC	95.9	95.3	95.9	95.0
modern w2v + SVC	95.9	95.1	95.1	95.1
modern ft + SVC	88.2	88.5	87.6	85.6
BERT classifier	**99.0**	**99.0**	**98.6**	**98.8**

Table 7: Comparing different data representations ran with SVC, and a fine-tuned BERT classifier. We use term frequencies, TF-IDF scores, word2vec vectors and fastText vectors for either historic or modern Swedish text, respectively. The results are presented as accuracy, and macro averaged precision, recall and F1 scores.

malised data set, we also include the results when using a pre-trained BERT model, fine-tuned for our classification task.

Even though we have a very limited amount of data, the BERT model is able to learn well from the fine-tuning, and outperforms all other data representations classified with SVC. Also, for the normalised data, both TF-IDF and word2vec representations get reasonably high scores. The use of fastText word embeddings gets one of the lowest results for the normalised data set, which is presumably explained by the fact this model is trained on a domain (Wikipedia data) relatively far from our historical data set. It is worth mentioning, though, that the BERT model may have had an advantage compared to the other models by only seeing the beginning of each text. It is possible that the first part of the documents provides the most beneficial information for a classification task, and this is a question we mean to follow up in future work.

For the raw data set, the use of historical fastText word embeddings performs the best with a F1 score at 93.9, though the use of TF-IDF values is not far behind with a F1 score at 92.7. The use of historical word2vec embeddings gets a rather low result, which is most likely explained by the number of OOV words for our data set matched with those embeddings (162,999 OOV words of the 676,000 tokens in our data set).

Top 30 features petitions
vy, vi, fõr, eder, nå, ödmjuk, nådig, hõga, baron, nådes, riddare, ûti, herr, hemman, ock, landshövding, tjänare, nåd, högvälborne, allra, jag, hög, herre, ed, kongl, ûnder, hõgvãlborne, ãr, nû, anhålla
[*we, we, for, your, grace/reach, humble, gracious, high, baron, grace, knight, in/within, mister, home, and, governor, servant, grace, "highness", the most, I, high, mister, oath, royal, under, "highness", is, now, request*]

Table 8: Top features for the petition class in Swedish (top) and with English translations (bottom).

5.2 Feature Importance

For this analysis, we will focus on the results for the class of petitions (the results for the other classes are displayed in Appendix B). We use a normalised and lemmatised version of our data set in order to get less inflected word forms and a more interpretable result. Even though the TC task benefits from only including content words (see Table 3), we here include all tokens in our data set so as not to exclude any part of speech.

As described in Section 1, writing petitions was a means for ordinary people to ask a social and economic superior for help or make complaints. This is also quite salient when inspecting the results from our feature importance experiment. Table 8 shows many tokens that express signs of someone inferior addressing someone superior (e.g. "grace", "humble", "servant", "highness"). Some of the features are redundant, since these are spelling variations of the same word (e.g. *vy/vi* 'we', *högvälborne/hõgvãlborne* 'highness') that failed to be normalised. Overall, we find that our chosen method for feature importance reveals highly relevant and interpretable characteristics of the petitions.

6 Conclusions

In this paper, we present a study of text classification and feature importance applied to historical Swedish text, with a special focus on petitions. We test the performance of both traditional and newer classification algorithms, and we examine how text pre-processing and different types of feature representation affect the result. We also analyze feature importance for our main class of interest: petitions.

The text classification results show that the statistical classification algorithms NB, RF, SVM, and kNN are indeed very able to distinguish between our different classes of historical text. We also find that pre-processing in the form of normalisation has a positive impact on the classification models, and that content words are particularly informative. Using a normalised and lemmatised version of our data set classified with an SVM classifier achieves a macro-averaged F1-score at 96.5, and only targeting content words with a kNN model pushes the score up to 97.0.

We also test how to best represent our data for a classification task. Using a more state-of-the-art method, a pre-trained BERT model, fine-tuned for our classification task and fed with a normalised version of our data set outperforms all other classification experiments with a macro average F1 score at 98.8. However, using much less computationally expensive methods with an SVM classifier also show quite good results for both a raw and a normalised version of our data set. For the raw data, using fastText embeddings, trained on historical Swedish texts, gave the best F1 score at 93.9. For the normalised data, fastText embeddings trained on contemporary Swedish resulted in a F1 score at 95.1. Even using such a simple approach as TF-IDF values in combination with an SVM classifier gave quite good results, both for the raw and normalised data set, with F1 scores at 92.7 and 95.0, respectively. We believe that this could be explained by the small amount of data used, and also that the classes in our data set have characteristics that the classifiers are able to differentiate quite effectively.

In the feature importance analysis, we make use of our text classification task and obtain the features most decisive for some of the classification models. We find that this method reveals features that are highly relevant and interpretable characteristics of the petitions, namely tokens that express signs of someone inferior addressing someone superior.

For future work, we are interested in further exploring text classification and feature importance as methods to analyse petitions. As mentioned in Section 1, research indicate that petitions follow a certain disposition. With this in mind, and given our results in this paper, we plan to investigate if petitions could be segmented by automatic means. If possible, we also want to examine where the most relevant features typically are placed. The main goal with these steps would be to facilitate and improve the task of information extraction for historians and other scholars interested in studying petitions further. Another area of improvement would be to test if other methods of classification would work better for a small, historical data set such as ours, in particular additional deep learning techniques. It would be interesting to make use of new generations of language models adapted to historical texts, if available.

References

Shlomo Argamon, Casey Whitelaw, Paul Chase, Sobhan Raj Hota, Navendu Garg, and Shlomo Levitan. 2007. Stylistic text classification using functional lexical features. *Journal of the American Society for Information Science and Technology*, 58(6):802–822.

Piotr Bojanowski, Edouard Grave, Armand Joulin, and Tomas Mikolov. 2017. Enriching word vectors with subword information. *Transactions of the association for computational linguistics*, 5:135–146.

Sidsel Boldsen and Fredrik Wahlberg. 2021. Survey and reproduction of computational approaches to dating of historical texts. In *Proceedings of the 23rd Nordic Conference on Computational Linguistics (NoDaLiDa)*, pages 145–156.

Marcel Bollmann. 2019. A large-scale comparison of historical text normalization systems. *arXiv preprint arXiv:1904.02036*.

Lars Borin, Markus Forsberg, Martin Hammarstedt, Dan Rosén, Roland Schäfer, and Anne Schumacher. 2016. Sparv: Språkbanken's corpus annotation pipeline infrastructure. In *SLTC 2016. The Sixth Swedish Language Technology Conference, Umeå University, 17-18 November, 2016.*

Lars Borin, Markus Forsberg, and Lennart Lönngren. 2013. Saldo: a touch of yin to wordnet's yang. *Language resources and evaluation*, 47(4):1191–1211.

Jacob Devlin, Ming-Wei Chang, Kenton Lee, and Kristina Toutanova. 2019. BERT: Pre-training of deep bidirectional transformers for language understanding. In *Proceedings of the 2019 Conference of the North American Chapter of the Association for Computational Linguistics: Human Language Technologies, Volume 1 (Long and Short Papers)*, pages 4171–4186.

Rosemarie Fiebranz, Erik Lindberg, Jonas Lindström, and Maria Ågren. 2011. Making verbs count: the research project 'gender and work' and its methodology. *Scandinavian Economic History Review*, 59(3):273–293.

Edouard Grave, Piotr Bojanowski, Prakhar Gupta, Armand Joulin, and Tomas Mikolov. 2018. Learning word vectors for 157 languages. In *Proceedings of the International Conference on Language Resources and Evaluation (LREC 2018)*.

Yaakov HaCohen-Kerner, Daniel Miller, and Yair Yigal. 2020. The influence of preprocessing on text classification using a bag-of-words representation. *PloS one*, 15(5):e0232525.

Simon Hengchen and Nina Tahmasebi. 2021. A collection of Swedish diachronic word embedding models trained on historical newspaper data. *Journal of Open Humanities Data*, 7(2):1–7.

Daniel Holmer and Arne Jönsson. 2020. Comparing the performance of various Swedish BERT models for classification. In *Eighth Swedish Language Technology Conference (SLTC2020). Organised by University of Gothenburgå, Sweden.*

Rab Houston. 2014. *Peasant petitions: social relations and economic life on landed estates, 1600-1850.* Springer.

Thorsten Joachims. 1998. Text categorization with support vector machines: Learning with many relevant features. In *European conference on machine learning*, pages 137–142. Springer.

Kamran Kowsari, Kiana Jafari Meimandi, Mojtaba Heidarysafa, Sanjana Mendu, Laura Barnes, and Donald Brown. 2019. Text classification algorithms: A survey. *Information*, 10(4):150.

Andrei Kutuzov, Murhaf Fares, Stephan Oepen, and Erik Velldal. 2017. Word vectors, reuse, and replicability: Towards a community repository of large-text resources. In *Proceedings of the 58th Conference on Simulation and Modelling*, pages 271–276. Linköping University Electronic Press.

Martin Malmsten, Love Börjeson, and Chris Haffenden. 2020. Playing with words at the National Library of Sweden – making a Swedish BERT.

Christopher D. Manning, Prabhakar Raghavan, and Hinrich Schütze. 2008. *Introduction to Information Retrieval.* Cambridge University Press, New York, NY, USA.

Andrew McCallum, Kamal Nigam, et al. 1998. A comparison of event models for naive bayes text classification. In *AAAI-98 workshop on learning for text categorization*, volume 752, pages 41–48. Citeseer.

Tomas Mikolov, Kai Chen, Greg Corrado, and Jeffrey Dean. 2013a. Efficient estimation of word representations in vector space. *arXiv preprint arXiv:1301.3781.*

Tomas Mikolov, Ilya Sutskever, Kai Chen, Greg S Corrado, and Jeff Dean. 2013b. Distributed representations of words and phrases and their compositionality. *Advances in neural information processing systems*, 26.

Vlad Niculae, Marcos Zampieri, Liviu P Dinu, and Alina Maria Ciobanu. 2014. Temporal text ranking and automatic dating of texts. In *Proceedings of the 14th Conference of the European Chapter of the Association for Computational Linguistics, volume 2: Short Papers*, pages 17–21.

F. Pedregosa, G. Varoquaux, A. Gramfort, V. Michel, B. Thirion, O. Grisel, M. Blondel, P. Prettenhofer, R. Weiss, V. Dubourg, J. Vanderplas, A. Passos, D. Cournapeau, M. Brucher, M. Perrot, and E. Duchesnay. 2011. Scikit-learn: Machine learning in Python. *Journal of Machine Learning Research*, 12:2825–2830.

Eva Pettersson and Lars Borin. 2022. *Swedish Diachronic Corpus*. Darja Fišer and Andreas Witt, CLARIN, Berlin: deGruyter.

Eva Pettersson, Jonas Lindström, Benny Jacobsson, and Rosemarie Fiebranz. 2. Histsearch-implementation and evaluation of a web-based tool for automatic information extraction from historical text. In *HistoInformatics@ DH*, pages 25–36.

Eva Pettersson, Beáta Megyesi, and Joakim Nivre. 2014a. A multilingual evaluation of three spelling normalisation methods for historical text. In *Proceedings of the 8th workshop on language technology for cultural heritage, social sciences, and humanities (LaTeCH)*, pages 32–41.

Eva Pettersson, Beáta Megyesi, and Joakim Nivre. 2014b. Verb phrase extraction in a historical context. In *The First Swedish National SWE-CLARIN Workshop, Swedish Language Technology Conference, 13th Nov 2014, Uppsala, Sweden.*

Peng Qi, Yuhao Zhang, Yuhui Zhang, Jason Bolton, and Christopher D. Manning. 2020. Stanza: A Python natural language processing toolkit for many human languages. In *Proceedings of the 58th Annual Meeting of the Association for Computational Linguistics: System Demonstrations*.

Chi Sun, Xipeng Qiu, Yige Xu, and Xuanjing Huang. 2019. How to fine-tune BERT for text classification? In *China national conference on Chinese computational linguistics*, pages 194–206. Springer.

Gongbo Tang, Fabienne Cap, Eva Pettersson, and Joakim Nivre. 2018. An evaluation of neural machine translation models on historical spelling normalization. In *Proceedings of the 27th International Conference on Computational Linguistics*, pages 1320–1331, Santa Fe, New Mexico, USA. Association for Computational Linguistics.

Thomas Wolf, Lysandre Debut, Victor Sanh, Julien Chaumond, Clement Delangue, Anthony Moi, Pierric Cistac, Tim Rault, Rémi Louf, Morgan Funtowicz, et al. 2019. Huggingface's transformers: State-of-the-art natural language processing. *arXiv preprint arXiv:1910.03771.*

Baoxun Xu, Xiufeng Guo, Yunming Ye, and Jiefeng Cheng. 2012. An improved random forest classifier for text categorization. *J. Comput.*, 7(12):2913–2920.

Yiming Yang and Xin Liu. 1999. A re-examination of text categorization methods. In *Proceedings of the 22nd annual international ACM SIGIR conference on Research and development in information retrieval*, pages 42–49.

Tianyi Zhang, Felix Wu, Arzoo Katiyar, Kilian Q Weinberger, and Yoav Artzi. 2020. Revisiting few-sample BERT fine-tuning. *arXiv preprint arXiv:2006.05987*.

A Hyperparameter Settings for Text Classification Task

When a random state is used, we set the seed to 11 to enable reproducible output. For all other hyperparameters, not specified here, we use the default settings.

MultinomialNB:	`alpha` = 0.5 `fit_prior` = False
RandomForestClassifier:	`bootstrap` = False `max_features` = 0.3
LinearSVC:	`C` = 5.0
KNeighborsClassifier:	`n_neighbors` = 1

Table 9: Hyperparameter settings for statistical text classification models.

B Top 30 Features for Classes Other than Petitions

Top 30 features letters
jag, du, vara, vi, gud, ha, hälsa, en, den, hjärta, väl, skriva, vÿ, kär, god, om, brev, vän, liv, skola, totus, stållhammar, vilja, fru, och, intet, att, hon, inte, han [*I, you, to be, we, God, to have, greet, one/a, it/that, hart, well, write, we(?), dear/in love, good, about, letter, friend, life, school, Totus, Stålhammar, will, wife, and, nothing/not, to/that, she, not, he*]
Top 30 features laws
eller, stånd, konung, riks, statsråd, rike, ej, man, domstol, böte, då, justitie, riksdag, äga, daler, kap, domare, sån, utskott, varda, lag, stats, miste, bo, särskild, ämbete, sätt, gälla, straffa, och [or, estate, king, national, minister, kingdom, not, one/man, court, fine, then, justice, parliament, own, daler, chapter, judge, such, committee, be/become, law, governmental, lost, live, specific/distinct, office, way/manner, apply/concern, penalise, and]
Top 30 features parish protocols
församling, att, församl, kyrka, på, socken, sexman, herr, st, sockenman, sockenstämma, pastor, uppläsa, icke, ock, person, barn, malm, år, uti, eric, per, maneck, av, gammal, ingen, sig, dr, fidem, man [*parish/assembly, to/that, parish/assembly, church, on, parish, elected representative in a parish, mister, Saint/pieces of, man of the parish/assembly, parish meeting, reverend, read, not, also, person, child, Malm, year, in/within, Eric, Per, Manech, of/off/by, old, no one, oneselfe, dr, (latin) faith, man*]
Top 30 features court records
och, ner, en, han, de, rådstuga, magistrat, där, niels, intet, borgmästare, rådman, rätt, ha, johan, 1709, sak, sal, stad, linköping, ordinarie, klingenberg, hon, 1710, samuel, pyttner, jöns, behm, här, haraldsson [*and, down, one/a, he, they/those, town hall, magistrate, there, Niels, nothing/not, mayor, district court judge, right/just/court, to have, Johan, 1709, think/matter/cause, ward, city, Linköping, ordinary, Klingenberg, she, 1710, Samuel, Pyttner, Jöns, Behm, here, Haraldsson*]

Table 10: Top features for genres other than petitions in Swedish (top) and with English translations (bottom).

Automatized Detection and Annotation for Calls to Action in Latin-American Social Media Postings

Wassiliki Siskou, Clara Giralt Mirón, Sarah Molina Raith, Miriam Butt
University of Konstanz
firstname.lastname@uni-konstanz.de

Abstract

Voter mobilization via social media has shown to be an effective tool (Savage et al., 2016). While previous research has primarily looked at how calls-to-action (CTAs) were used in Twitter messages from non-profit organizations (Guidry et al., 2014) and protest mobilization (Rogers et al., 2019), we are interested in identifying the linguistic cues used in CTAs found on Facebook and Twitter for an automatic identification of CTAs. The work is part of an on-going collaboration with researchers from political science, who are investigating CTAs in the period leading up to recent elections in three different Latin American countries. We developed a new NLP pipeline for Spanish to facilitate their work. Our pipeline annotates social media posts with a range of linguistic information and then conducts targeted searches for linguistic cues that allow for an automatic annotation and identification of relevant CTAs. By using carefully crafted and linguistically informed heuristics, our system so far achieves an F1-score of 0.85.

1 Introduction

We here report on a NLP pipeline designed to automatically identify and annotate "calls-to-action" (CTAs). We focus specifically on the mobilization of potential voters via social media as part of an on-going collaboration with partners from political science. CTAs are of interest for political science because recent years have seen social movements and political parties working with CTAs via social media as an effective tool for social mobilization (Savage et al., 2016; Guidry et al., 2014).

Guided by the interests of our project partners from political science (Haiges and Zuber, 2021), who are investigating the expression of grievances in the context of ethnic political parties, we focus on Facebook and Twitter posts leading up to the recent (2020) elections across Latin America and aim to support their research by automatically detecting and annotating CTAs. We faced several challenges in doing this. For one, we cannot build on very much previous NLP work. Although initial work has been done to identify CTAs for Russian (Rogers et al., 2019), no research had as yet been done on the linguistic expression of CTAs in Spanish. We were also faced with severe issues of data scarcity — in 31,229 social media postings contained in the corpus, only 2,542 were found to contain CTAs. In addition, the corpus collected by our partners is inherently unbalanced, as it differs across countries and elections.

As such we decided to implement a primarily rule-based NLP pipeline for the automatized detection and annotation of CTAs. Our pipeline is based on previous efforts focusing on English and German and is designed particularly to identify deep morphosyntactic, semantic and pragmatic linguistic features that are relevant for analysis at the discoursal level (Biber et al., 1998; Biber and Conrad, 2009) and for the linguistic framing of utterances (cf. Druckman's frames of communication (Druckman, 2011; Chong and Druckman, 2007)). While other studies have focused on analyzing the effects of such CTAs on voters (Heiss and Matthes, 2016; Kligler-Vilenchik et al., 2021), in this use case we are concerned with how these mobilizations are linguistically expressed. We therefore aim at automatically identifying CTAs via linguistic cues.

2 Related Work

As already noted, there is limited previous work we can build on. Guidry et al. (2014) showed that Twitter messages from non-profit organizations framed as a CTA were retweeted more often and generated more interaction between users than other messages, while they were simultaneously the least used strategy for messages. Rogers et al. (2019) worked on historical data of Bolotnaya protests (2012) in Russia to demonstrate the possibility of automatically detecting CTAs in social

Proceedings of the 6th LaTeCH-CLfL Workshop, pages 65–69
October 16, 2022. ©2022 International Conference on Computational Linguistics

media posts. Their classification task yielded an F1-score of 0.77, thus showing that CTAs in Russian can be successfully detected automatically to some degree. While their focus lies on the detection of CTAs in a protest setting, where movements use social media to mobilize people and convince them to join the protests, we are focusing on CTAs that are targeting voter mobilization.

3 Characterization of Calls to Action

Our specific use case is the analysis of social media posts published in the period leading up to an election and aimed at mobilizing voters. We therefore restricted an identification of CTAs to sentences in social media posts that directly or indirectly call upon the addressees for political participation in an election setting. Typical examples are (1) and (2).

(1) *Cumplamos nuestra responsabilidad de votar.*
'Let us fulfill our responsibility to vote.'

(2) *¡Sal a votar!* 'Get out to vote!'

(3) *Es momento de poner fin a décadas de los mismos de siempre. Llegó el momento del pueblo.*
'It is time to put an end to decades of the same old ones. The time has come for the people.'

Whereas the CTAs in the first two examples are directly encoded and expressed via an imperative, the more indirect example (3) also falls under our definition of a CTA. Here, the message to politically participate is covertly encoded and does not involve a direct use of an imperative. In order to automatically identify such indirect CTAs, it is necessary to implement linguistically informed rules (see §6). We exclude CTAs that aim at getting readers to click on a specific link, support an organization with donations or attend events or demonstrations, even though they are linguistically similarly framed as direct CTAs. This exclusion is motivated by the research interests of our partners, who are not interested in these other types of CTAs, but in voter mobilization.

4 NLP pipeline LiAnS

For the automatic detection and annotation of CTAs we used LiAnS, a rule-based NLP pipeline. LiAnS (Linguistic Annotation Service) has been built on the basis of *VisArgue* (Gold et al., 2015), a NLP pipeline initially designed for analyzing linguistic features in spoken dialogs and debates in English and German. We built a Spanish version of the pipeline in the context of the CTA project.[1] The automated linguistic feature identification in *VisArgue* is realized in a rule-based fashion: For each feature, a list of relevant cues (lexical items and constructions) is defined by language experts, and rules are created for the disambiguation according to the context they are found in. This has a clear advantage over a naive and decontextualized application of static word lists. The linguistic features covered by *VisArgue* were selected by experts of theoretical and computational linguistics and are strongly grounded in theoretical linguistic insights. We used the existing features and categories as a blueprint for the Spanish LiAnS. Carefully crafted feature sets and disambiguation rules were added to ensure the reliable annotation of CTAs.

The main workflow of LiAnS consists of two steps: 1) preprocessing; 2) annotation with prior disambiguation. We first convert the raw posts into standardized XML files, which are then further preprocessed using the *Stanza* NLP kit (Qi et al., 2020). Stanza conducts sentence splitting, tokenization and lemmatization on the input files, and adds POS-tags, morphological features and dependency relations of each token (lexeme) as XML attributes. LiAnS further adds *discourse unit splitting*. Approximating the definition of a *basic discourse unit* (Polanyi et al., 2004), each clause is defined as one discourse unit (DU), e.g., if a sentence is comprised of one matrix clause and one embedded clause, the sentence is defined as containing two DUs.

After preprocessing, rule-based annotation is applied on the basis of pre-defined disambiguation rules for linguistic features as in Table 1. By considering the position of the linguistic cue and the POS of the surrounding lexemes, we implement any ambiguity resolution that might be necessary. Annotations are initially applied to the lexemes. Based on the particular type of use cases, aggregated, context-aware feature calculation on higher levels, e.g., DU-, sentence- or document-level can be defined. LiAnS allows for a modular usage of the features, which means that users can select their own customized subset of features that are of interest to the specific use case. LiAnS will then

[1] Our Spanish pipeline is based on a refined and extended German and English LiAnS version of VisArgue, designed and built by Qi Yu and Marina Janka at the University of Konstanz.

exclusively annotate these features.[2]

5 Data

The overall corpus is still in the process of being compiled by our political science partners (Haiges and Zuber, 2021), and currently consists of around 30,000 posts on Twitter and Facebook published by political parties, indigenous associations and presidential candidates before and during the three most recent elections in Latin America, which took place in Bolivia (18 October 2020), Ecuador (7 February 2021) and Peru (11 April 2021). Table 2 shows the exact number of posts in our current corpus per country. As can be seen the data set is not only unbalanced, but also fairly small for Bolivia, motivating our rule-based approach, which is not data hungry, but instead relies on linguistic knowledge.

6 Methodology

All posts in the dataset were annotated with LiAnS using the features available for the Spanish version. To only extract DUs and sentences that thematically deal with elections from the dataset, we manually compiled a list of voting-related keywords such as *democracia* 'democracy' and *elecciones* 'elections', including their synonyms and semantically related nouns, verbs and adjectives. Corresponding DUs and sentences were then extracted.

Direct CTAs can be detected very straightforwardly based simply on the identification of imperative forms, so one easy way of proceeding is to search for instances of imperatives of verbs like *votar* 'vote' as well as the participle of *votar* 'voting'. In a further step, we searched for sentences which contain imperatives and election-related keywords from our hand-defined list. In this way, we are able to detect CTAs as in example (2). Additionally, sentences containing the election date (e.g. *este 7 de febrero*), or count downs to the election day (*faltan 5 días para*) were also considered as CTAs since they aim at reminding voters about when to exercise their right to vote.

Moving on to more indirect and emotive CTAs, we established rules that search for the noun *voto* 'vote' preceded by the pronoun *tú* 'your' or *nuestro* 'our' to identify posts that directly aimed at motivating voters through the use of more appellative expressions by directly addressing them. CTAs as in (4) are often followed by a phrase describing the expected (positive) change that may occur after voting for a specific candidate or voting in general.

(4) *Pido tu voto para...*
'I ask for your vote to...'

Furthermore, we looked for modal phrases and expressions that imply obligations and were used in combination with election-related vocabulary to identify voter-mobilization.

While the identification of direct CTAs is relatively straight-forward and can be pinned down to the use of imperatives and the different forms of the verb *votar* mainly, implicit calls to action require deeper linguistic knowledge, as their surface coding is indirect. For the annotation of implicit CTAs, we perused the dataset manually and tracked down cues that were used to frame the call without using similar formulations to those mentioned above. We found that implicit calls to action were often encoded in sentences implying that it is time *for change* (as in example (3)), *to change the future of the country, to rescue the country, to stand up for the country* or *to take the country forward*, and thus intend to bring people to the polls to actively engage in the act of change. In addition, implicit CTAs often appeal to voters' sense of *'us'* vs. *'them'*. For example, some CTAs read "*juntos + Verb*" (*'together + verb'*) and aim to create a sense of belonging to the community by giving the impression to voters that the common goals can only be achieved if they become part of this community by casting their vote for the candidate. To automatically detect those implicit CTAs we implemented rules that search for those key phrases together with election-related vocabulary and tag the posting as such.

7 Results and Discussion

A randomly selected subset of 800 Facebook and 200 Twitter posts from Ecuador was manually annotated by two Spanish speaking annotators, both co-authors of the paper, in order to evaluate the results from our NLP pipeline. We decided to evaluate on data from Ecuador, as the majority of our corpus comes from there. Out of 800 Facebook posts 156 (16 implicit and 140 explicit) and 29 (10 implicit and 19 explicit) of 200 Tweets were identified as CTAs. With the help of a more detailed analysis of the linguistic features found in CTAs we found that 49 % of them include at least one

[2] Access to the Spanish version of LiAnS and the CTA annotation can be requested via e-mail.

Dimension	Feature	Examples
Discourse Relation	adversative	*pero* (but); *al contrario* (on the contrary)
	causal	*porque* (because); *ya que* (since) ; *puesto que* (since)
	conditional	*cuando* (if); *en caso que* (in the event that)
	consecutive	*pues* (for); *consecuentemente* (consequently)
Modality	modal	*deber* (must); *querer* (want); *poder* (can)
Sentence Modifier	intensifier	*muy* (very); *de hecho* (in fact)
	negation	*no* (no); *nunca* (never) ; *jamás* (never)
Information Exchange	accommodation	AGREEMENT: *prometer* (promise); *consentir* (agree); *reconocer* (acknowledge) DISAGREEMENT: *rechazar* (reject); *disputar* (dispute); *degradar* (degrade)
	speech act	INFORMATION GIVING: *decir* (say); *aclarar* (clarify) INFORMATION SEEKING: *preguntar* (ask); *consultar* (consult)
Politeness	polite items	*por favor* (please); *gracias* (thank you)

Table 1: Available features Spanish LiAnS version. The column *Examples* provides a few examples in Spanish as they are implemented in LiAnS. Small caps indicate different subcategories within the feature.

Source	Bolivia	Peru	Ecuador
Twitter	526	1,667	4,959
Facebook	991	1,252	21,834

Table 2: Overview of data set by country and source.

imperative to mobilize voters, while 57 % contain at least one of the different forms of the verb *votar*, 40 % contain the election date, and around 10% include more indirect means of CTAs which can not be pinned down to specific linguistic features but depend more on the pragmatic context of the posting.

Based on the above mentioned subset of 1000 social media posts, our system shows an overall precision of 0.95, a recall of 0.77 and a F1-score of 0.85 for the automatic identification of CTA types. For the Twitter data, precision is 0.92, recall 0.78 and F1 0.84, while the scores for Facebook data show a precision score of 0.81, a recall 0.83 and a F1 score of 0.81. These values allow us to draw the conclusion that our system performs almost equally good across different social media platforms albeit the differing posting format used on both platforms. We attribute the differences between the manual and automatic CTA annotation to the fact that the used rules for CTA identification in our pipeline need to be further refined in order to identify certain linguistic features that are being used to mobilize voters.

An overview of our results for the automatic detection of explicit and implicit CTAs across the whole corpus is presented in Table 3. While the majority of CTAs are formulated as imperatives and were thus identified based on their morphology, a portion of the voter mobilizations were identified by the LiAnS feature *modal*, specifically the subcategory of *obligation*. In addition to *modal*, the feature *polite items* of LiAnS helped to identify more covert CTAs as in (4), where the appellative character of the sentence comes through the use of a polite phrase.

Source	Bolivia		Peru		Ecuador	
Type	Imp	Exp	Imp	Exp	Imp	Exp
Twitter	0	39	19	43	53	217
Facebook	4	70	8	94	121	2,303

Table 3: # of identified CTAs per country, source and type (Explicit *vs* Implicit).

Overall our results show that LiAnS can help to annotate small corpora that are unsuitable for machine learning approaches due to their small size and unbalanced nature, therefore reducing the manual annotation effort for our collaboration partners.

8 Limitations

The results of our evaluation show that there is still some room for improvement. First, the currently unbalanced nature of the corpus is not just a problem for machine learning approaches, it also poses challenges for the development of the NLP pipeline, as regional language varieties of all countries must be considered equally when creating the annotation rules. Second, our annotations rely on the morphological features provided by the *Stanza* NLP kit. This means that our pipeline struggles when the morphological analysis delivered by Stanza is erroneous. For example, this was the case for *voto* 'vote', which can be a verb or a noun. All instances of *voto* were analyzed as nouns by Stanza, which makes it difficult to identify DUs such as *voto por un futuro mejor* 'vote for a better future'. We adjusted the pipeline to correct for errors of this type.

9 Conclusion and Future work

In conclusion, we have implemented an automated approach to identify explicit and implicit election-related CTAs in Spanish social media. While a few previous studies have looked at the identification of CTAs in tweets related to protests, to the best of our knowledge our work is the first to look at the linguistic patterns that can be found in such attempts at voter mobilization.

Our next steps are, first, to annotate more CTA posts from Peru and Bolivia in order to create a more balanced gold standard corpus; and, second, to create our own balanced corpus. Third, we aim to expand our set of rules to allow especially more implicit CTAs to be annotated automatically.

We plan on adding a more sophisticated scoring system that assigns an aggregated score to the identified CTA cues. Thus, the classification as a CTA of a post will depend on how many linguistic cues that indicate a CTA are present and how heavily they are weighted. The word *vota* 'vote', for instance, should receive a greater weight than a modal like *tenemos que* 'we have to', since the former is a clear cue for a CTA, while the latter could also be used in other political contexts. We are confident that we can improve our overall results even further with these extensions of the pipeline and the introduction of a sophisticated scoring system. Finally, we also intend to experiment with machine learning approaches once the data set has grown large enough via boot-strapping through CTA clas-sifcations and annotations via our pipeline.

Acknowledgement

The work reported on in this paper was funded by the Deutsche Forschungsgemeinschaft (DFG – German Research Foundation) under Germany's Excellence Strategy – EXC-2035/1 – 390681379 as part of the project "Mobilizing Inequality".

References

Douglas Biber and Susan Conrad. 2009. *Register, Genre, and Style*. Cambridge University Press, Cambridge.

Douglas Biber, Susan Conrad, and Randi Reppen. 1998. *Corpus Linguistics: Investigating Language Structure and Use*. Cambridge University Press, Cambridge.

Dennis Chong and James N. Druckman. 2007. Framing public opinion in competitive democracies. *American Political Science Review*, 101(4):637–655.

James N. Druckman. 2011. What's it all about?: Framing in political science. In Gideon Keren, editor, *Perspectives on Framing*, pages 279–301. Taylor and Francis.

Valentin Gold, Mennatallah El-Assady, Annette Hautli-Janisz, Tina Bögel, Christian Rohrdantz, Miriam Butt, Katharina Holzinger, and Daniel Keim. 2015. Visual linguistic analysis of political discussions: Measuring deliberative quality. *Digital Scholarship in the Humanities*, 32(1):141–158.

Jeanine Guidry, Richard Waters, and Gregory Saxton. 2014. Moving Social Marketing Beyond Personal Change to Social Change. *Journal of Social Marketing*, 4:240–260.

Lea Haiges and Christina Isabel Zuber. 2021. Movements, Parties and the Making of Indigenous Politics in Ecuador and Peru. *2021 ECPR General Conference*.

Raffael Heiss and Jörg Matthes. 2016. Mobilizing for some. *J. Media Psychol. Theor. Methods Appl.*, 28:123–135.

Neta Kligler-Vilenchik, Maya de Vries Kedem, Daniel Maier, and Daniela Stoltenberg. 2021. Mobilization vs. Demobilization Discourses on Social Media. *Political Communication*, 38(5):561–580.

Livia Polanyi, Chris Culy, Martin Van Den Berg, Gian Lorenzo Thione, and David Ahn. 2004. Sentential structure and discourse parsing. In *Proceedings of the Workshop on Discourse Annotation*, pages 80–87.

Peng Qi, Yuhao Zhang, Yuhui Zhang, Jason Bolton, and Christopher D. Manning. 2020. Stanza: A Python Natural Language Processing toolkit for many human languages. In *Proceedings of the 58th Annual Meeting of the Association for Computational Linguistics: System Demonstrations*, pages 101–108.

Anna Rogers, Olga Kovaleva, and Anna Rumshisky. 2019. Calls to action on social media: Detection, social impact, and censorship potential. In *Proceedings of the Second Workshop on Natural Language Processing for Internet Freedom: Censorship, Disinformation, and Propaganda*, pages 36–44.

Saiph Savage, Andres Monroy-Hernandez, and Tobias Höllerer. 2016. Botivist: Calling Volunteers to Action Using Online Bots. In *Proceedings of the 19th ACM Conference on Computer-Supported Cooperative Work and Social Computing*, page 813–822, New York, NY, USA. Association for Computing Machinery.

The Distribution of Deontic Modals in Jane Austen's Mature Novels

Lauren E. Levine
Georgetown University
lel76@georgetown.edu

Abstract

Deontic modals are auxiliary verbs which express some kind of necessity, obligation, or moral recommendation. This paper investigates the collocation and distribution within Jane Austen's six mature novels of the following deontic modals: *must*, *should*, *ought*, and *need*. We also examine the co-occurrences of these modals with name mentions of the heroines in the six novels, categorizing each occurrence with a category of obligation if applicable. The paper offers a brief explanation of the categories of obligation chosen for this investigation. In order to examine the types of obligations associated with each heroine, we then investigate the distribution of these categories in relation to mentions of each heroine. The patterns observed show a general concurrence with the thematic characterizations of Austen's heroines which are found in literary analysis.

1 Introduction

Jane Austen is a celebrated British author whose classic works have endured over the centuries. From 1811 to 1818, her six mature novels: *Northanger Abbey* (NA), *Sense and Sensibility* (S&S), *Pride and Prejudice* (P&P), *Mansfield Park* (MP), *Emma* (E), and *Persuasion* (P) were published, *Northanger Abbey* and *Persuasion* being published posthumously.

In recent years, efforts in the area of digital humanities have grown, and the interest for having accessible tools and methodologies for approaching a quantitative analysis of Jane Austen's writings has increased (Runge, 2019). Analytical techniques such as keyword analysis, phraseological research, and distribution analysis have been performed on the works of Jane Austen in order to gain literary, structural, and linguistic insights into the texts (Fischer-Starcke, 2010). This includes investigation into modal verbs: Wijitsopon (2013) has noted modal auxiliary verbs to be a linguistic feature particularly characteristic of Jane Austen's novels, and argued that an analysis of clusters containing the modal auxiliary *must* provided evidence of literary critics' claims that Austen's novels are framed more by the internal thoughts and perspectives of the characters rather than by the physical events of the stories. Previously, Burrows (1986) also explored the differing frequency patterns of modal auxiliary verbs, finding differences of statistical significance between different modes of narrative as well as between different characters within Jane Austen's works. There have also been less quantitative discussions of Jane Austen's use of modals, such as Boyd (1984), which offers a close analysis of the character intricacies and social commentary expressed by Austen's masterful use of modals.

We aim to continue such investigation into modal auxiliary verbs in Austen's work, specifically looking at a selection of deontic modals. Deontic modality is a linguistic mode that expresses how the world ought to be relative to some normative standard, such as moral norms, and frequently carries a sense of necessity or obligation. Deontic modals can narrowly be defined as the set of modal auxiliary verbs, such as *can* and *should*, which have the potential to express deontic modality (Carr, 2017). In this paper, we examine the distribution in Jane Austen's mature novels of the following deontic modals: *must*, *should*, *ought*, and *need*.

All six of Jane Austen's mature novels embody themes of obligation, propriety and duty, but the presentation of these themes is not uniform across the novels. While *Pride and Prejudice* has a heroine who balances propriety and wit in Elizabeth Bennet, *Mansfield Park*'s heroine Fanny Price is so obliging to her position in society that the book is often considered to be "moral at the cost of comedy and vigour" (Todd, 2006). Deontic modals can be used by an author to stylistically incorporate themes such as societal obligation and duty into the prose. By investigating the deontic modals that Austen employs in relation to her heroines, we aim

Proceedings of the 6th LaTeCH-CLfL Workshop, pages 70–74
October 16, 2022.

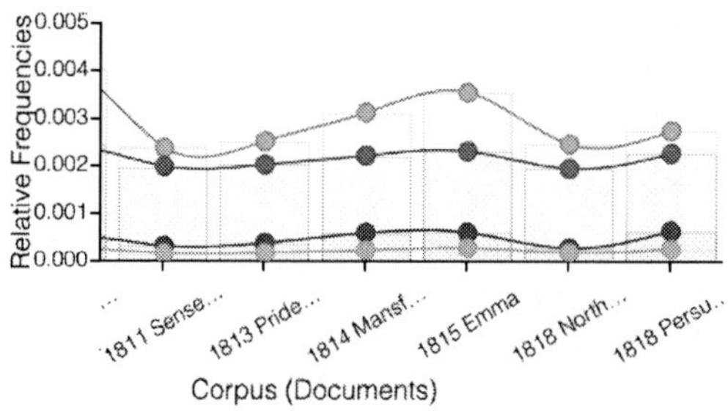

Figure 1: Relative frequencies of deontic modals in Jane Austen's novels. (From top to bottom) Orange: *must*, Pink: *should*, Purple: *ought*, Blue: *need*

to characterize how different aspects of the theme of obligation are associated with each of Austen's heroines.

For the purposes of this investigation, we leverage *Voyant Tools*, an open access web-based suite of text analysis tools that allow for easy visualization of corpus data, including relative frequency of terms, collocations, and occurrence contexts (Sinclair and Rockwell, 2021). *Voyant Tools* contains a Jane Austen corpus compiled from digital texts freely available from Project Gutenberg.

Voyant Tools was selected to be used in this investigation for its ability to provide easy access to a full corpus of Jane Austen's works, as well as for the particular analysis functions included in its interface, such as the collocates tool and the relative frequency tool, which provide adequate functionality to engage in meaningful analysis through relatively simple corpus linguistic methods. In addition to providing specific literary analysis, in this paper, we demonstrate how accessible digital tools, such as *Voyant Tools*, allow for researchers without significant technical expertise to leverage relatively simple corpus-based methods of analysis in order to gain literary insights.

2 Relative Frequency of Deontic Modals

The relative frequency of a term in a corpus refers to the ratio between the number of times the term occurs in the corpus and the total number of tokens in the corpus. A high relative frequency is typically taken to be an indicator that the linguistic feature (or term) under investigation is of significance in the corpus (Fischer-Starcke, 2010).

Using *Voyant Tools*, the relative frequencies of the modal verbs *must*, *should*, *ought*, and, *need* were calculated for each of Austen's six novels.

Obligation Modal	Top Collocates (Verbs)
must	think, know, said, make, feel
should	think, like, said, know, come
ought	know, think, feel, say, make
need	fear/be afraid, say, tell, ask, think

Table 1: Top verbal collocates of deontic modals.

The visualization of this data is presented in Figure 1. We note that *must* and *should* have higher relative frequencies across the board (the highest being *most* in *Emma* with a relative frequency of 0.0035218), reflecting that they are more common words than *ought* and *need*.

The figure proceeds in order of publication of the novels, but it should be noted that the manuscript for *Northanger Abbey* was actually completed around 1803, making it the earliest of Austen's novels. With this in mind, we see that there is a general increase in the relative frequency of all four deontic modals investigated as time moves forward. This could indicate that the use of deontic modals to express obligation became more of a characteristic feature in Austen's later works: *Mansfield Park*, *Emma*, and *Persuasion*.

3 Collocates of Deontic Modals

Collocates of a given term are other terms that appear with greater than random probability in proximity to that term in a corpus. This greater than random probability indicates that the co-occurrence of two collocates depends on a relationship between the lexical terms, and examining such collocational patterns can reveal meaningfully ways in which terms are related in texts such as Austen's novels (Wijitsopon, 2013).

Leveraging the *Voyant Tools* collocates function using a window size of 5 tokens, we examined the collocates for the four deontic modals previously mentioned. As we are investigating auxiliary verbs, some of the top verbal collocates for each modal are highlighted in Table 1. As we can see, the top collocates for all of the modals are relatively similar verbs. They revolve around thoughts, communication, feelings, and perception, which supports the notion that Austen's stories are more strongly framed around feelings and perceptions than actions.

When further examining the collocates of the modals within each of Austen's novels, we found that the top collocates between novels were also fairly similar, with the exception that the name of each heroine was also a top collocate within her own novel. This presents an opportunity to investigate how the distribution and usage of deontic modals differ between the heroines of Austen's novels.

4 Relative Modal Obligation per Heroine

As the heroines of all of Austen's novels were shown to have a high level of co-occurrence with the deontic modals being investigated, we set out to examine the occurrences of these modal verbs and if/how they were used in context to convey a sense of obligation in the narrative.

First, we looked to establish what proportion of deontic modals co-occurring with the mentions of the heroines' names were actually relevant to the given heroine in the discourse. This required a manual evaluation of all of the instances of a deontic modal that occur within 5 tokens to the left or 5 tokens to the right of a mention of one of the heroines' names in all six novels to determine whether or not they had some relevance to the heroine in question. This manual evaluation was completed by the author of this paper. This filtering brought the total number of occurrences of deontic modals to be further investigated from 244 occurrences down to 154 occurrences. (It should be noted that only co-occurrences with heroines' names/nicknames were investigated. There are many more co-occurrences with pronoun mentions of the heroines which could be examined in future work.)

After establishing for each heroine which occurrences of deontic modals were directly relevant, we then reviewed those occurrences to determine whether or not their usage introduced some intent of obligation into the discourse. This was a subjective annotation based on review of the surrounding context in the novel for each occurrence. The cases that remained (116 in total) were then compared to the total number of relevant modal occurrences for each heroine in order to determine the ratio of how many of the relevant co-occurrences of deontic modals actually introduced some element of obligation in the discourse for each heroine. The proportions for each heroine are listed in Table 2.

Looking at Table 2, we see that most of the heroines are around the same level, with Elinor and Marianne (S&S) on the lower end, and Fanny (MP) very much on the high end with a proportion of 0.97 of co-occurring deontic modals conveying some intent of obligation into the discourse that is relevant to Fanny. This tracks with literary critics' understanding of Fanny as a character that is largely propelled by other (generally male) characters (Todd, 2006). However, based on the relative frequencies of deontic modals across the novels that were presented earlier in the paper, one might expect the proportions in Table 2 to be uniformly higher of Austen's later heroines. In order to understand why this is not the case, we must also investigate the different types of obligation being introduced into the discourse by the these modals.

Heroine	Relative Modal Obligation
Catherine (NA)	0.85
Elinor (S&S)	0.59
Marianne (S&S)	0.63
Elizabeth (P&P)	0.8
Fanny (MA)	**0.97**
Emma (E)	0.75
Anne (P)	0.75

Table 2: A ratio of the occurrences of deontic modals which are (1) co-occurring with the heroine name (2) relevant to the heroine in the discourse and (3) express some intention of obligation in the discourse relative to the occurrences of deontic models that just fulfill (1) and (2)

5 Categories of Obligation

For the purpose of this investigation, a small set of 5 categories for differentiating senses of obligation was developed in order to sort the 116 occurrences of deontic modals that were judged to invoke some sense of obligation in the discourse. The categorizations were developed from examining those 116 cases and considering what groupings might be relevant to character analysis. A brief description of each category and an accompanying example are listed below:

Obligation of Action (OA): Some obligation is placed on the action or the potential action of the heroine (either by another party or by the heroine herself).

> e.g.: *You have had a long run of amusement, and now you **must** try to be useful." Catherine took up her work directly...* (NA)

Obligation of Feeling (OF): Some obligation is placed on the feelings or the potential feelings

Category	Catherine (NA)	Elinor (S&S)	Marianne (S&S)	Elizabeth (P&P)	Fanny (MP)	Emma (E)	Anne (P)
OA	**0.73**	0.4	0.7	0.5	0.38	0.5	0.33
OF	0	**0.3**	0.1	0.06	0.24	0.21	0.17
OO	0.18	0.2	0.1	0.13	**0.21**	0.07	0.08
OE	0.09	0.1	0.2	0.31	0.15	0.11	**0.42**
O	0	0	0	0	0.02	**0.11**	0

Table 3: This table shows the proportional distribution of obligation categories associated with each heroine. The highest proportion among the heroines for each obligation category is highlighted in bold.

of the heroine (either by another party or by the heroine herself).

> e.g.: *He was evidently oppressed, and Fanny **must** grieve for him...* (MP)

Object of Obligation (OO): The heroine is the object of some sense of obligation that is placed (not by the heroine) on another party.

> e.g.: *... that Elinor's merit **should** not be acknowledged by every one who knew her, was to her comprehension impossible.* (S&S)

Expression of Obligation (EO): The heroine expresses some obligation or moral judgment on another party or a state of affairs. (If the expression is directed towards the heroine herself, first choose OA or OF if applicable.)

> e.g.: *...Mr and Mrs Musgrove," exclaimed Anne, "**should** be happy in their children's marriages.* (P)

Other (O): There is a sense of obligation expressed that does not fit into one of the above categories.

6 Distribution of Obligation Categories amongst Heroines

The categories described above were used to manually annotate the deontic modals occurring with each heroine. These manual annotations were completed by the author of this paper. Once these annotations had been made, the number of modal occurrences annotated with each obligation category were totaled for each heroine. Each of these category totals was then divided by the total number of modal occurrences associated with the heroine in order to get the proportional distribution of obligation categories associated with each heroine. The results of these calculations are presented in Table 3. Each column of the table shows the proportional breakdown for how the obligation categories are distributed for a single heroine.

Looking at Table 3, we see that Catherine (NA) has the highest Obligation of Action (OA) proportion. This is fitting, as Catherine is one of Austen's younger heroines, whose character at the outset of the novel is considered to be naive. As such, she is frequently instructed in her behavior. Throughout the course of the story, she learns what behavior is proper and what is not. Elinor (S&S) has the highest Obligation of Feeling (OF) proportion, which is also fitting because Elinor's central story line in *Sense and Sensibility* revolves around how she is obligated to suppress her feelings because the man she loves is already engaged to another woman. The highest Object of Obligation (OO) proportion comes from Fanny (MP), whose character is commonly criticized for being overly moralistic and lacking in agency (Todd, 2006). In *Mansfield Park*, Fanny's feelings are rarely consulted on any matter and she is often treated as an object. Finally, Anne (P) has the highest proportion for Expression of Obligation (EO). Anne is Austen's final heroine, and arguably her most mature. Anne is the oldest heroine, and she is also the most self-reflective and self-controlled. As such, it is fitting that Anne is the heroine who has the highest proportion in the category for expressing her own understanding of how things should be. Overall, we see that the breakdown of obligation categories amongst the modal occurrences for each heroine have a resemblance to the characterizations of Jane Austen's heroines that are understood through literary analysis.

7 Conclusion

In this paper we examined how deontic modals are distributed in Jane Austen's novels, and how they contribute to elements of Austen's style and themes. We found that the relative frequencies of deontic modals are higher in Austen's later novels, and that the verbal collocates of these modals generally revolve around perceptions and communication, which support the literary notion that the framing of Austen's novels favors perception over physical action.

Upon examination of the co-occurrences of these modals with name mentions of the heroines of Austen's novels, we found that the proportion of deontic modals that worked to convey a sense of obligation in the discourse varied from heroine to heroine, and we found that the type of obligation most commonly conveyed by these modals also varied from heroine to heroine. As discussed above, these distributions reflect some general characterizations of Austen's heroines.

As these findings corroborate existing literary perspectives, we see that there is merit in engaging in quantitative corpus analysis to gather supporting evidence for literary claims, as well as to potentially seek out new patterns of interest for literary analysis. In addition these specific insights, this paper provides a methodology for gaining literary insights through the use of simple corpus linguistic methods. This paper also serves to demonstrate how accessible digital tools, such as *Voyant Tools*, allow for researchers without advanced programming skills to leverage quantitative methods of analysis to engage with literary texts.

References

Zelda Boyd. 1984. Jane austen's" must": The will and the world. *Nineteenth-Century Fiction*, 39(2):127–143.

J. F. Burrows. 1986. Modal verbs and moral principles: An aspect of jane austen's style. *Literary and Linguistic Computing*, 1(1):9–23.

Jennifer Carr. 2017. Deontic modals. In *The Routledge handbook of metaethics*, pages 194–210. Routledge.

Bettina Fischer-Starcke. 2010. *Corpus Linguistics in Literary Analysis Jane Austen and Her Contemporaries*. Continuum.

Laura L. Runge. 2019. Austen and computation 2.0. *Texas Studies in Literature and Language*, 61(4):397–415.

S. Sinclair and G. Rockwell. Voyant tools [online]. 2021.

Janet Todd. 2006. *The Cambridge Introduction to Jane Austen*. Cambridge University Press.

Raksangob Wijitsopon. 2013. A corpus-based study of the style in jane austen's novels. *MANUSYA*, 16(1):41–64.

Man vs. Machine: Extracting Character Networks from Human and Machine Translations

Aleksandra Konovalova
University of Turku
aleksandra.a.konovalova@utu.fi

Antonio Toral
University of Groningen
a.toral.ruiz@rug.nl

Abstract

Most of the work on Character Networks to date is limited to monolingual texts. Conversely, in this paper we apply and analyze Character Networks on both source texts (English novels) and their Finnish translations (both human- and machine-translated). We assume that this analysis could provide some insights on changes in translations that could modify the character networks, as well as the narrative. The results show that the character networks of translations differ from originals in case of long novels, and the differences may also vary depending on the novel and translator's strategy.

1 Introduction

Character Networks (CNs) building can be considered as a part of Social Networks Analysis (SNA) research. The main difference between SNA and CNs extraction has to do with the type of datasets to which these methods are applied: CNs extraction is typically used for different works of art (mainly literary texts of different genres as well as films), while SNA is usually performed on more structured datasets, e.g. online social networks, such as YouTube or LiveJournal (Mislove et al., 2007).

Most of the work on CNs to date applies them to monolingual texts. The main novelty of our work stems from the fact that we apply these techniques not only to original texts but also to their translations (both by human translators and by Machine Translation (MT) systems). In doing so, we aim to unveil whether the connections between characters (represented by CNs), modified by human or machine translator, differ, which can point to narrative differences between original texts and translations.

There are different tasks that could benefit from the extraction of CNs in this bilingual setting, namely MT. MT could be enhanced with the contextual information, namely the global context of the whole text that could be in a form of a graph (Xu et al., 2020). We consider the task of CNs extraction in the scope of enhancing MT of literary texts. In this framework, we consider the extraction of CNs as a valuable first step, so that we can find out how the CNs of Human Translation (HT) and MT compare to the CN of the original.

In this paper we take a look at the CNs of English originals and Finnish translations thereof. The structure of the paper is as follows: first we provide an overview of the related work (Section 2), subsequently we describe our data (Section 3), after which we discuss the creation of the list of the characters' names that we will use for our methods (Section 4). We continue the paper with describing the method (Section 5) that we used. Finally, we present our results of both qualitative analyses and quantitative assessment and analyze them (Section 6). We conclude our paper in Section 7.

2 Related work

Character Networks extraction is a broad problem, so there have been many attempts to tackle it from different angles. It can be the main focus of the research (John et al., 2019; Kubis, 2021), or only a step towards a broader goal, e.g. learning representations of stories based on character networks (Lee and Jung, 2019, 2020). It can be automated (Chen et al., 2019) or not (Moretti, 2011). The data for character networks extraction can also vary from movies (Agarwal et al., 2014) to novels (Agarwal et al., 2012) and fairytales (Schmidt et al., 2021). The most thorough overview of character network extraction so far has been done by Labatut and Bost (Labatut and Bost, 2019). Also Schmidt et al. (2021), aside from their original topic of research, raised an issue regarding the evaluation of character networks: according to them, currently there is no standardized approach for such evaluation and most research on this topic evaluates the extracted networks by proxy or using SNA metrics (Schmidt et al., 2021).

Proceedings of the 6th LaTeCH-CLfL Workshop, pages 75–82
October 16, 2022. ©2022 International Conference on Computational Linguistics

The novelty of our research with respect to previous work lies mainly in three points: firstly, we are taking a look at CNs of translations; secondly, we are looking at CNs of machine-translated texts; and thirdly, we are looking at an uncommon language pair (English-Finnish), since, as far as we know, there is no related work for character networks based on Finnish texts to date.

3 Data

The main dataset is made up of corpora of English and Finnish literary texts. The English part of the dataset was gathered from Project Gutenberg (`https://www.gutenberg.org/`), while the Finnish human-translated subcorpus is available at the Language Bank of Finland as The Downloadable Version of Classics of English and American Literature in Finnish (`https://www.kielipankki.fi/corpora/ceal-2/`).

The English subcorpus contains two novels (*Pride and Prejudice* by Jane Austen, *Bleak House* by Charles Dickens) and a short story (*The Washington Square* by Henry James). The Finnish human-translated corpus contains the corresponding Finnish translations of these works carried out by Kersti Juva, while the Finnish machine-translated subcorpus was created by DeepL Translator (`https://www.deepl.com/translator`) from the English originals on May 26, 2022. Table 1 contains some statistics about the corpora.

English and Finnish human-translated subcorpora and English and Finnish machine-translated subcorpora were sentence-aligned for consistency and for the purpose of doing close reading. The alignment was done using InterText (Vondricka, 2014). In case of Human Translations, the alignment was done semi-automatically (we had to go through the whole texts and align problematic sentences manually), but for MT it was done automatically, because the sentence splitting of the output translations of DeepL corresponded to the one of the original texts.

4 Creation of character names' list

Before applying our methods (see Section 5), we had to create a character names' list, so that we could use this list for implementation of our methods. To perform this task, we got the information from different internet sources that contain information about characters from the novels in our dataset (see Appendix A).

While creating a list of characters' names as a basis for our CNs, we also faced many questions about characters, such as: what is a literary character? Who do we consider a character from the point of the narrative? Do we take into consideration off-screen characters (characters that are only mentioned in the text and do not participate in the plot)? To answer these questions, we needed to define what / who the character is.

The literary character can be seen as a construct which definition and features depend on the study area (Margolin, 1990). Jannidis (2013) considered a character "a text- or media-based figure in a storyworld, usually human or human-like" or "an entity in a storyworld". Overall, characters are interconnected with both narrative and storyworld and contribute to their development from many aspects.

Based on this notion, we considered a literary character every figure that was relevant for the narrative development (thus, e.g. names of famous persons that are mentioned but do not appear in the novel directly were not included). So we decided to include both onscreen (entities that are actively participating in the storyworld) and off-screen (entities that are passively contributing to the construction of the storyworld) characters (e.g. in case of *Washington Square*, it was the mother of the main character that was mentioned only twice, but never participated in the story herself).

We also included all possible names that can be used for naming a certain character by splitting the full name (e.g. *Elizabeth Bennet* would also get versions *Elizabeth* and *Bennet*) and by analyzing possible versions (*Lizzy* for *Elizabeth Bennet*) that were mentioned in the internet sources (see Appendix A). We also included full names (if applicable) even if they were not used for naming a character in the text just for reference (e.g. in case of *Catherine Sloper*). So *Elizabeth Bennet* would get the following names: *Bennet*, *Eliza*, *Eliza Bennet*, *Elizabeth*, *Elizabeth Bennet*, *Lizzy*, and *Catherine Sloper* would get the names *Catherine*, *Catherine Sloper* and *Sloper*. The creation of the characters' names list was carried out only by one annotator.

As a result, we would have a list of all possible characters' names. For this research we decided not to link different names of the same characters, because there were relatives and namesakes which were impossible to distinguish from the context.

Corpus	Characters (without newline characters)	Sentences	Words
English subcorpus	2,956,068	28,360	549,383
Finnish subcorpus (Human Translations)	2,861,687	23,153	387,734
Finnish subcorpus (Machine Translations)	3,069,732	23,518	410,767

Table 1: Statistics for the corpora used in our study

5 Methods

We extracted the character networks from English, Finnish human-translated and Finnish machine-translated texts using the same workflow. The workflow was implemented using Python with the help of the NetworkX library (`https://networkx.org/`) for CN-related quantitative metrics and visualization.

The workflow proceeds sequentially as follows:

1. Splitting texts by chapters (we searched in the text for the expressions that contained the chapters' names and split the text by them) and transforming each novel into a list of chapters;

2. Searching for the names from characters' names list in every chapter and producing a list of character relationships for each chapter; Iterating through a list of chapters and producing the final results for character relationships in the novel.

We decided to use chapters as the units to build the CNs for several reasons. Firstly, using smaller units (e.g. paragraphs) may have led to unexpected results, since the texts also contained dialogues and letters which may have zero characters in one paragraph despite having a clear link between the characters outside the dialogue or the letter. Secondly, we consider a novel chapter as an autonomous part of narrative which may provide a more finalized view into characters' relationships.

We consider our approach to be semi-automated, since we had to build lists of characters' names manually. We also decided to introduce some limitations to our research.

For this paper, we decided not to link different versions of the names and their references, such as pronouns, due to the complexity of such a task, especially regarding Finnish translations. For example, in *Pride and Prejudice* we would have 5 characters that could be linked to "Miss Bennet", namely all five Bennet sisters: Jane, Elizabeth, Mary, Catherine and Lydia. Moreover, it is used in plural - there are "younger Miss Bennets" and "older Miss Bennets". As per our knowledge, there is also no coreference model for Finnish language, and training such a model would require from us creation of the annotated corpus, which could be a topic for a paper on its own. For a similar reason we also decided not to use Named Entity Recognition (NER) state-of-the-art tools, because our previous research has shown the need to further refine the results of NER pipeline: namely the results of lemmatization step for foreign names in Finnish texts needed to be polished further (Konovalova et al., 2022).

6 Evaluation and results

After implementing our workflow, we used it on our corpus, producing CNs for English original texts, Finnish Human Translations and Finnish MT outputs. For our assessment, we performed both qualitative and ative analyses. Quantitative analysis was done by analysing the CNs' metrics and qualitative analysis was done to provide some insights and possible reasons for such results of quantitative analysis.

6.1 Qualitative Analysis (close reading)

We performed close reading for English originals and Finnish Human Translations while doing sentence alignment. We also performed close reading for Finnish MT outputs.

We grouped the changes in translations in two groups: changing the pronoun into the proper noun and changing names completely.

6.1.1 Changing the pronoun into the proper noun

Human Translations

Close reading showed that in some cases in

Finnish Human Translations names of the characters were used instead of the pronouns in English originals: for example, in different interactions between *Elizabeth Bennet* and *Mr. Darcy* in *Pride and Prejudice* translation (see Table 2).

We assume that there could be two possible reasons for this: firstly, the translator's own style, and secondly, the nature of the target language (in Finnish there is one third-person pronoun, *hän*, that corresponds both to *he* and *she*, so the use of the character's name could be the attempt to avoid ambiguity. The other way to avoid ambiguity is to use notions like *mies* (*man*) and *nainen* (*woman*)). Since the last reason is tied to the target language, it could also be linked to the normalization strategy used by the translator (namely, adapting the translations to target language norms (Baker and Somers, 1996)).

We assume that such translator's decisions affected the quantitative results for the Character Networks that we present in the next subsection (6.2) on Quantitative Assessment.

Machine Translations

Similarly to Human Translations, there were cases when the pronoun would be replaced with the name. The possible reason for it could also be connected to the normalization principle that was learnt and used by the MT model during MT.

In Table 2 we present several examples where, surprisingly, both Human Translation and MT use the same normalization technique.

There was also an interesting example where it seems that coreference went wrong in the MT output, as "she" in original text is another character, *Mrs. Phillips* (referenced by *"täti"* (*aunt* in Finnish) in Human Translation):

Original: She received him with her very best politeness, which he returned with as much more, apologising for his intrusion, without any previous acquaintance with **her**, which he could not help flattering himself, however, might be justified by his relationship to the young ladies who introduced him to **her** notice.

MT: Jane otti miehen vastaan parhaalla mahdollisella kohteliaisuudellaan, ja mies vastasi kohteliaasti ja pyysi anteeksi tunkeutumistaan, koska hän ei tuntenut **Janea** aikaisemmin, mutta hän ei voinut olla imartelematta itseään, että hänen suhteensa niihin nuoriin neitoihin, jotka esittelivät miehen **Janeen**, saattaisi kuitenkin oikeuttaa tämän tunkeutumisen.

Human Translation: Täti otti herran vastaan kaikin tavoin kohteliaasti, mihin mies vastasi samalla mitalla ja pannen paremmaksi, pyysi anteeksi, että tunkeutui näin kylään ilman aikaisempaa tuttavuutta, mutta tahtoi kuitenkin uskoa sukulaisuussuhteen hänet esitelleisiin nuoriin naisiin antavan sille oikeutuksen.

6.1.2 Changing names completely

Human Translations

There was one case when the name that has a distinctive meaning in the original text has to be changed in the Human Translation to save and convey this meaning to the reader. On the contrary, it was not changed in MT. Compare:

Original: <...>, Mr. Snagsby mentions to the 'prentices, "I think my little woman is a-giving it to **Guster**!" This proper name, so used by Mr. Snagsby, has before now sharpened the wit of the Cook's Courtiers to remark that it ought to be the name of Mrs. Snagsby, seeing that she might with great force and expression be termed a **Guster**, in compliment to her **stormy** character.

HT: <...>, herra Snagsby sanoo oppipojilleen: "Siellä taitaa pikkurouva kurittaa **Mollya**!" Herra Snagsbyn mainitsema etunimi on aikaa sitten saanut naapurit letkauttamaan, että se olisi sopiva nimi rouva Snagsbylle, sillä nimi **Möly** istuisi hänelle kuin nyrkki silmään hänen **äänekkään** luonteensa ansiosta.

MT: <...>, herra Snagsby sanoo apulaisille: "Luulen, että pikku naiseni antaa sen **Gusterille**!". Tämä herra Snagsbyn käyttämä nimi on ennenkin saanut Cookin hovimiehet huomauttamaan, että sen pitäisi olla rouva Snagsbyn nimi, koska häntä voisi nimittää hyvin voimakkaasti ja ilmeikkäästi **Gusteriksi**, kohteliaisuutena hänen **myrskyisälle** luonteelleen.

Guster has a *stormy* personality, and her name sounds like *gust* - sudden rush of the wind. In Finnish Human Translation the translator faced two problems: first - how to convey the name's meaning to the Finnish reader and second - how to still have the English name in the translation. It was solved by linking the existing name - Molly - to Finnish word *möly* (*noise*) and saying that Molly/Möly has a *noisy* character.

Machine Translations

We noticed that in machine-translated texts there were also changes in the names: some of them were sometimes domesticated, for example, *Catherine* would be changed to *Katariina* (Finnish version

Original	Machine Translation	Human Translation
Elizabeth listened with delight to the happy, though modest hopes which **Jane** entertained of Mr. Bingley's regard, and said all in her power to heighten **her** confidence in it.	Elizabeth kuunteli ihastuneena **Janen** iloisia, vaikkakin vaatimattomia toiveita herra Bingleyn kunnioituksesta ja sanoi kaiken voitavansa vahvistaakseen **Janen** luottamusta siihen.	Elizabethille oli ilo kuulla onnellisista joskin kainoista haaveista, joita **Janella** oli herra Bingleyn tunteisiin nähden, ja hän sanoi kaiken, mitä pystyi sanomaan, vahvistaakseen **Janen** luottamusta niihin.
She could not help frequently glancing her eye at **Mr. Darcy**, though every glance convinced her of what she dreaded; for though **he** was not always looking at her mother, she was convinced that **his** attention was invariably fixed by her.	Hän ei voinut olla vilkaisematta usein **herra Darcyyn**, vaikka jokainen vilkaisu sai hänet vakuuttuneeksi siitä, mitä hän pelkäsi; sillä vaikka **Darcy** ei aina katsonutkaan äitiä, hän oli vakuuttunut siitä, että **Darcy** kiinnitti hänen huomionsa aina äitiinsä.	Hän ei voinut olla vähän väliä vilkaisematta syrjäsilmällä **herra Darcyyn** siitä huolimatta, että jokainen vilkaisu vahvisti hänen pelkonsa; sillä vaikka **Darcy** ei katsonut äitiin koko ajan, hän oli varma, että äiti oli **Darcyn** hellittämättömän huomion kohteena.
So I thought it a good opportunity to hint to Richard that if he were sometimes a little careless of himself, I was very sure he never meant to be careless of **Ada**, and that it was a part of his affectionate consideration for **her** not to slight the importance of a step that might influence both their lives.	Ajattelin, että nyt oli hyvä tilaisuus vihjata Richardille, että vaikka hän oli joskus hieman huolimaton itseään kohtaan, olin aivan varma, ettei hän koskaan aikonut olla huolimaton **Adaa** kohtaan ja että oli osa hänen hellästä huomaavaisuudestaan **Adaa** kohtaan, ettei hän vähättelisi sellaisen askeleen merkitystä, joka saattoi vaikuttaa heidän molempien elämään.	Niin minä katsoin tilaisuuden sopivaksi vihjata Richardille, että jos hän joskus olikin hiukan huoleton oman itsensä suhteen, hän ei toki koskaan voisi olla huoleton **Adan** suhteen, ja että hänen kiintymykseensä **Adaan** kuului osana se, ettei hän vähätellyt minkään askelen merkitystä, millä saattaisi olla vaikutusta heidän yhteiseen elämäänsä.

Table 2: Examples of changing pronouns into proper nouns in Human and Machine Translations.

of the name) or *Elizabeth* would be changed to *Elisabet* (also Finnish version of the name). So in the MT output there could be two versions for the same name: *Catherine* would correspond to both *Catherine* and *Katariina*, and *Elizabeth* - to *Elizabeth* and *Elisabet*.

Original: It pleased **Catherine** to think that she should be brave for his sake, and in her satisfaction she even gave a little smile.

MT: **Katariinaa** ilahdutti ajatus siitä, että hänen piti olla rohkea hänen vuokseen, ja tyytyväisyydessään hän jopa hymyili hieman.

Compare to:

Original: "It will be easy to be prepared for that," **Catherine** said.

MT: "Siihen on helppo valmistautua", **Catherine** sanoi.

Overall the results of close reading show that both Human and Machine Translation tend to use normalization techniques. In the case of MT, the domestication of the names was used sporadically, which created several versions of one name in translation.

6.2 Quantitative Assessment (metrics)

We used the following metrics for assessing and comparing our results:

1. Different centrality metrics which are the main ones for the analysis of character networks (Newman, 2010):
   (a) Betweenness centrality (how much each character connects other characters between themselves); we took a look at the first 5 results with the highest values for this metric;
   (b) Degree centrality (how many connections one node (character) has to others); we also took a look at the first 5 results with the highest values for this metric;
2. Density (what is the level of connections of the whole graph)
3. Diameter (how big the network is).

Text type	Betweenness centrality (max, n=5)	Degree centrality (max, n=5)	Density	Diameter
Original / Human Translation / Machine Translation	Almond: 0.037, Catherine: 0.037, Penniman: 0.037, Sloper: 0.037, Morris Townsend: 0.22	Almond: 1.0, Catherine: 1.0, Penniman: 1.0, Sloper: 1.0, Morris Townsend: 0.94	0.77	2

Table 3: Results of different metrics for *Washington Square*.

We present our results in the tables below (one table per novel) and we also provide visualization for the characters that have the highest values for the metrics. The nodes of the graphs represent characters, and the edges represent relationships between characters.

Washington Square (Table 3)

Probably because of the size of the *Washington Square* (35 chapters, length of the original text: 354,440 characters) and because we split the texts by chapters, the CNs were the same for all three versions (original, HT and MT). The five characters with maximum betweenness centrality and degree centrality correspond to the main characters: *Mrs. Almond, Catherine Sloper, Mrs. Penniman, Dr. Austin Sloper* and *Morris Townsend.*

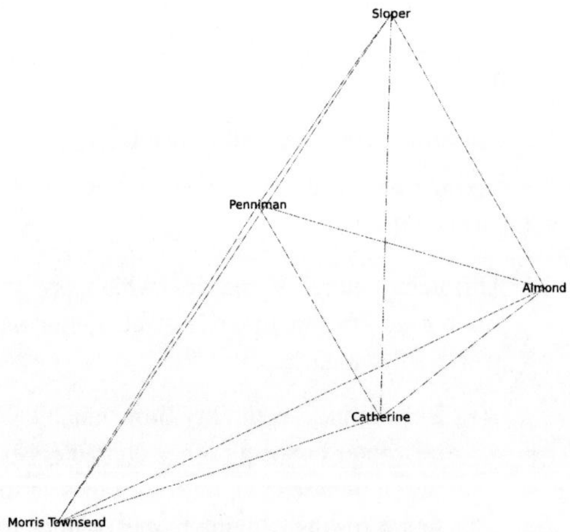

Figure 1: Example for the CN for *Washington Square* for 5 characters with maximum scores.

Pride and Prejudice (Table 4)

The main characters, according to the metrics, are *Bennet* (could be anyone from the family, but most probably it is either *Mr. Bennet* or *Mrs. Bennet*), *Bingley* (most probably *Mr. Bingley* than his sister, *Miss Bingley*), *Elizabeth Bennet* and *Mr. Darcy*. The fifth character varies: in original and machine-translated text it is *Mr. Wickham*, in human-translated text it is *Jane Bennet*. The difference in the mentions could also be attributed to the aforementioned translation strategy to use a character's name instead of the pronoun for better clarity. It is also interesting that in Human Translation *Jane Bennet* becomes a more important character than *Mr. Wickham* which could be attributed to the translator's strategy of using more proper nouns in the *Jane Bennet-Mr.Bingley* or *Jane Bennet-Elizabeth Bennet* interactions.

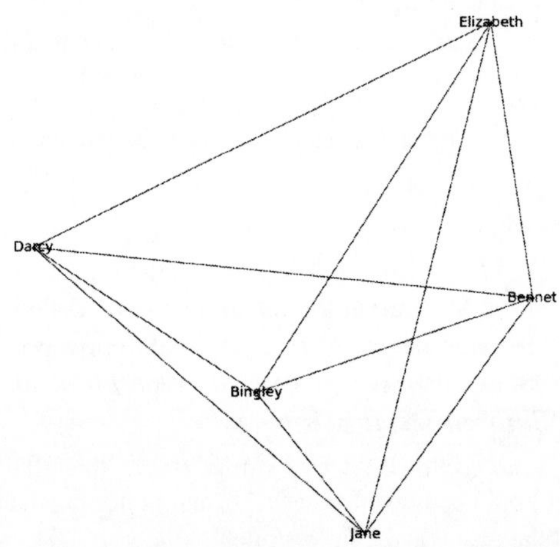

Figure 2: Example for the CN for *Pride and Prejudice* for 5 characters with maximum scores.

Bleak House (Table 5)

There are two narratives in *Bleak House*: one is done from third-person perspective, and the other is narrated by *Esther Summerson*, which may affect her appearance in the text. According to the metrics, the main characters are *Dedlock* (probably *Lady Dedlock*), *Esther Summerson, John Jarndyce, Richard Carstone* and *Mr. Tulkinghorn*. It is also

Text type	Betweenness centrality (max, n=5)	Degree centrality (max, n=5)	Density	Diameter
Original	Bennet: 0.013, Bingley: 0.013, Elizabeth: 0.013, Darcy: 0.013, Wickham: 0.012	Bennet: 1.0 Bingley: 1.0, Elizabeth: 1.0, Darcy: 1.0, Jane: 0.98	0.79	2
Human Translation	Bennet: **0.015**, Bingley: **0.015**, Elizabeth: **0.015**, Darcy: **0.015**, Jane: **0.013**	Bennet: 1.0 Bingley: 1.0, Elizabeth: 1.0, Darcy: 1.0, Jane: 0.98	**0.76**	2
Machine Translation	Bennet: 0.013, Bingley: 0.013, Elizabeth: 0.013, Darcy: 0.013, Wickham: 0.012	Bennet: 1.0 Bingley: 1.0, Elizabeth: 1.0, Darcy: 1.0, Jane: 0.98	0.79	2

Table 4: Results of different metrics for *Pride and Prejudice*. Scores in translations that differ from the original text shown in bold.

Text type	Betweenness centrality (max, n=5)	Degree centrality (max, n=5)	Density	Diameter
Original	Dedlock: 0.02, Summerson: 0.03, Jarndyce: 0.05, Tulkinghorn: 0.02, Richard: 0.02	Dedlock: 0.79, Summerson: 0.86, Jarndyce: 0.94, Richard: 0.76, Tulkinghorn: 0.77	0.4	**3**
Human Translation	Dedlock: 0.02, Summerson: 0.03, Jarndyce: 0.05, Richard: 0.02, Tulkinghorn: 0.02	Dedlock: 0.79, Summerson: 0.86, Jarndyce: 0.94, Richard: **0.78**, Tulkinghorn: **0.76**	**0.39**	2
Machine Translation	Dedlock: 0.02, Summerson: 0.03, Jarndyce: **0.04**, Lady Dedlock: 0.02, Tulkinghorn: 0.02	Dedlock: 0.79, Jarndyce: **0.93**, Richard: 0.76, Summerson: **0.85**, Tulkinghorn: **0.76**, Lady Dedlock: **0.76**	0.4	2

Table 5: Results of different metrics for *Bleak House*. Scores in translations that differ from the original text shown in bold.

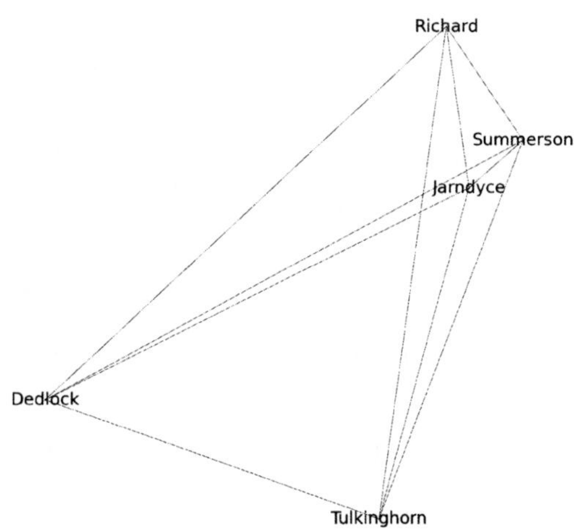

Figure 3: Example for the CN for *Bleak House* for 5 characters with maximum scores.

interesting that the diameter of the original network changes in both translations (original diameter was 3, while in translations it was reduced to 2). *Bleak House* also has the lowest density compared to other texts, which could be due to the size of the text (359,426 words, with the whole subcorpus being 548,383 words).

7 Conclusion

We have created Character Networks for original texts, for Human Translations and Machine Translations for three novels. Results show that for longer novels there are changes in Character Networks both in Human and Machine which may be attributed to the translator style or the target language features in human translations and to the models used in machine translations. One of the most interesting results is that the main 5 characters of *Pride and Prejudice* change in human translations with *Jane Bennet* replacing *Mr. Wickham*. We assume that our research could be enhanced further e.g. by using coreference which would require the creation of an annotated corpus, by grouping different versions of character names together (either manually or automatically) and by studying different language pairs as source-target languages for originals and translations.

References

Apoorv Agarwal, Sriramkumar Balasubramanian, Jiehan Zheng, and Sarthak Dash. 2014. Parsing screenplays for extracting social networks from movies. In *Proceedings of the 3rd Workshop on Computational Linguistics for Literature (CLFL)*, pages 50–58, Gothenburg, Sweden. Association for Computational Linguistics.

Apoorv Agarwal, Augusto Corvalan, Jacob Jensen, and Owen Rambow. 2012. Social network analysis of alice in wonderland. In *CLfL@NAACL-HLT*.

Mona Baker and Harold Somers. 1996. *'Corpus-based Translation Studies: The Challenges that Lie Ahead'*. John Benjamins Publishing Company, Netherlands.

R.H.-G. Chen, C.-C. Chen, and C.-M. Chen. 2019. Unsupervised cluster analyses of character networks in fiction: Community structure and centrality. *Knowledge-Based Systems*, 163:800–810.

Fotis Jannidis. 2013. Character. In Peter Hühn et al., editor, *the living handbook of narratology*. Hamburg University, Hamburg.

Markus John, Martin Baumann, David Schuetz, Steffen Koch, and Thomas Ertl. 2019. A visual approach for the comparative analysis of character networks in narrative texts. In *2019 IEEE Pacific Visualization Symposium*, IEEE Pacific Visualization Symposium, pages 247–256, Piscataway, NJ. IEEE.

Aleksandra Konovalova, Antonio Toral, and Kristiina Taivalkoski-Shilov. 2022. Dr. Livingstone, I presume? polishing of foreign character identification in literary texts. In *Proceedings of the 2022 Conference of the North American Chapter of the Association for Computational Linguistics: Human Language Technologies: Student Research Workshop*, pages 123–128, Hybrid: Seattle, Washington + Online. Association for Computational Linguistics.

Marek Kubis. 2021. Quantitative analysis of character networks in Polish 19th- and 20th-century novels. *Digital Scholarship in the Humanities*, 36(Supplement$_2$) : $ii175 - -ii181$.

Vincent Labatut and Xavier Bost. 2019. Extraction and analysis of fictional character networks: A survey. *CoRR*, abs/1907.02704.

O-Joun Lee and Jason J. Jung. 2019. Integrating character networks for extracting narratives from multimodal data. *Information Processing Management*, 56(5):1894–1923.

O-Joun Lee and Jason J. Jung. 2020. Story embedding: Learning distributed representations of stories based on character networks. *Artificial Intelligence*, 281:103235.

Uri Margolin. 1990. The what, the when, and the how of being a character in literary narrative. *Style*, 24:453–68.

Alan Mislove, Massimiliano Marcon, Krishna P. Gummadi, Peter Druschel, and Bobby Bhattacharjee. 2007. Measurement and analysis of online social networks. In *Proceedings of the 7th ACM SIGCOMM Conference on Internet Measurement*, IMC '07, page 29–42, New York, NY, USA. Association for Computing Machinery.

Franco Moretti. 2011. Network theory, plot analysis. *Stanford Literary Lab 2.*

M. E. J. Newman. 2010. *Networks: an introduction*. Oxford University Press, Oxford; New York.

David Schmidt, Albin Zehe, Janne Lorenzen, Lisa Sergel, Sebastian Düker, Markus Krug, and Frank Puppe. 2021. The FairyNet corpus - character networks for German fairy tales. In *Proceedings of the 5th Joint SIGHUM Workshop on Computational Linguistics for Cultural Heritage, Social Sciences, Humanities and Literature*, pages 49–56, Punta Cana, Dominican Republic (online). Association for Computational Linguistics.

Pavel Vondricka. 2014. Aligning parallel texts with intertext. In *LREC*, pages 1875–1879. European Language Resources Association (ELRA).

Mingzhou Xu, Liangyou Li, Derek. F. Wong, Qun Liu, and Lidia S. Chao. 2020. Document graph for neural machine translation.

A Sources

1. The 5 Least Important Characters in Pride and Prejudice, accessed 09.01.2022. https://theseaofbooks.com/2016/04/29/the-5-least-important-characters-in-pride-and-prejudice/

2. Austenopedia, accessed 09.01.2022. http://austenopedia.blogspot.com/p/entry-number-1.html

3. Bleak House Characters | Course Hero, accessed 09.01.2022. https://www.coursehero.com/lit/Bleak-House/characters/

4. Washington Square Character Analysis | LitCharts, accessed 09.01.2022.https://www.litcharts.com/lit/washington-square/characters

The COVID That Wasn't: Counterfactual Journalism Using GPT

Sil Hamilton
McGill University
sil.hamilton@mcgill.ca

Andrew Piper
McGill University
andrew.piper@mcgill.ca

Abstract

In this paper, we explore the use of large language models to assess human interpretations of real world events. To do so, we use a language model trained prior to 2020 to artificially generate news articles concerning COVID-19 given the headlines of actual articles written during the pandemic. We then compare stylistic qualities of our artificially generated corpus with a news corpus, in this case 5,082 articles produced by CBC News between January 23 and May 5, 2020. We find our artificially generated articles exhibits a considerably more negative attitude towards COVID and a significantly lower reliance on geopolitical framing. Our methods and results hold importance for researchers seeking to simulate large scale cultural processes via recent breakthroughs in text generation.

1 Introduction

The rush to cover new COVID-19 developments as the virus spread across the world over the first half of 2020 induced a variety of editorial mandates from public broadcasters. Chief among these was a desire to mitigate shock from a public unaccustomed to large-scale public health emergencies of the calibre COVID-19 presented. This desire translated into systematic underreporting together with a reluctance to portray COVID-19 as the danger it was (Quandt et al., 2021; Boberg et al., 2020). Broadcasters in the United States (Zhao et al., 2020), the United Kingdom (Garland and Lilleker, 2021), and Italy (Solomon et al., 2021) all exhibited this phenomenon.

Although many studies have verified the above effects, few if any studies to date have considered *alternative* approaches the media could have taken in their portrayal of COVID-19. Evaluating these alternatives is critical given the close relationship between media framing, public opinion, and government policy (Ogbodo et al., 2020; Lopes et al., 2020).

In this paper we present a novel method of simulating media coverage of real world events using Large Language Models (LLMs) as a means of interpreting news industry biases. LLMs have been used in a variety of settings to generate text for real-world applications (Meng et al., 2022; Drori et al., 2021). To our knowledge, they have not yet been used as a tool for critically understanding the interpretation of events through media coverage or other forms of cultural framing.

To do so, we use Generative Pre-trained Transformer 2 (GPT-2), which was trained on text produced prior to the onset of COVID-19, to explore how the Canadian Broadcasting Corporation (CBC) covered COVID and how else they might have reported on these breaking events. By generating thousands of simulated articles, we show how such "counterfactual journalism" can be used as a tool for evaluating real-world texts.

2 Background

The COVID-19 pandemic has given researchers a variety of opportunities to study human behavior in response to a major public health crisis. One core dimension of this experience is reflected in the changing role that the media has played in communicating information to the public in a quickly changing health environment (Van Aelst, 2021; Lilleker et al., 2021). Times of crises enshrine the media as a valuable mediator between the public and government.

This changing role registers itself in the editorial policies at news corporations across the world. Research published over the past two years has confirmed that public news broadcasters in Australia, Sweden, and the United Kingdom all significantly altered their editorial style in response to both societal and governmental pressures (Holland and Lewis, 2021; Shehata et al., 2021; Birks, 2021) during COVID-19.

What this research has so far lacked is the ability

Proceedings of the 6th LaTeCH-CLfL Workshop, pages 83–93
October 16, 2022. ©2022 International Conference on Computational Linguistics

to infer what *could* have been communicated, i.e. what losses were entailed in these editorial shifts. While a great deal of recent work has studied the biases intrinsic to large language models[1], no work to date has used LLMs to study the biases of human generated text. Reporting on real-world events inevitably requires complex choices of selection and evaluation, i.e. which events and which actors to focus on along with modes of valuation surrounding those choices. Simulating textual production given similar prompts such as headlines can provide a means of better understanding the editorial choices made by news agencies.

In using a language model as a simulative mechanism, we draw on a long research tradition of using simulation to understand real-world processes. Simulation has proven a boon for those working in the sciences, including climate science and physics (Winsberg, 2010), and for those working in the social sciences, where agent-based social modelling has led to advances in understanding complex social phenomena (Squazzoni et al., 2014). We seek to bring these techniques to the study of cultural behavior, where simulation has historically seen less of an uptake (Manovich, 2016).

3 Method

Our project consists of the following principal steps:

1. Create a news corpus drawn from our target time-frame (15 January to 5 May 2020) whose content is COVID-19 related.

2. Fine-tune a language model whose generative output is statistically similar to a random sampling of our news source published *before* our target time-frame, i.e. prior to COVID.

3. Using this model, generate full-length text articles using various prompts, including headlines and associated metadata.

4. Compare generated text articles with the original news corpus across key stylistic metrics.[2]

3.1 Corpus

We first obtain a comprehensive collection of CBC News' online articles concerning COVID-19 published between January and May 2020 from Kaggle (Han, 2021). Our corpus contains 5,114 articles all in the form of a headline, subheadline, byline, date published, URL, and article text. Deduplicating and cleaning the corpus with a series of `regex` filters leaves 5,082 articles spread across the first four months of COVID-19.

3.2 Language Model

We use a Transformer-based large language model (LLM) as our CBC simulacrum. We formalize our model as follows: we define an article as a chain of k tokens. Let $X(d, \theta)$ be a probability distribution representing the pulling of a token out from the language model, where d is the article metadata and θ are the prior weights. The probability of drawing k tokens is then

$$\Pr(\bar{x}_k) = \prod_{i=1}^{k} \Pr(X(d, \theta) = x^i | \bar{x}_i) \quad (1)$$

where $\bar{x}^i$ is the ith element of the vector $\bar{x}$, and $\bar{x}_i$ is the vector consisting of the first i elements of the vector $\bar{x}$.

Selecting a pretrained language model suitable for use as a base with which to further train with specific writing samples is a non-trivial task given the plurality of large language models released in the past four years (HuggingFace, 2022). We surveyed models for candidates possessing the following qualities:

- the model must be neither egregious nor lacking in parameter count;

- domain-relevant samples must have been present in the pretraining corpus;

- and most importantly, the model must not be aware of COVID.

Keeping with the above requirements, we select the medium-sized Generative Pre-trained Transformer-2 (GPT-2) as distributed by OpenAI as our candidate model. We found the medium-sized GPT-2 model desirable because it is light enough to be fine-tuned with a single consumer-level GPU; CBC News was the 21st most frequent data source OpenAI used in producing its training set (Clark, 2022) and the model was trained in 2018, two years before the beginning of COVID-19.

[1]See Garrido-Muñoz et al. (2021) for a recent survey of works investigating latent biases present within large language models.

[2]We make our code available here.

3.2.1 Fine-tuning

Provided with sufficient context in the prompt, a freshly obtained GPT-2 model produces qualitatively convincing news article text. It will, however, periodically confuse itself with exactly which publication it is imitating, e.g. it can switch from sounding like CNN to CBC to BBC in a single text. For the purposes of comparison with a single news source, it is thus necessary to fine-tune the model with example texts encapsulating the desired editorial and writing style.

Fine-tuning is a two-step process. We first gather a sequence of texts best representing our target writing mode before fine-tuning a stock GPT-2 model with the training dataset.

Training Dataset We use a web scraper to extract a random selection of news articles published between 2007 and 2020 from CBC News' website. We configure our scraper to pull the same metadata as our COVID-19 dataset: headline, subheadline, date, URL, and article text. We again deduplicate to reduce the possibility of overfitting our model. With this method we collect 1,368 articles with an average length of 660 words per article.

We next construct a dictionary structure to formalize both our generation targets and to provide GPT-2 a consistent interface with which to aid it in logically linking together pieces of metadata. Previous research has indicated fine-tuning LLMs with structured data aids the model in both understanding and reacting to meaningful keywords (Ueda et al., 2021). We therefore structure our fine-tuning data in a dictionary. We provide a template of our structure below.

```
{
 'title': 'Lorem ipsum...',
 'description': 'Lorem ipsum...',
 'text': 'Lorem ipsum...'
}
```

We produce one dictionary per article in our training set. We convert each dictionary to a string before appending it to a final dataset text file with which we train GPT-2.

Training With our training dataset in hand, we proceed to configure our training environment. We use an Adam optimizer with a learning rate of $2e^{-4}$ and run the process (Kingma and Ba, 2014). Training the model for 20,000 steps over six hours results in a final model achieving an average training loss of 0.10.

3.2.2 Model Hyperparameters

In addition to fine-tuning our model, we experiment with different hyperparameters and prompt strategies. Numerous prior studies have described the effects hyperparameter tuning has on the token generation process (van Stegeren and Myśliwiec, 2021; Xu et al., 2022). For our purposes, we use three prompting strategies when generating our synthetic news articles along with one further parameter (*temperature*):

Standard Context Only title and description metadata are used as context d for the model.

Static Context In addition to the standard context, we supply the model with an additional `framework` key containing a brief description of the COVID-19 pandemic found on the website of the Centre for Disease Control (CDC) in May 2020. All generation iterations use the same description.

Rolling Context We again supply the model with an additional `framework` key, but keep the description of COVID-19 contemporaneous with the date of the real article in question. We again use the CDC as a source but instead use the Internet Archive's Way Back Machine API to scrape dated descriptions.[3]

Temperature We manipulate the temperature hyperparameter during generation with half-percentage steps shifting the temperature between $0.1 \ldots 1$. The temperature value is a divisor applied on the `softmax` operation on the returned probability distribution, the affect of which effectively controls the overall likelihood of the most probable words. A high temperature results in a more dynamic and random word choice, while a lower temperature encourages those words which are most likely according to the model's priors.

Models Manipulating the above hyperparemeters gives us the following model framework:

- Model 1: headline-only, temperature between 0.1 and 1
- Model 2: static context, temperature between 0.1 and 1
- Model 3: rolling context, temperature between 0.1 and 1

[3]https://archive.org/help/wayback_api.php

We find that manipulating the `softmax` temperature hyperparameter has no measurable effect on our measures described below. We thus proceed using only three primary models for article generation using a temperature of 0.50, which we refer to in the remainder of the paper as Models 1, 2, and 3. When we rely on a single model to exhibit results Model 3 will be the model we choose to illustrate.

3.3 News Article Generation

Having now obtained both our models and our real-world corpus, we proceed with the text-generation step by prompting our model with metadata taken from CBC's COVID-19 articles. The generation process takes the following form:

1. For each article dictionary, extract the `title` and `description` keys.

2. For each pair of keys, create a new dictionary and add an empty `text` key.

3. Convert all new dictionaries to strings and tokenize using GPT-2's Byte Pair Encoder (BPE).

4. Have GPT-2 predict the contents of the `text` key using the title and description as context, generating 750 tokens in the process.

5. Collect generated tokens and insert into the `text` key.

Doing so generates 5,082 counterfactual news articles that temporally correspond to our CBC News corpus for each of our three primary models. Each article pair in each model thus shares metadata but differs in content, with one being original and the other generated.

We provide here examples drawn from our simulated-actual article pairs to illustrate the performance of our models. Further examples may be found in Appendix A.

Headline 1: "China confirms human-to-human transmission of new coronavirus."

CBC: "Human-to-human transmission has been confirmed in an outbreak of a new coronavirus, the head of a Chinese government expert team said Monday, as the total number of cases more than tripled and the virus spread to other cities in China."

GPT: "An outbreak of a new coronavirus has been confirmed in southern China's Hebei Province, the lead author of a scientific paper said Thursday. The total number of cases more than triples the number of cases in the area, which corresponds to the Beijing and Shanghai hot spots..."

Headline 2: "Quebec travel agencies feel the heat as local travellers cancel flights to China."

CBC: "[Name omitted for privacy] has dreamed of heading to Thailand with her partner for years. But with a five-month-old baby in tow and 14 cases of the coronavirus reported in the area so far..."

GPT: "Quebec travel agencies are feeling the heat as local travellers cancel flights to China. China remains the most dangerous place on Earth for travellers..."

3.4 Measures

To assess the stylistic differences between our simulated and real-world corpora we use the following measures:

Measure 1: Sentiment We measure the sentiment of each article with the open-source Python library *VADER* (Hutto and Gilbert, 2014). Prior studies have validated the use of VADER on journalistic texts, finding the model to be superior to various alternatives in detecting sentiment (Castellanos et al., 2021). We additionally validate a small sample of measured sentences to ensure the accuracy of the tool.

We measure sentiment by first splitting a given article into s sentences, obtain the compound polarity score $(-1...1)$ for each s, then average all s into a final score for the article. The resulting real number represents the overall sentiment of the article.

We apply a number of heuristics to ensure the sentiment score accurately reflects the reality of COVID-19. Words that would previously represent a positive sentiment (such as a "'positive' test") become negative in actuality during a pandemic. It is the same for certain negative terms like "testing 'negative.'" Our heuristics appropriately shift such terms as they appear, allowing for a more accurate measurement. As we later show, our heuristics demonstrate a strong correlation between our simulated and actual corpora.

Sentence	Sentiment
"Thousands of cyclists pedalled along empty Toronto highways today, enjoying the good weather and raising money for charity."	0.8074
"'They're good at running them and we have to create the right environment for them,' she said."	0.6124
"She said it's not good enough to say there's a strategy — that the province needs a strategy in action."	-0.3412
"Transportation Minister Clare Trevena said the incident is 'obviously' worrisome."	-0.4019

Table 1: A subset of sentences and their VADER sentiment score from the control dataset.

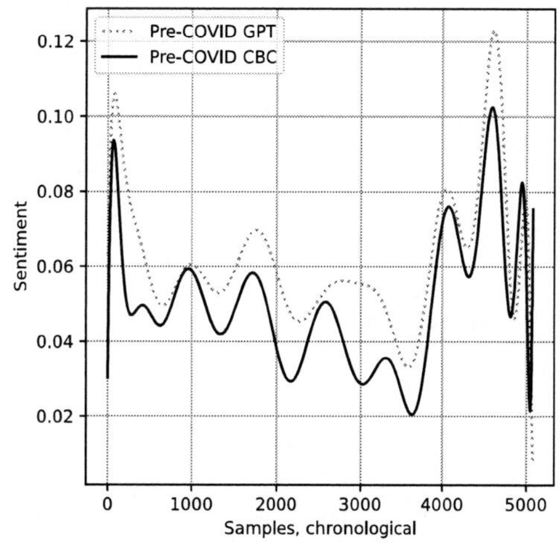

Figure 1: Correlation of sentiment in pre-COVID CBC and GPT articles over a ten year period.

Measure 2: Named Entity Recognition We detect and track named entities in each article with the use of the Python library *spaCy* and their `en_core_web_sm` model (Montani et al., 2022) given prior studies found the model is effective in recognizing named entities (Schmitt et al., 2019). We specifically tally all entities tagged as being a person, geopolitical entity, or organization on an intra-article basis.

Measure 3: Focus We take the ratio of total unique named entities e over article length l and call it *focus*, a novel measure for how focused a given article x is around a given set of entities:

$$focus(x) = \frac{e}{l} \quad (2)$$

We see focus as a measure of concentration around prominent agents in the news.

Measure 4: Key Words We conduct a key word test on each respective corpus to identify repeatedly used terms bearing sentimental weight as per VADER. Following best practices, we only rank significant words in reference to each other rather than assigning significance to any term in isolation. We use the two formulae presented below for determining key words in a given corpus, as provided by Rayson (2012).

We first calculate the averaged frequency E_i for each word in our corpus with

$$E_i = \frac{N_i \sum_i O_i}{\sum_i N_i} \quad (3)$$

where N is the total word count and O is the frequency for the word.

Having now obtained a list of frequencies, we proceed with modifying our frequencies with a log-likelihood (LL) test:

$$LL = 2 \sum_i O_i \ln(\frac{O_i}{E_i}) \quad (4)$$

We then rank our key words according to their respective LL values before comparing our two respective key word lists.

4 Results

4.1 Fine-Tuning Validation

Validating artificial text generation is a challenging task as there is no "right" answer when it comes to creating artificially generated text. Our primary goal in this case is to disambiguate whether our results are an effect of GPT-2 behavior (i.e. a result of model bias) or an effect of our fine-tuning and prompt engineering (i.e. a result of COVID-specific information). To do so, we first create a control dataset consisting of 5,077 randomly sampled CBC articles published prior to COVID between 14 January 2010 and 31 December 2019 ("pre-COVID CBC"). We then generate artificial articles with a standard context and a temperature of 0.5. As shown below, our pre-COVID model produces articles whose distributions are highly statistically similar to the pre-COVID CBC data across our three primary measures, suggesting that any deviation from these levels of correlation in

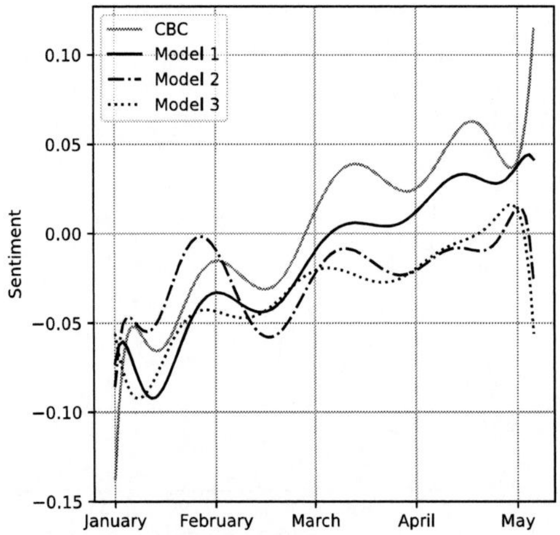

Figure 2: Averaged weekly article sentiment over the first four months of the pandemic.

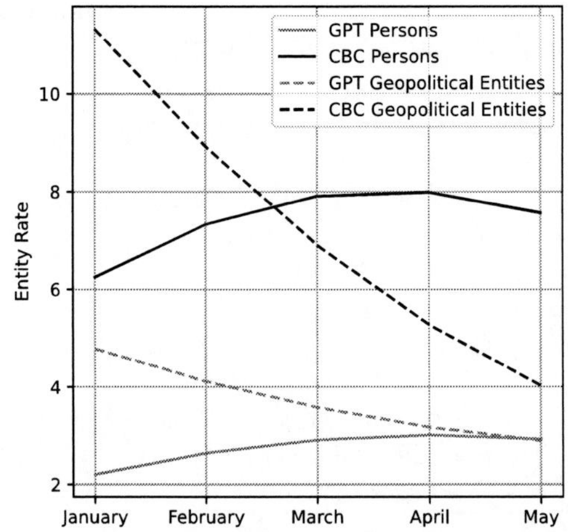

Figure 3: Average values of given entity types in CBC & GPT articles over the first four months of the pandemic for Model 3.

subsequent models is an effect of the COVID fine-tuning and not a default behavior of the model.

Sentiment We find fine-tuning GPT-2 with pre-COVID CBC data produces a model whose textual output is sentimentally similar to pre-COVID CBC articles as may be observed in Figure 1. The sentiment distributions measured in our generated and real-world control datasets share an overlap of 97.7% (Cohen's $d \approx 0.06$) and a moderately positive correlation coefficient of $r \approx 0.57$. We furthermore note GPT-2 is typically more positive in tone than CBC when examining the two distributions as a whole. A selection of validated sentences together with their respective sentiment values are presented in Table 1.

Focus When measuring focus values for the control dataset, we again note a large overlap between GPT-2 and CBC at 93.6% ($d \approx 0.16$) together with a weakly positive correlation or $r \approx 0.17$. These values suggest GPT-2 has learned focus trends latent in the pre-COVID CBC training set.

Key words Our final validation metric is a key words test using the process described in section 3.4. The mean log-likelihood of key words deployed by GPT-2 is 9.61 (95th percentile ≈ 42), indicating such terms are only marginally more likely to be used by GPT than by pre-COVID CBC.

4.2 Measure 1: Sentiment

We begin by noting that CBC News' treatment of COVID-19 during our period of inquiry develops in two stages (Figure 2): articles prior to early March register overall as negative in their sentiment valence (stage 1), while articles written after the first two months become increasingly positive (stage 2). Note that in the pre-COVID data sentiment values were uniformly positive for both CBC and GPT.

When comparing our simulated texts to CBC, we find that our simulated corpora all demonstrate similar trends over time, but with significantly lower levels of positivity than the actual corpus, which is a direct reversal of the pre-COVID baseline. The headline-only model (Model 1) exhibits the highest level of correlation with the CBC corpus at $r \approx 0.28$, while the rolling context model (Model 3) exhibits the starkest overall difference in terms of generating more negative sentiment with an overall effect size of $d \approx -0.28$ (more than double what we see for Model 1 at $d \approx -0.12$). In general, we note that Model 1 adheres most strongly to CBC practices, while adding the CDC context, whether rolling or static, tends to make the models diverge more strongly from CBC practices.

4.3 Measure 2: Named Entity Recognition

Tracking entities classified as persons, geopolitical entities (e.g., countries), and organizations (e.g., the World Health Organization), we find a similar two-stage process as we did when observing sentiment. As is observable in Figure 3, we see a significant decline of geopolitical entities after March in the CBC corpus replaced by a slight increase in notable persons. While the rolling context model exhibits decent correlation with the CBC corpus at $r \approx 0.27$, we find a very strong discrepancy in the relative reliance on geopolitical entities in the GPT corpus compared to CBC with an overall effect size of $d \approx -0.63$.

4.4 Measure 3: Focus

Measuring the personal focus of articles reveals a number of trends. Predominant among these is a clear upwards trend over time in the CBC articles. Continuing the split stage analysis of the past measurements, we find focus increases linearly as the months of the pandemic pass. Higher focus values indicate that fewer entities are being discussed at greater length (i.e. are centralized more strongly). We also note a low correlation between article sentiment and article focus ($r \approx 0.18$), suggesting that focalization around fewer persons is associated with more positive messaging. We explore this effect further in subsection 5.3.

In terms of our simulated corpus, we see that GPT-2 remains relatively consistent in both focus and sentiment over the course of our time window. While there remains an extremely weak positive correlation between sentiment and focus in the Model 3 corpora ($r \approx 0.02$), this is likely an artifact carrying over from the headlines themselves becoming more positive over time.

4.5 Measure 4: Key Words

When we observe the likelihood of a given word's appearance in one corpus or the other, here too we observe some notable trends.[4] We present a subsection of our results in Table 2 using Model 3.

Conducting a qualitative analysis on the top key words underscores two points. First, we find Model 3 (and other models) routinely interpret COVID-19 as a flu, reflected in the model deploying terms like "flu" and "strain" more regularly than CBC News. This interpretation likely accounts for a majority of the discrepancies between the two corpora. Second, we find CBC is more likely to describe societal responses to COVID-19 ("emergency," "crisis"), whereas GPT-2 draws on imagery to convey the medical threat of the disease ("sickened," "infected").

[4]We condition only on VADER vocabulary and not the full set of words.

CBC News	LL	**GPT-2**	LL
"crisis"	475	"flu"	2465
"care"	431	"strain"	871
"cancelled"	371	"infected"	855
"isolation"	363	"great"	558
"emergency"	264	"sickened"	400
"anxiety"	170	"threat"	317
"support"	158	"cancer"	302
"sick"	149	"natural"	249
"critical"	138	"killed"	189
"vulnerable"	134	"dangerous"	167

Table 2: A selection of the ten most prevalent sentimentally-charged terms in either corpus.

5 Discussion

In this section we identify three noteworthy discrepancies between the behavior of our models and the real-world CBC corpus and discuss their potential implications.

5.1 Effect 1: Positivity Bias ("Rally-Around-The-Flag")

We note that all of our simulated models trained on the COVID data generated news that was far more negative than actual coverage, which grew increasingly positive over time. This result is especially notable given that pre-COVID models were uniformly more positive than actual CBC articles.

A relevant theory that can help make sense of this is the "rally-around-the-flag" effect, which posits that national discourse trends in favour of reigning governments during times of crisis (Van Aelst, 2021). Theorists in communication studies note news media do not remain neutral during crises, but instead work to assuage public fears by promoting trust in local leaders (Quandt et al., 2021).

The "rally-around-the-flag" effect could help explain why CBC News articles became more positive as lockdowns began and why our language models, which were not subject to such pressures, nevertheless remained more negative. Regardless of the cause of this discrepancy between our models and CBC, it is worth noting our language models consistently interpreted COVID in more negative terms than this particular public broadcaster. An important aspect to underscore is that we do not see the same effect when we run the same process on a random assortment of pre-COVID arti-

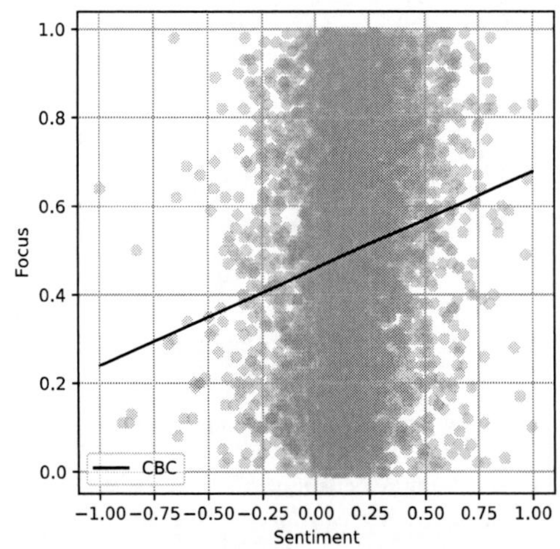

Figure 4: Relationship between focus and sentiment in CBC articles. Focus values are normalized.

cles, meaning our GPT models are not intrinsically more negative but rather interpret these particular events more negatively than CBC.

5.2 Effect 2: Early Geopolitical Bias

As we saw in Figure 3, CBC News relied on considerably more geopolitical entities in the early weeks of the pandemic than in the latter weeks, an effect our models only mildly reproduced. The strong decline of geopolitical entities in the CBC data past February suggests an editorial re-orientation away from understanding the pandemic in global geopolitical terms and towards a local health emergency that is more in line with what our models were producing from the beginning.

5.3 Effect 3: Person versus Disease Centredness

While the rate of geopolitical entities in the CBC data eventually converges with our GPT models, we see that the reliance on individual persons is consistently stronger in the CBC , something we did not see in the pre-COVID models. In conjunction with our key-word findings, this suggests that GPT's interpretation of the pandemic is far more medical and health-oriented ("infected," "sickened") than CBC, whose treatment remained more focused on people. As we show in Figure 4, this person-centredness is also associated with higher levels of positivity. Future work will want to explore whether this personal focalization was unique to the CBC, COVID, or the experience of social upheaval more generally.

6 Conclusion

The aim of our paper has been to develop a framework for using the text-generation affordances of large language models to better understand the interpretive perspectives of the news media when covering major social events. We rely on a simulative process whereby the generation of thousands of alternative views of a real world event can provide a framework for understanding the interpretive perspectives employed by news organizations.

Given that language models can approximate human discourse (Radford et al., 2018), they can be used to generate a distribution of possible responses to an event to better understand the actual selection mechanisms used by real-world actors. Key to this process is validating the extent to which the qualities of artificially generated text are a function of model parameters or the process of fine-tuning, i.e. an effect of the real-world event we aim to simulate. Our aim in doing so is to illustrate how language models can be used as diagnostic tools for human behavior. Given no prior knowledge of a major event, what would a language model say? And what might this tell us about our own human reactions?

Based on the results we have obtained here, we see the following possible avenues for further research using LLMs for textual simulation:

Further Domain Exploration. What other scenarios might LLMs be analytically useful for? In this paper, we have explored LLMs as a tool to assess media coverage, but future work will want to observe how they behave in other domains. News is a particularly well-structured form of textual communication and thus we expect LLMs to perform more adequately in this domain given prior research (Ueda et al., 2021). We await future work exploring other textual domains.

Modeling Audience Expectations. We have used GPT as a tool to assess the interpretive frameworks of the news media, specifically the CBC. However, we might also consider the ways in which LLMs can provide us with population-level expectations about an event. For example, the strong reliance on the "flu" in our models could be seen as a faithful mirror of how laypeople generally have thought about COVID (in distinction from public health experts). While one might argue that this is "erroneous" from a public health perspective, such semantic frameworks may be useful resources in fashioning public communication during times of crisis or upheaval. LLMs may be able to help us better understand what biases audiences are bringing to novel events thus helping experts craft more appropriate messaging that aligns with audience expectations.

Predicting Future Outcomes. While we have used GPT as a tool to assess past behavior, future work could explore the predictive power of LLMs, while exercising a great deal of caution when it comes to their application. For example: Can LLMs identify future valuable research questions? Financial or economic events given changing real-world information? Or potential political crises given the communicative behavior of principal actors (e.g. politicians)? An equally potent line of research will want to explore the dangers of such approaches as in past experiences of predictive policing. New technologies always bring an admixture of analytical affordance and risk that needs to be better understand with respect to LLMs. More experimentation with respect to the efficacy of textual simulation is definitely warranted.

References

Jen Birks. 2021. Just following the science: Fact-checking journalism and the government's lockdown argumentation. In *Power, Media and the Covid-19 Pandemic*, pages 139–158. Routledge.

Svenja Boberg, Thorsten Quandt, Tim Schatto-Eckrodt, and Lena Frischlich. 2020. Pandemic populism: Facebook pages of alternative news media and the Corona crisis – a computational content analysis. Technical Report arXiv:2004.02566, arXiv. ArXiv:2004.02566 [cs] type: article.

Eric Castellanos, Hang Xie, and Paul Brenner. 2021. Global news sentiment analysis. In *Proceedings of the 2019 International Conference of The Computational Social Science Society of the Americas*, pages 121–139, Cham. Springer International Publishing.

Jack Clark. 2022. GPT-2 domains. Original-date: 2019-02-11T04:21:59Z.

Iddo Drori, Sunny Tran, Roman Wang, Newman Cheng, Kevin Liu, Leonard Tang, Elizabeth Ke, Nikhil Singh, Taylor L. Patti, Jayson Lynch, Avi Shporer, Nakul Verma, Eugene Wu, and Gilbert Strang. 2021. A neural network solves and generates mathematics problems by program synthesis: Calculus, differential equations, linear algebra, and more. *CoRR*.

Ruth Garland and Darren Lilleker. 2021. From consensus to dissensus: The UK's management of a pandemic in a divided nation. In *Political communication in the time of coronavirus*, pages 17–32. Routledge.

Ismael Garrido-Muñoz, Arturo Montejo-Ráez, Fernando Martínez-Santiago, and L. Alfonso Ureña-López. 2021. A survey on bias in deep NLP. *Applied Sciences*, 11(7):3184.

Ryan Han. 2021. COVID-19 News articles open research dataset.

Kate Holland and Monique Lewis. 2021. Mapping national news reports on COVID-19 in Australia: Topics, sources, and imagined audiences. In Monique Lewis, Eliza Govender, and Kate Holland, editors, *Communicating COVID-19*, pages 59–81. Springer International Publishing, Cham.

HuggingFace. 2022. Models - Hugging Face.

Clayton Hutto and Eric Gilbert. 2014. Vader: A parsimonious rule-based model for sentiment analysis of social media text. In *Proceedings of the international AAAI conference on web and social media*, volume 8, pages 216–225.

Diederik P. Kingma and Jimmy Ba. 2014. Adam: A method for stochastic optimization.

Darren Lilleker, Ioana A Coman, Miloš Gregor, and Edoardo Novelli. 2021. Political communication and COVID-19: Governance and rhetoric in global comparative perspective. In *Political Communication and COVID-19*, pages 333–350. Routledge.

Bárbara Lopes, Catherine Bortolon, and Rusi Jaspal. 2020. Paranoia, hallucinations and compulsive buying during the early phase of the COVID-19 outbreak in the United Kingdom: A preliminary experimental study. *Psychiatry Research*, 293:113455.

Lev Manovich. 2016. The science of culture? social computing, digital humanities and cultural analytics. *Journal of Cultural Analytics*.

Yu Meng, Jiaxin Huang, Yu Zhang, and Jiawei Han. 2022. Generating training data with language models: Towards zero-shot language understanding. *CoRR*.

Ines Montani, Matthew Honnibal, Matthew Honnibal, Sofie Van Landeghem, Adriane Boyd, Henning Peters, Paul O'Leary McCann, Maxim Samsonov, Jim Geovedi, Jim O'Regan, Duygu Altinok, György Orosz, Søren Lind Kristiansen, Daniël De Kok, Lj Miranda, Roman, Explosion Bot, Leander Fiedler, Grégory Howard, Edward, Wannaphong Phatthiyaphaibun, Richard Hudson, Yohei Tamura, Sam Bozek, Murat, Ryn Daniels, Peter Baumgartner, Mark Amery, and Björn Böing. 2022. explosion/spaCy: New span ruler component, JSON (de)serialization of doc, span analyzer and more.

Jude Nwakpoke Ogbodo, Emmanuel Chike Onwe, Joseph Chukwu, Chinedu Jude Nwasum, Ekwutosi Sanita Nwakpu, Simon Ugochukwu Nwankwo, Samuel Nwamini, Stephen Elem, and Nelson Iroabuchi Ogbaeja. 2020. Communicating health crisis: a content analysis of global media framing of COVID-19. *Health Promotion Perspectives*, 10(3):257–269.

Thorsten Quandt, Svenja Boberg, Tim Schatto-Eckrodt, and Lena Frischlich. 2021. Stooges of the system or holistic observers?: A computational analysis of news media's facebook posts on political actors during the coronavirus crisis in Germany. In *Political Communication in the Time of Coronavirus*, pages 101–119. Routledge.

Alec Radford, Jeffrey Wu, Rewon Child, David Luan, Dario Amodei, and Ilya Sutskever. 2018. Language models are unsupervised multitask learners.

Paul Rayson. 2012. *Corpus Analysis of Key Words*. John Wiley & Sons, Ltd.

Xavier Schmitt, Sylvain Kubler, Jérémy Robert, Mike Papadakis, and Yves LeTraon. 2019. A replicable comparison study of NER software: StanfordNLP, NLTK, OpenNLP, SpaCy, Gate. In *2019 Sixth International Conference on Social Networks Analysis, Management and Security*.

Adam Shehata, Isabella Glogger, and Kim Andersen. 2021. The Swedish way: How ideology and media use influenced the formation, maintenance and change of beliefs about the coronavirus. In *Political Communication in the Time of Coronavirus*. Taylor & Francis.

Sheldon Solomon, Daniele Rostellato, Ines Testoni, Fiorella Calabrese, and Guido Biasco. 2021. Journalistic denial of death during the very first traumatic period of the Italian COVID-19 pandemic. *Behavioral Sciences*, 11(3):41.

Flaminio Squazzoni, Wander Jager, and Bruce Edmonds. 2014. Social simulation in the social sciences: A brief overview. *Social Science Computer Review*, 32(3):279–294.

Alberto Ueda, Rodrygo L. T. Santos, Craig Macdonald, and Iadh Ounis. 2021. Structured fine-tuning of contextual embeddings for effective biomedical retrieval. In *Proceedings of the 44th International ACM SIGIR Conference on Research and Development in Information Retrieval*, pages 2031–2035, Virtual Event Canada. ACM.

Peter Van Aelst. 2021. COVID-19 as an ideal case for a rally-around-the-flag?: How government communication, media coverage and a polarized public sphere determine leadership approvals in times of crisis. In *Political Communication in the Time of Coronavirus*, pages 1–13. Routledge.

Judith van Stegeren and Jakub Myśliwiec. 2021. Fine-tuning GPT-2 on annotated RPG quests for NPC dialogue generation. In *The 16th International Conference on the Foundations of Digital Games (FDG) 2021*, pages 1–8, Montreal QC Canada. ACM.

Eric Winsberg. 2010. Science in the age of computer simulation. In *Science in the Age of Computer Simulation*. University of Chicago Press.

Frank F. Xu, Uri Alon, Graham Neubig, and Vincent Josua Hellendoorn. 2022. A systematic evaluation of large language models of code. In *Proceedings of the 6th ACM SIGPLAN International Symposium on Machine Programming*, pages 1–10, San Diego CA USA. ACM.

Erfei Zhao, Qiao Wu, Eileen M Crimmins, and Jennifer A Ailshire. 2020. Media trust and infection mitigating behaviours during the COVID-19 pandemic in the USA. *BMJ Global Health*, 5(10):e003323.

A Article Samples

We present further samples of both CBC and GPT-written articles concerning COVID-19:

Headline 3: "Air Canada suspends all flights to Beijing and Shanghai amid coronavirus outbreak."

CBC: "Airlines around the world have started to cancel more flights to China as coronavirus fears have dragged down demand for air travel in the area. Air Canada normally runs 33 flights a week to China out of Toronto, Vancouver and Montreal but on Wednesday the airline announced it would halt all flights to Beijing and Shanghai until the end of February at least. "Air Canada's last flights departing Canada will operate today and the return flights will operate from Beijing and Shanghai tomorrow, January 30, 2020," the airline said. "Affected customers will be notified and offered options, including travel on other carriers where available, or a full refund. Air Canada regrets this situation and apologizes for the serious disruption to our customers' travel plans," the airline said in a statement. It isn't the only airline scaling back. British Airways on Wednesday suspended all direct flights to and from mainland China through to the end of February, although it will maintain limited service to Hong Kong..."

GPT: "Toronto's processing plant for large appliances grounded all Air Canada flights heading to and from Shanghai after Shanghai Municipal Airport in China confirmed that there has been a record number of cases of coronavirus there this year. The grounding applies to all international flights including incoming and outgoing Air Canada and Air Canada Plus flights to and from Shanghai. China is seeing a soaring number of avian coronavirus infections at one point making it the top of the list of infectious diseases to watch out for. There is a recent trend of high-pathients experiencing shedding of viral loads, Peter Clark, assistant regional director of the Shanghai Centers for Disease Control and Prevention, told CBC News. This could be a result of sharing among regions of the same influenza virus circulation area...'"

Headline 4: "Officials in northern Sask. link COVID-19 cases with travel to Alberta."

CBC: "Provincial and Indigenous health officials in northern Saskatchewan are investigating COVID-19 cases they say are linked to travel to Alberta. A statement from the Saskatchewan Health Authority says it and the Northern Inter-Tribal Health Authority have begun a contact tracing investigation into new cases of the novel coronavirus in the province's north that are linked to cross-boundary travel. The statement notes there have been reports of a number of COVID-19 cases at an oil sands facility north of Fort McMurray, Alta., although it doesn't specify whether any of the new cases in Saskatchewan are believed to be connected to that outbreak...."

GPT: "Northern Saskatchewan officials are linking travel to Alberta to clusters of a cluster infection. Health officials in Edmonton and Calgary are also investigating cases that are linked to travel to the Alberta province. Officials in northern Sask. are linking travel to Alberta to clusters of COVID-19, a coronavirus that's ravaged South Asia in the last 30 years. Health officials in Edmonton and Calgary are also investigating cases that are linked to travel to the Alberta province. (CBC) Minister of Health Emily Lackord says all of Canada is susceptible, but the outbreak is most aggressive yet. Saskatchewan's northern boundary is the only place with the disease, she says...'"

War and Pieces: Comparing Perspectives About World War I and II Across Wikipedia Language Communities

Ana Smith
Dept. of Computer Science
Cornell University
alsmith@cs.cornell.edu

Lillian Lee
Dept. of Computer Science
Cornell University
llee@cs.cornell.edu

Abstract

Wikipedia is widely used to train models for various tasks including semantic association, text generation, and translation. These tasks typically involve aligning and using text from multiple language editions, with the assumption that all versions of the article present the same content. But this assumption may not hold. We introduce a methodology for approximating the extent to which narratives of conflict may diverge in this scenario, focusing on articles about World War I and II battles written by Wikipedia's communities of editors across four language editions. For simplicity, our unit of analysis representing each language communities' perspectives is based on national entities and their subject-object-relation context, identified using named entity recognition and open-domain information extraction. Using a vector representation of these tuples, we evaluate how similarly different language editions portray how and how often these entities are mentioned in articles. Our results indicate that (1) language editions tend to reference associated countries more and (2) how much one language edition's depiction overlaps with all others varies.

1 Introduction

Wikipedia's expansive content and multiple language editions have made it an invaluable resource, particularly for the training of large language models and translation models in natural language processing (NLP). Less work has gone into quantifying the *differences* among language editions though. In particular, military conflicts, with their political implications and charged nature due to casualties, may be described in distinct ways by different language editions. While community guidelines ensure some quality control and consistency across articles, Table 1 shows that in descriptions from German (DE), English (EN), French (FR), and Italian (IT) Wikipedia articles about the World War I battle at Verdun, there is still disagreement about whether the German objective was to "bleed" the French army. Instead of glossing over this difference, we aim to quantitatively measure it.

There are challenges to measuring these differences, though. Language editions may differ because of (1) linguistic differences in expression; (2) lack of information access, especially due to language barriers; and (3) an author's subjective preferences for sources. There is work on identifying subjectivity in Wikipedia (Recasens et al., 2013; Pavalanathan et al., 2018). But these supervised approaches, while successful, are limited by their need for explicit annotations. This work instead uses unsupervised methods to measure reporting tendencies of Wikipedia articles about battles in World Wars I and II from four language versions — German (DE), English (EN), French (FR), and Italian (IT).

We narrow our scope of analysis to national entities and their contexts, posing the following computationally-amenable question about the representation of such entities:

> *RQ1: How do combatant entity distributions vary among articles from different language editions about the same event?*

Although an author's preferred writing language is not equivalent to an author's nationality, language editions are known to reflect geopolitics in images (He et al., 2018), cultural topics (Tian et al., 2021), and community participation (Shi et al., 2019). Therefore, we hypothesize the following:

> *H1: Languages associated with particular combatants will emphasize that combatant more than others.*

While entity distributions alone facilitate comparisons, the context in which those entities appear may also contribute to subtle differences in perspective. We incorporate context by using (subject,

Proceedings of the 6th LaTeCH-CLfL Workshop, pages 94–104

DE	*Summary: Germany did* not *intend to "bleed" France*
	In contrast to subsequent representations by the Chief of Staff of the German Army, Erich von Falkenhayn , [3] the original intention of the attack was not to "bleed" the French army without spatial targets. With this assertion made in 1920, Falkenhayn tried to give the unsuccessful attack and the negative German myth of the "blood mill" an alleged meaning.
EN	*Summary: Germany* did *intend to inflict mass casualties on France*
	Falkenhayn wrote in his memoir that he sent an appreciation of the strategic situation to the Kaiser in December 1915, "...French General Staff would be compelled to throw in every man they have. If they do so the forces of France will bleed to death." The German strategy in 1916 was to inflict mass casualties on the French, a goal achieved against the Russians from 1914 to 1915, to weaken the French Army to the point of collapse.
FR	*Summary: Germany did* not *intend to "bleed" France*
	According to the version that Falkenhayn gives of his plan in his Memoirs after the war 15 , the goal is to engage in a battle at the loss ratio favorable to the German army, and therefore to discourage France to obtain the stop of the fights... Recent historical works, notably those of the German historian Holger Afflerbach, cast doubt on the version of Falkenhayn who claimed to want to "bleed dry" the French army.
IT	*Summary: Germany* did *intend to "bleed" France*
	... [I]n Verdun the purpose of the Falkenhayn offensive was to "bleed the French army to death drop by drop." In the plans of the German Chief of General Staff , the moral and propaganda importance of an attack on Verdun would have meant that all the French effort was poured into the defense of a stronghold considered to be of primary importance for France.

Table 1: Segments of different-language articles that provide contrasting accounts of a supposed German strategy to "bleed" France in the Battle of Verdun. (Google Translate was used for German (DE), French (FR), and Italian (IT); English (EN) is the original.)

relation, object) *tuples* filtered for the geopolitical entities used above, asking the second question:

> *RQ2: How are tuples from different language editions grouped or separated when clustered?*

Differences between language editions are expected, but the gap between languages associated with Germany and Italy and the languages associated with the United States, Britain and France might be expected to have more overlap in their accounts of battles, given wartime alliances:

> *H2: The German (DE) and Italian (IT) language editions of Wikipedia will overlap more in facts than the English (EN) and French (FR) language editions.*

Contributions. In a quantitative analysis of entity distributions related to language-country association, we find a language edition associated with a particular country does tend to emphasize that country more than other language editions do (H1 validated). An additional contribution is an approach to reveal conflicting or corroborating tuples by using a downstream diagnostic *battle outcome* inference task. The results of this task indicate that several factors discussed in more detail below affect representation quality.

We demonstrate that though there are more instances of standalone tuples, clustering facts based on similarity across language editions and averaging their representation yields a representation that is more linearly correlated with battle outcome. The results of our outcome prediction task suggest that different language editions provide complementary information and models benefit from using all language versions rather than just one.

In this work, we describe multilingual Wikipedia articles. But there are parallels to news articles from different broadcasters and countries that produce documents covering the same events. A possible extension is to identify domain-specific indicators of differences in opinion in scenarios where a pre-built lexicon is not immediately available, but multiple perspectives are. Another possible application of this methodology is as a diagnostic tool to identify potential sources of bias in Wikipedia datasets.

2 Related work

There is prior work extracting relations between and events involving geopolitical entities from text (O'Connor et al., 2013; Chambers et al., 2015; Makarov, 2018; Han et al., 2019; Stoehr et al., 2021); see Hürriyetoğlu et al. (2021) for a recent collection of papers. We focus on managing and comparing descriptions of such relations across different language communities (McCarthy et al., 2021; Scharf et al., 2021). (Of course, multilingual parallel and comparable corpora have been a mainstay of machine translation since its beginnings.)

2.1 Multilingual Wikipedia

Our research is primarily a study of the relationship between a Wikipedia article's content and its relationship to the corresponding article in another language edition. Other work compares Wikipedia language editions from the perspective of the geography associated with an article (Lieberman and Lin, 2009), the imagery of articles (He et al., 2018; Porter et al., 2020), and perspectives of colingual groups on common topics (Tian et al., 2021). Our project is closely aligned in spirit with other analyses of how wars are described across different language communities in Wikipedia (Gieck et al., 2016; Zhou et al., 2015; Bridgewater, 2017; Kubś, 2021)

2.2 Wikipedia and information extraction

Wikipedia has served various purposes outside of its obvious role as an open-edited, free encyclopedia. After years of studies on Wikipedia's information quality (Stvilia et al., 2007; Arazy et al., 2011; Kumar et al., 2016), more recent work focuses more on leveraging it to answer questions (Chen et al., 2017), populate knowledge bases (Hoffmann et al., 2011; Wu and Weld, 2008), and generate summary tables (Liu et al., 2019). The former line of work more directly questions the quality of Wikipedia content. We do not assess the quality of information directly, but rather assess the prevalence of certain pieces of information. Our work is similar to the latter line of work in that we attempt to simplify Wikipedia content to a few phrases for analysis. Our work differs from prior work in that it does not extract snippets from a larger body of text to fill in answers. Rather, it compares snippets from multiple language editions.

3 Data Collection

Our corpus of battle descriptions is collected from multiple language editions of Wikipedia. To identify potential candidate articles for download, we take the names of articles listed under the English language categories "Battles of World War I" and "Battles of World War II"[1] and corresponding categories in other language editions (e.g., Battaglie_della_prima_guerra_mondiale) identified by interlanguage Wikilinks for German, French, and Italian. These languages were selected because they are the primary languages employing Latin script used by combatant countries with the largest recorded casualties.[2]

	WWI			WWII		
Rank	Lang	No.	≉ En	Lang	No.	≉ En
1	EN	606	—	EN	2958	—
2	FR	373	23%	FR	1358	10%
3	IT	327	7%	IT	888	10%
4	DE	225	16%	DE	788	5%

Table 2: Number of retrieved distinct identifiers for Wikipedia articles listed under the WWI or WWII battle categories. (Recall that we restricted attention to Latin-script languages for countries with the most casualties.) "≉ En" columns: % of articles in that language without an English-language equivalent.

Different language editions do encompass different sets of articles, with some articles available in only a subset of data. So even if the communities are comprised of the same individuals with the same aims in every language edition, the output is non-equivalent for all languages. In total, our dataset has 765 distinct WWI battles and 3430 distinct WWII battles. See Table 2 for the distribution across language editions.

After the names of battle articles in different languages are collected, they are disambiguated by linking them to a Wikidata item identifier known as a QID, obtained by querying the WikiData API. QIDs link articles across different language editions, and we use the reduced set of QIDs to identify all language editions of each article. Though there is still a bias for articles grouped under the "Battles of World War I" and "Battles of World War II" categories, this additional step reduces the likelihood that we are collecting data only visible from English Wikipedia. For example, the DE version of Wikipedia tends to have fewer articles, possibly because they conceptualize warfare differently (e.g., campaigns instead of actions).

Full-text content is then downloaded from Wikipedia using the PetScan interface[3]. The next section discusses how this data is further cleaned

[1] https://en.wikipedia.org/wiki/Category:Battles_of_World_War_I, https://en.wikipedia.org/wiki/Category:Battles_of_World_War_II

[2] We repeat that the restriction to Latin script is an attempt to minimize processing differences between languages. Moving to a larger set of more diverse languages is a direction for future work.

[3] https://en.wikipedia.org/wiki/Wikipedia:PetScan

WWI				WWII			
DE	EN	FR	IT	DE	EN	FR	IT
german	german	german	german	german	german	german	german
british	british	british	british	japanese	japanese	japanese	japanese
french	french	french	french	british	british	british	british
russian	germans	germans	germans	soviet	italian	french	italian
army	russian	france	russian	american	soviet	germans	soviet
germans	ottoman	russian	italian	us	french	soviet	germans
division...	france	ottoman	germany	allied	germans	american	french
...(german empire				germans	allied	us	american
italian	russians	germany	france	italian	us	germany	us
german empire	belgian	italian	russians	french	american	france	allied
austria	germany	armenian	russia	army	germany	allied	germany
france	allied	austro	austrian	americans	france	italian	italy
hungary	armenian	austria	austro	france	japan	japan	france
reserve division	italian	hungary	ottoman	infantry...	axis	americans	americans
army corps	russia	turkish	turkish	...division			
russians	austria	somme	army	category	united states	united states	japan
category	belgium	allied	belgian	polish	dutch	soviets	soviets
austrian	uk	russians	allied	dutch	chinese	polish	polish
reserve corps	hungary	ottomans	italy	germany	the united states	dutch	axis
weblinks	romanian	italy	meuse	japan	italy	italy	army
germany	turkish	serbian	belgium	the red army	italians	category	chinese

Table 3: Top 20 most frequent non-pronoun, non-individual-human terms per language (after →Spanish→English translation) automatically tagged as geopolitical named entities in our World War I (left) and World War II (right) corpora.

and partitioned.

4 Associated Languages and Entities

Initially, all battle articles listed under the battle categories in each of the four languages are collected. But because this work compares language editions, only the intersection of the four language editions is used. This results in 131 articles for World War I and 414 articles for World War II. This subset is then processed as described below.

4.1 Processing articles

Our approach requires the use of open domain information extraction, which has until recently been largely restricted to English, so all articles must be translated to English for our method. To compensate for translation noise in our non-English articles, all articles (including English articles) are translated to "new", fifth language, Spanish, and then to English using Google Translate.[4] Importantly, we subject English to potential translation errors to avoid privileging it as the only language under consideration that would not have undergone translation otherwise.

[4]We employed only European languages to stay within a family of relatively related languages; future work can be more ambitious about language choices.

Translation. Using different language revisions enables us to probe differences across groups of editors employing the same language. On the other hand, although the original language of the articles is expected to give the most accurate distinctions, we choose to work with translated versions of the articles so that we can apply a standardized set of NLP tools developed for English. To avoid privileging the originally-English articles, all language versions are first translated to a *new* language (Spanish, given that there are many high-quality machine translation models between Spanish and other languages) before being then retranslated into English via Google Translate.

Text cleaning The collected articles are in xml format, complete with internal links, templates, and other artifacts. The article text is sentence- and word-tokenized; then, internal links are simplified to the alt-text only, and we remove templates including infoboxes, inline references, and text starting from the section headers "References" and "See also".

Named entity tagging. Though there are two major sides in these wars, there are numerous combatants. We use the named entity tagger to identify geopolitical entities and persons. Manual inspection of the entities in the context of the article is used to identify ties to a single political entity. Al-

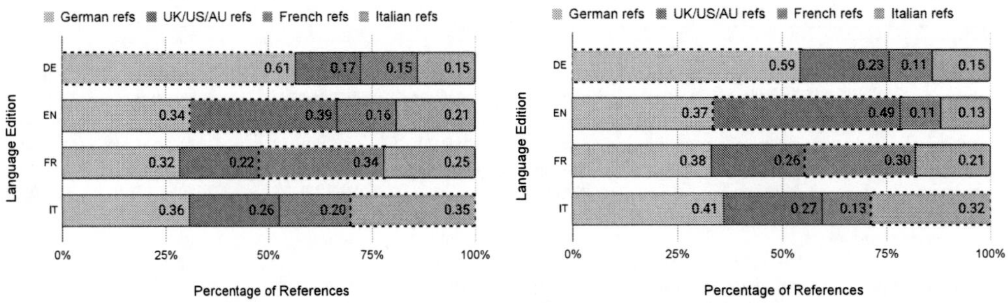

(a) WWI

(b) WWII

Figure 1: Comparison of per-article proportions of self-references vs. other-references, as discussed in §4.3.

liances of entities (e.g., Allied Powers) are considered separately.

Associating entities with nations/alliances. Recall our first research question is related to the combatant distributions across language editions. One difficulty is associating a particular entity with a combatant nation, due to issues with granularity and type of reference: American entities may be referred to as *the United States* (nation name), *Eisenhower* (leadership), *333rd Field Artillery Battalion* (military unit), or *they* (pronoun). To address this issue, a list of nations, leaders grouped by nation, and military units by nation are collected for each article from English Wikipedia categories and pages. (We exclude pronouns and entities not clearly identified by nationality as existing coreference tools did not prove reliable enough on our data.) Though this does not encompass all entities mentioned in our corpus, it does capture prominent entities.

4.2 Entity-count statistics

In total, there are 88,317 entities in our WWI corpus and 274,713 entities in our WWII corpus. Table 3 lists the most common non-pronoun non-person grammatical subjects in our World War I and World War II data. The most prominent national entity across all language editions by far is Germany. This is to be expected given that in both wars Germany was engaged with combatants on both the Eastern Front and the Western Front, whereas most other combatants only appear on one Front. In the World War I corpus, the British are the second most common national entity subject. In the World War II corpus, the Japanese are the second most prominent national entity. Not shown here is a list of PERSON entities. The most frequent persons listed in those tables are, surprisingly, *battle* in WWI and, unsurprisingly, *Hitler* in WWII. Our tags do contain noise. The word *battle* should *not* be tagged as a person, but it was tagged so across all language editions. The spaCy (Honnibal and Montani, 2017) en_core_web_sm model was used to obtain named entity and part-of-speech information.

4.3 Associated-language test (RQ1)

In the introduction, we hypothesized that languages associated with a combatant country would reference that combatant as a subject more than any other combatant. To evaluate our hypothesis, we compare the relative proportion of counts per article of *self-references* (i.e., references to a nation by its associated language) to *other-references* (i.e., references to a nation by other languages). Each other-reference is normalized by the number of other languages (i.e., 3) for a more balanced comparison to other self-references. Though doing so reduces statistical power, instances are grouped by war for better analysis.

Figure 1 is a stacked barplot of the self-reference and other-reference proportions in our dataset. To test significance between populations, we use the Mann-Whitney U test implementation in scipy (Virtanen et al., 2020), as our population sizes differ between the "self" country reference group and the "other" countries reference group and are non-normally distributed. When using a Bonferroni correction of 2 on a p-value threshold of 0.01 since a test was run for each war, our p-values for both WWI (5.46e-6) and WWII (8.61e-4) are significant at <0.005. Though the data are not normally distributed, the self-reference distribution suggests that our hypothesis H1 is supported (i.e., languages associated with particular nations are more likely to mention those nations than ones that are not).

A breakdown of references by language edition and country reveals more nuance, with self-references highlighted by the dashed borders. The significance of the above test may be attributed in part to DE's many self-references and other language editions' many other-references to DE. This is likely because Germany's engagement on both Eastern and Western fronts made it a more common reference overall. That said, for every language version, the proportion of self-references is greater than references to that country in other language editions. This indicates there is indeed a tendency to emphasize the countries commonly associated with these languages. We consider H1 validated.

5 Tuple Clusters

While the entities alone indicate a preference for language editions to reference their associated countries more, the context in which they occur may aid our understanding of why these differences in distribution occur. We hypothesized that overlap among languages may be more likely between English and French accounts and German and Italian accounts than any combination of the two. But overlap alone says little about why accounts may differ.

We simplify article text to (subject, object, relation) tuples. Solely as a means to validate the quality of representation, a domain-specific outcome inference task is used. The intuition is that a better representation should enable a linear classifier to learn a correlation between outcome and text, among other properties.

5.1 Extracting tuples and clustering

Tuple extraction. Once all articles are translated, (subject, relation, object) tuples are extracted with the Stanford NLP Toolkit's OpenIE implementation (Angeli et al., 2015). This system was chosen instead of a neural approach to limit the possibility that information is hallucinated or generated that was not in the original text (such problems are known to occur in neural models such as Imojie (Kolluru et al., 2020)).

One problem is that essentially redundant tuples may be considered distinct. Consider the following tuples:

1. EN: ('sides', 'suffered casualties with', 'numbers of soldiers succumbing to freezing')
2. EN: ('sides', 'suffered casualties with', '**large** numbers of soldiers succumbing to freezing')

The only difference between (1) and (2) is the adjective "large" in the object. To address this problem, we group tuples by subject and relation per article section (e.g., == *Aftermath* ==) and take only the tuple within each group with the longest object (in tokens). No subject should be a substring of another subject, and no relation should be a substring of another relation. Hence, tuple (2) would be retained and (1) discarded.

Tuple representation. Following Kristof et al. (2021), averaged word embeddings are used to represent text content. As a baseline, we compare this against a 1- to 3-gram bag-of-words.

We begin with a basic representation of tuple t that doesn't distinguish between subject, object, and verb (relation) status:

$$v_{sro} = \frac{1}{|t|}\sum_{w \in t} \text{emb}(w) \quad (1)$$

where emb() is a mapping of w to a pretrained vector. This reflects our naive hypothesis that treating an entity (e.g., France) as an object is not distinct from treating it as the subject. We also compare a pretrained embedding (GLoVe (Pennington et al., 2014)) and an embedding trained on our corpus (using fasttext) only to assess the extent to which the context of World War conflict influences a model. Though GLoVe is trained on more data, the nature of conflict may contravene typical associative assumptions and domain-specific words (especially entities) may be dropped. Both vectors are of dimension 100. This dimension was chosen because previous studies suggest that dimensions on the order of 100 are relatively similar in performance but better than those with dimensions on the order of 10 (Rodriguez and Spirling, 2021). In the case of GLoVe, a random vector was assigned to out-of-vocabulary words. The fasttext embeddings were trained using a character n-gram of maximum size 3 and a learning rate of 0.05. These embeddings are trained over the combined corpus (both WWI and WWII). Words appearing in fewer than 0.1% of tuples are excluded to manage the number of features and prevent overfitting.

The first representation neglects the structure denoted by the tuple. But this may be harmful in cases where distinguishing the subject and the object tuple matters (e.g., (France, defeated, Germany) is

1st lang	Tuples contributed to cluster
DE	('German armed forces', 'lost will', 'resist')
DE	('German positions', 'against Army is', 'United Kingdom')
DE	('British troops', 'Only announced', 'their victory at Battle of Havrincourt')
DE	('German forces', 'lost will', 'resist')
EN	('Germans', 'could consolidate', 'their positions')
EN	('American forces', 'face', 'difficult task')
EN	('Germans', 'encouraged', 'Allies')
EN	('Germans', 'were', 'weakening')
FR	('German divisions', '6 at', 'least')
FR	('German army', 'withdraw until', 'November 11 1918')
IT	('advance', 'would', 'would also backed by 300 machine guns')

Table 4: An example multilingual (s, r, o) cluster obtained from articles on the 1918 Battle of Havrincourt. The component tuples, while from four distinct languages, generally correspond to the "tuple" that the Germans were unable to hold their position against British troops.

distinct from (Germany, defeated, France)). To address this, a 300 dimensional representation is concatenated to v_{sro}. The mean vector for each word in the subject (s), relation (r), and object (o) is calculated as above and concatenated as follows:

$$v^{(t)} = [v_s; v_r; v_o] \quad (2)$$

Though the structure of $v^{(t)}$ ensures that the word *France* as an object is distinct from *France* as a subject, similar tuples may be written in the passive voice in one language and not another. To combat the issue of word order, $v^{(t)}$ is concatenated to v_{sro} to form the second feature vector used:

$$v^{(t)}_{final} = [v_s; v_r; v_o; v_{sro}] \quad (3)$$

Clustering tuples into tuples. The ultimate goal is to group similar tuples from different language versions in such a way that we minimize the size of the clusters — so that the included tuples should be more similar — while maximizing heterogeneity of within-cluster source languages, that is, the number of source languages represented in the cluster. To address both limits, we implement a hierarchical K-means clustering algorithm with thresholds for cluster sizes. Euclidean distance is used to measure (dis)similarity among instances. Clusters are recursively split until they contain fewer than 16 instances. Table 4 shows an example cluster.

Because word embeddings may associate words by type (e.g., tuples with *Germany* and *France* as subjects appear in the same cluster), an additional one-hot vector is prepended to $v^{(t)}_{final}$ to split tuple clusters along country lines when clustering.

$$v^{(t)}_{cluster} = [a_{\text{de}}; a_{\text{en}}; a_{\text{fr}}; a_{\text{it}}; v^{(t)}_{final}] \quad (4)$$

Here, $a_{<\text{language}>}$ is 1 if the associated language occurs in the subject of the tuple, otherwise 0. A single cluster can be represented by the mean of all $v^{(t)}_{cluster}$ tuple representations in the cluster. It is this mean vector that is used in the following experiments.

5.2 Validating representation quality

To assess the quality of the proposed representations, we use the outcome of the battle as a target to evaluate the extent these representations implicitly attribute advantages to (or minimize disadvantages of) combatants. For this task, the input is a tuple representation and the output is the *outcome* (e.g., 0 if Germans won, otherwise 1). Not every tuple is expected to directly correspond to the outcome, but any tuple that does should benefit from a better representation as indicated by an increase in model precision. In our experiments, we employ 3-fold cross-validation; for each fold, we fit a logistic regression model using the scikit-learn implementation (Pedregosa et al., 2011). The regularization parameter C is tuned over the range [0.01, 0.1, 0.5, 1.0, 3.0]. The results of evaluating the model on a held-out test set are shown in Table 5.

Results. The bag-of-words (*bow*) representation presents a competitive baseline, particularly for WWI, as do the smaller $v_s ro$ representations. The WWII corpus benefits from the word embedding representation across the board, though. (Bear in mind that it is approximately 4 times larger than the WWI corpus.) Additionally, averaging the tuple representations per cluster yields even better outcome inference results — for example, on WWII using fasttext, F1 goes from .567 for unclustered to .662 for clustered — likely because of the larger context on which it draws in comparison to a single tuple.

Though there are fewer instances, using clusters is more advantageous in outcome inference than using individual tuples suggesting that the context derived from grouping similar tuples is useful for corroborating outcomes. Part of this effect may be due to complementary information from different language editions. Using $v^{(t)}_{cluster}$, we turn

feature	WWI tuples F1	WWI tuples recall	WWI tuples prec	WWI clusters F1	WWI clusters recall	WWI clusters prec	WWII tuples F1	WWII tuples recall	WWII tuples prec	WWII clusters F1	WWII clusters recall	WWII clusters prec
majority	0.372	0.500	0.297	0.286	0.500	0.201	0.378	0.500	0.304	0.317	0.500	0.232
$\#words$	0.372	0.500	0.297	0.375	0.500	0.299	0.378	0.500	0.304	0.349	0.500	0.268
$\#tuples$	0.372	0.500	0.297	0.375	0.500	0.299	0.378	0.500	0.304	0.349	0.500	0.268
bow_{sro}	0.467	0.523	0.560	**0.609**	**0.610**	**0.635**	0.502	0.545	0.617	0.573	0.586	0.608
bow_{final}	**0.475**	0.520	0.545	0.604	0.605	0.622	0.508	0.547	0.611	0.583	0.591	0.607
v_{sro} (G)	0.392	0.506	**0.616**	0.536	0.555	0.585	0.468	0.533	0.636	0.602	0.616	0.650
v_{final} (G)	0.431	0.516	0.581	0.531	0.539	0.548	0.512	0.553	0.638	0.606	0.621	0.660
v_{sro} (F)	0.435	0.521	**0.616**	0.562	0.573	0.604	0.537	0.569	0.658	0.633	0.642	0.675
v_{final} (F)	0.468	**0.533**	0.613	0.602	0.602	0.616	**0.567**	**0.586**	**0.663**	**0.662**	**0.669**	**0.706**

Table 5: Battle outcome inference results using several representations. (F) denotes the use of fasttext vectors, while (G) denotes GLoVe. On the left side of each table are the results obtained when using individual tuples as instances. On the right side are the results obtained when using the mean of a cluster's tuple representations as instances.

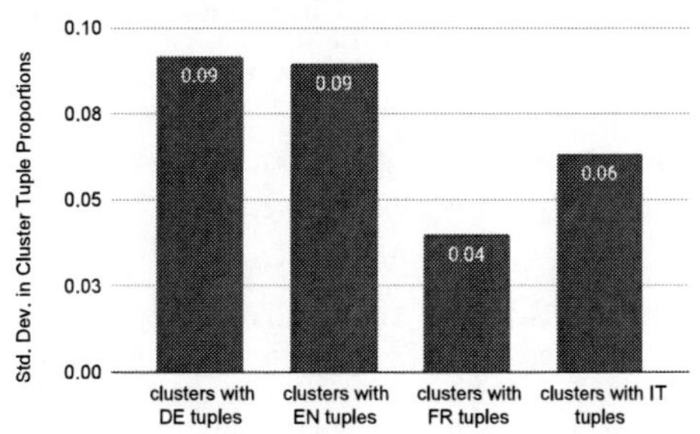

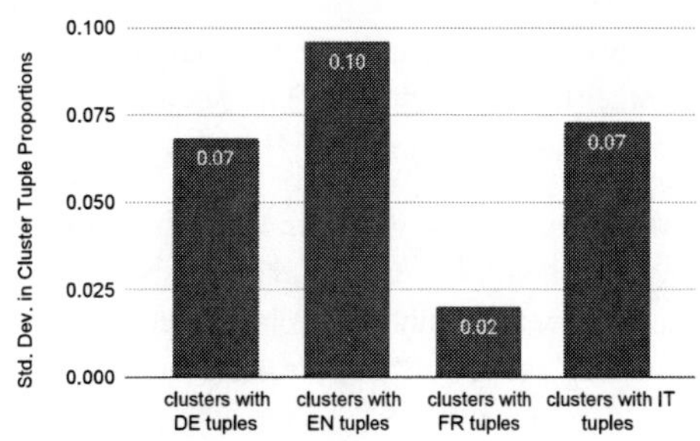

Figure 2: Bar chart showing the standard deviation in the proportion of language tuples in a subset of clusters defined by the presence of at least one tuple of a particular language. The cluster subsets defined by the presence of FR tuples in both WWI and WWII tend to have a balanced mix of tuples from DE, EN, and IT.

to our second research question regarding overlap between language editions with clusters.

5.3 Measuring cluster composition (RQ2)

To measure language heterogeneity in the tuples, each language (l_1) is paired with every other unique language (l_2) counted in the cluster. The count of occurrences of l_2 is then divided by the total number of tuples for that language. Correcting in this way, rather than using simple overlap, is intended to reduce the effects of population size (e.g., there being more EN tuples than FR tuples means the former are more likely to end up in any cluster by chance). This in turn helps us to better assess semantic (dis)agreement among language editions.

Figure 2 shows that the tuples with FR language tend to co-exist in a balanced manner with tuples from other languages in both the WWI and WWII data; this is true even though FR has the fewest tuples of all the language editions. One possible explanation may be that though the French language version contains fewer tuples, each tuple tends to be corroborated by other language versions. See Table 6 for the total number of tuples. In contrast, EN tends to be the most variable in its proportions. Though FR clusters include EN tuples in a similar proportion () to all other tuples, EN includes a much smaller proportion of FR tuples (). These results partially contradict our hypothesis that the overlap would be greatest between FR and EN and between DE and IT. We consider H2 as not validated.

6 Conclusion

In this work, we introduced a methodology for identifying information upon which language editions agree and disagree by applying open-domain information extraction and unsupervised learning to English translations of articles. Our results indicate that (1) language editions tend to mention their associated country more than other language editions mention the same country and (2) the FR language

Lang	WWI		WWII	
	Tuples	Clusters	Tuples	Clusters
DE	181,456	78.5%	526,290	77.5%
EN	184,795	81.0%	504,085	69.8%
FR	107,879	69.6%	376,489	69.8%
IT	133,041	69.5%	532,223	76.3%

Table 6: Counts and cluster coverage of tuples extracted from the World War I and World War II corpora using the Stanford OpenIE system. The "Clusters" columns indicate the proportion of clusters in which the languages appear.

edition align with other language editions' accounts more than the reverse. Result (1) confirms other work on geopolitical tendencies of multilingual Wikipedia. Result (2) implies that FR Wikipedia may have a more limited though balanced account than other language editions. More qualitative analysis is needed though.

Limitations There are limitations to using machine translation for historical analysis. To avoid issues regarding nuance, articles are reduced to a set of simple (subject, relation, object) tuples. The vector representations used were also evaluated on downstream tasks before use in our second experiment.

Future work There are several possible directions for future work. Regarding tasks, it may be of interest to NLP practitioners to understand the impact the information imbalances have on downstream tasks such as translation. For the language communities themselves, it may be useful to be aware of the gaps in the accounts they are writing. To make this more useful for them, an important step would be to expand to other languages; our analysis is limited to four languages. Future work should include articles from languages correlated with combatants on the Western and Pacific front.

Ultimately, more conclusive results will require a better model of the community dynamics and citation practices of editors, especially over time as well as more qualitative analysis of the differences between language editions. We aim to continue this work with the hope it encourages interest and advances in the overlap of computational, historical, and cultural analysis.

7 Acknowledgments

We thank the anonymous reviewers, Austin Benson, Tianze Shi, Arthur Spirling, and the Cornell NLP group for helpful comments. This work was supported in part by a Cornell Provost Diversity Fellowship.

References

Gabor Angeli, Melvin Jose Johnson Premkumar, and Christopher D. Manning. 2015. Leveraging linguistic structure for open domain information extraction. In *Proceedings of the 53rd Annual Meeting of the Association for Computational Linguistics and the 7th International Joint Conference on Natural Language Processing (Volume 1: Long Papers)*, pages 344–354.

Ofer Arazy, Oded Nov, Raymond Patterson, and Lisa Yeo. 2011. Information quality in wikipedia: The effects of group composition and task conflict. *Journal of Management Information Systems*, 27(4):71–98.

Matt Bridgewater. 2017. History writing and Wikipedia. *Computers and Composition*, 45:36–50.

Nathanael Chambers, Victor Bowen, Ethan Genco, Xisen Tian, Eric Young, Ganesh Harihara, and Eugene Yang. 2015. Identifying political sentiment between nation states with social media. In *Proceedings of the 2015 Conference on Empirical Methods in Natural Language Processing*, pages 65–75, Lisbon, Portugal. Association for Computational Linguistics.

Danqi Chen, Adam Fisch, Jason Weston, and Antoine Bordes. 2017. Reading wikipedia to answer open-domain questions. In *Proceedings of the 55th Annual Meeting of the Association for Computational Linguistics (Volume 1: Long Papers)*, pages 1870–1879.

Robin Gieck, Hanna-Mari Kinnunen, Yuanyuan Li, Mohsen Moghaddam, Franziska Pradel, Peter A. Gloor, Maria Paasivaara, and Matthäus P. Zylka. 2016. Cultural differences in the understanding of history on Wikipedia. In *Designing Networks for Innovation and Improvisation*, pages 3–12, Cham. Springer International Publishing.

Xiaochuang Han, Eunsol Choi, and Chenhao Tan. 2019. No permanent Friends or enemies: Tracking relationships between nations from news. In *Proceedings of the 2019 Conference of the North American Chapter of the Association for Computational Linguistics: Human Language Technologies, Volume 1 (Long and Short Papers)*, pages 1660–1676, Minneapolis, Minnesota. Association for Computational Linguistics.

Shiqing He, Allen Yilun Lin, Eytan Adar, and Brent J Hecht. 2018. The_tower_of_babel. jpg: Diversity of visual encyclopedic knowledge across wikipedia language editions. In *ICWSM*, pages 102–111.

Raphael Hoffmann, Congle Zhang, Xiao Ling, Luke Zettlemoyer, and Daniel S Weld. 2011. Knowledge-based weak supervision for information extraction of overlapping relations. In *Proceedings of the 49th Annual Meeting of the Association for Computational Linguistics: Human Language Technologies-Volume 1*, pages 541–550. Association for Computational Linguistics.

Matthew Honnibal and Ines Montani. 2017. spaCy 2: Natural language understanding with Bloom embeddings, convolutional neural networks and incremental parsing. To appear.

Ali Hürriyetoğlu, Hristo Tanev, Vanni Zavarella, Jakub Piskorski, Reyyan Yeniterzi, Osman Mutlu, Deniz Yuret, and Aline Villavicencio. 2021. Challenges and applications of automated extraction of socio-political events from text (CASE 2021): Workshop and shared task report. In *Proceedings of the 4th Workshop on Challenges and Applications of Automated Extraction of Socio-political Events from Text (CASE 2021)*, pages 1–9, Online. Association for Computational Linguistics.

Keshav Kolluru, Samarth Aggarwal, Vipul Rathore, Soumen Chakrabarti, et al. 2020. Imojie: Iterative memory-based joint open information extraction. In *Proceedings of the 58th Annual Meeting of the Association for Computational Linguistics*, pages 5871–5886.

Victor Kristof, Aswin Suresh, Matthias Grossglauser, and Patrick Thiran. 2021. War of words II: Enriched models of law-making processes. In *Proceedings of the Web Conference 2021*, WWW '21, page 2014–2024, New York, NY, USA. Association for Computing Machinery.

Jakub Kubś. 2021. Historical narratives in different language versions of wikipedia. *Academic Journal of Modern Philology*, (12):83–94.

Srijan Kumar, Robert West, and Jure Leskovec. 2016. Disinformation on the web: Impact, characteristics, and detection of wikipedia hoaxes. In *Proceedings of the 25th international conference on World Wide Web*, pages 591–602. International World Wide Web Conferences Steering Committee.

Michael Lieberman and Jimmy Lin. 2009. You are where you edit: Locating Wikipedia contributors through edit histories. In *Proceedings of the International AAAI Conference on Web and Social Media.*

Tianyu Liu, Fuli Luo, Pengcheng Yang, Wei Wu, Baobao Chang, and Zhifang Sui. 2019. Towards comprehensive description generation from factual attribute-value tables. In *Proceedings of the 57th Annual Meeting of the Association for Computational Linguistics*, pages 5985–5996.

Peter Makarov. 2018. Automated acquisition of patterns for coding political event data: Two case studies. In *Proceedings of the Second Joint SIGHUM Workshop on Computational Linguistics for Cultural Heritage, Social Sciences, Humanities and Literature*, pages 103–112, Santa Fe, New Mexico. Association for Computational Linguistics.

Arya D. McCarthy, James Scharf, and Giovanna Maria Dora Dore. 2021. A mixed-methods analysis of western and Hong Kong–based reporting on the 2019–2020 protests. In *Proceedings of the 5th Joint SIGHUM Workshop on Computational Linguistics for Cultural Heritage, Social Sciences, Humanities and Literature*, pages 178–188, Punta Cana, Dominican Republic (online). Association for Computational Linguistics.

Brendan O'Connor, Brandon M. Stewart, and Noah A. Smith. 2013. Learning to extract international relations from political context. In *Proceedings of the 51st Annual Meeting of the Association for Computational Linguistics (Volume 1: Long Papers)*, pages 1094–1104, Sofia, Bulgaria. Association for Computational Linguistics.

Umashanthi Pavalanathan, Xiaochuang Han, and Jacob Eisenstein. 2018. Mind your POV: Convergence of articles and editors towards Wikipedia's neutrality norm. *Proceedings of the ACM on Human-Computer Interaction*, 2(CSCW):1–23.

F. Pedregosa, G. Varoquaux, A. Gramfort, V. Michel, B. Thirion, O. Grisel, M. Blondel, P. Prettenhofer, R. Weiss, V. Dubourg, J. Vanderplas, A. Passos, D. Cournapeau, M. Brucher, M. Perrot, and E. Duchesnay. 2011. Scikit-learn: Machine learning in Python. *Journal of Machine Learning Research*, 12:2825–2830.

Jeffrey Pennington, Richard Socher, and Christopher D. Manning. 2014. Glove: Global vectors for word representation. In *Empirical Methods in Natural Language Processing (EMNLP)*, pages 1532–1543.

Emily Porter, P. M. Krafft, and Brian Keegan. 2020. Visual narratives and collective memory across peer-produced accounts of contested sociopolitical events. *Trans. Soc. Comput.*, 3(1).

Marta Recasens, Cristian Danescu-Niculescu-Mizil, and Dan Jurafsky. 2013. Linguistic models for analyzing and detecting biased language. In *Proceedings of the 51st Annual Meeting of the Association for Computational Linguistics (Volume 1: Long Papers)*, pages 1650–1659.

Pedro Rodriguez and Arthur Spirling. 2021. Word embeddings: What works, what doesn't, and how to tell the difference for applied research. *Journal of Politics*.

James Scharf, Arya D. McCarthy, and Giovanna Maria Dora Dore. 2021. Characterizing news portrayal of civil unrest in Hong Kong, 1998–2020. In *Proceedings of the 4th Workshop on Challenges and Applications of Automated Extraction of Socio-political Events from Text (CASE 2021)*, pages 43–52, Online. Association for Computational Linguistics.

Feng Shi, Misha Teplitskiy, Eamon Duede, and James A Evans. 2019. The wisdom of polarized crowds. *Nature human behaviour*, 3(4):329–336.

Niklas Stoehr, Lucas Torroba Hennigen, Samin Ahbab, Robert West, and Ryan Cotterell. 2021. Classifying dyads for militarized conflict analysis. In *Proceedings of the 2021 Conference on Empirical Methods in Natural Language Processing*, pages 7775–7784, Online and Punta Cana, Dominican Republic. Association for Computational Linguistics.

Besiki Stvilia, Les Gasser, Michael B Twidale, and Linda C Smith. 2007. A framework for information quality assessment. *Journal of the American society for information science and technology*, 58(12):1720–1733.

Yufei Tian, Tuhin Chakrabarty, Fred Morstatter, and Nanyun Peng. 2021. Identifying distributional perspectives from colingual groups. In *Proceedings of the Ninth International Workshop on Natural Language Processing for Social Media*, pages 178–190.

Pauli Virtanen, Ralf Gommers, Travis E Oliphant, Matt Haberland, Tyler Reddy, David Cournapeau, Evgeni Burovski, Pearu Peterson, Warren Weckesser, Jonathan Bright, et al. 2020. Scipy 1.0: fundamental algorithms for scientific computing in python. *Nature methods*, 17(3):261–272.

Fei Wu and Daniel S Weld. 2008. Automatically refining the wikipedia infobox ontology. In *Proceedings of the 17th international conference on World Wide Web*, pages 635–644. ACM.

Yiwei Zhou, Alexandra Cristea, and Zachary Roberts. 2015. Is Wikipedia really neutral? A sentiment perspective study of war-related Wikipedia articles since 1945. In *Proceedings of the 29th Pacific Asia Conference on Language, Information and Computation*, pages 160–168, Shanghai, China.

Computational Detection of Narrativity: A Comparison Using Textual Features and Reader Response

Max Steg and **Karlo Slot*** and **Federico Pianzola**
University of Groningen / Oude Kijk in Het Jatstraat 26, 9712 EK Groningen, Netherlands
m.steg@student.rug.nl, k.h.r.slot@student.rug.nl, f.pianzola@rug.nl

Abstract

The task of computational textual narrative detection focuses on detecting the presence of narrative parts, or the degree of narrativity in texts. In this work, we focus on detecting the local degree of narrativity in texts, using short text passages. We performed a human annotation experiment on 325 English texts ranging across 20 genres to capture readers' perception by means of three cognitive aspects: suspense, curiosity, and surprise. We then employed a linear regression model to predict narrativity scores for 17,372 texts. When comparing our average annotation scores to similar annotation experiments with different cognitive aspects, we found that Pearson's r ranges from .63 to .75. When looking at the calculated narrative probabilities, Pearson's r is .91. We found that it is possible to use suspense, curiosity and surprise to detect narrativity. However, there are still differences between methods. This does not imply that there are inherently correct methods, but rather suggests that the underlying definition of narrativity is a determining factor for the results of the computational models employed.

1 Introduction

Storytelling is and has been a big part of the daily lives of many. People learn from stories, get inspired by stories, relate to stories and *feel* stories. We as humans can be seen as story-interpreting machines. However, how we perceive and interpret storytelling elements has been a point of discussion in the field of narratology for a number of years. Previous research has attempted to define narrativity by means of cognitive processes (Genette and Levonas, 1976; Herman, 2009; Willis, 2021). A notable way to define narrativity is discussed extensively by Herman (2009), who uses four perceptive elements to define what makes a text narrative: situatedness, event sequencing, world-making and, as he describes it, "feltness".

Another important change in narratology concerns the shift from an idea of narrativity as a binary class, i.e. a text is a narrative or not, to narrativity as "a local, multidimensional scalar property" (Piper et al., 2021; Sternberg, 2001). Accordingly, Piper et al. (2021) have attempted to use the definition of narrativity as a scalar property to computationally detect narrativity, emulating human judgement using statements regarding the elements defined by Herman (2009).

However, there are still a lot of aspects of narrativity detection left unexplored. Alternative definitions heavily focus on readers' perception of texts (Sternberg, 2003, 2011; Passalacqua and Pianzola, 2016). For instance, Sternberg (2011) illustrates that narrativity can be defined by inherent human interpretation, which he refers to as the three "narrative universals": suspense, curiosity, and surprise. This research will attempt to explore the possibility of using this form of readers' perception as a way to detect narrativity, and will thus answer the questions:

To what extent can suspense, surprise and curiosity as a form of readers' perception be employed to detect narrativity?

Is there a relation between textual features associated to narrativity and reader response identified by narrative universals?

To answer these questions, we improve a text-based approach to detect the local narrativity of documents (Piper et al., 2021), provide new reader-response-based annotations for an existing corpus (Piper and Bagga, 2022), and discuss the results and implications of detecting narrativity using two different theoretical frameworks.

2 Related works

The goal to define the concept of narrativity in order to detect said concept within literary texts has

*The first two authors contributed equally.

Proceedings of the 6th LaTeCH-CLfL Workshop, pages 105–114
October 16, 2022. ©2022 International Conference on Computational Linguistics

been a main drive within the study of narratology. One of the fundamental definitions of narrative has been proposed by Genette and Levonas (1976), stating that the minimum requirements of a narrative should be that they represent a sequence of events by means of one or more characters.

Over time, researchers have elaborated on the aforementioned definition utilising two paradigms related to narrativity, as described by Herman (2009): "etic" and "emic". Etic approaches to narrativity regard the concept as definable and detectable by means of textual and structural elements. Whereas emic approaches utilise cognitive processes to classify texts by means of their degree of narrativity. A similar dichotomy has been described by Passalacqua and Pianzola (2016) by comparing objectivist and constructivist paradigms in the context of narrative theory. Passalacqua and Pianzola (2016) describe the objectivist paradigm as viewing textual aspects, such as semantics and syntactics, as defining features of a narrative. Constructivist theory, however, regards the relation between the audience and the text as a way to detect narrativity, which Passalacqua and Pianzola (2016) described as being "the result of a process of construction and combination of certain processes and properties whose specificity is also dependent on extra-objectual factors". One approach grounded within constructivist narrative theory, that can thus be considered an emic approach, is the concept of "readers' perception".

Readers' perception, or often called "reader response" and "reception" in literary studies, depicts the way a reader interprets textual elements on an emotional or cognitive level (Willis, 2021). Several researchers have attempted to define narrativity by means of readers' perception. These definitions have been employed by other research to detect narrativity in a handful of manners, including computational methods.

Herman (2009) suggests that the degree of narrativity in stories can be defined by the means of four perceptive elements:

1. *Situatedness*. In what context the narrative is presented.

2. *Event sequencing*. How events within a narrative are ordered, i.e. in a temporal fashion.

3. *World-making*. How the narrative presents a fictional or realistic world.

4. *"Feltness"*. How the reader is affected by the experiences presented in texts.

Metilli et al. (2019) have used the perceptive elements by Herman (2009)—mainly event sequencing—to propose a framework with technological challenges and requirements regarding the extraction of narratives from text. This framework consists of a combination of techniques to detect events using textual elements, such as temporal and named entity recognition, human annotation, and deep learning. Metilli et al. (2019) defined events as being "set in space and time, endowed with factual components" and having "semantic relations" with each other. Based on this definition, human annotators were assigned to identify sentences as being events or not. Simultaneously, a similar framework was proposed by Rodrigues et al. (2019), who provided guidelines to be used when aiming to visualise narratives by means of spatio-temporal relations. This vision described the concept of time and space in storytelling as something intuitive and inherently human. Both approaches by Metilli et al. (2019) and Rodrigues et al. (2019) indicate that human interpretation, or readers' perception, as described by Herman (2009) can be utilised to detect and visualise narrativity within texts by means of annotation and construction of classification models.

This idea has been successfully implemented by Piper et al. (2021) as well. While utilising etic, objectivist approaches to detect narrativity across long time scales, such as extracting narrativity by means of lexical and syntactic features, Piper et al. (2021) also utilized emic, constructivist approach similar to Metilli et al. (2019) and Rodrigues et al. (2019) using the perceptive elements by Herman (2009). Piper et al. (2021) assembled a team of three trained annotators to annotate 5-sentence-long passages spanning across four "discursive domains": (1) non-fiction, (2) fiction, (3) poetry and (4) science. The annotators were assigned to rate the passages on a 5-point Likert scale based on three elements: (1) "feltness", reworded as "agency", (2) event sequencing and (3) world-making. These elements have been explained in a codebook including annotation guidelines. While their approach to quantify readers' perception by means of Herman's elements and human annotation as a way to detect narrativity within texts is valid, their data lacks linguistic and stylistic differences. Piper and Bagga (2022) uses an expanded dataset spanning across 19 genres, ranging from legal documents to Aesop's fables, and from 19th century literature to Reddit stories. This extensive dataset is extremely helpful for narrativity detection, due to its divergent nature, and can also be used to detect narrativity by means of different forms of readers' perception.

One other theory, also mentioned by Piper et al. (2021), which acknowledges the human interpretative aspects of narratives, has evolved over several years (Sternberg, 2011). Sternberg (2011) views narrativity as having the possibility to be defined by the effect that it can have on the reader, a view grounded within readers' perception. Sternberg states that the degree of narrativity of literary texts can be defined through three "master effects", or "universals": (1) suspense, (2) curiosity, and (3) surprise:

- *Suspense*. An event can be experienced as having suspense when the reader is presented with information that can eventually guide the reader to a sense of closure, or fulfilment (Sternberg, 2003). An example of this can be that the reader of a story is given the information that character A has a knife behind their back, but character B, with whom character A is having a conversation, is not aware of it; the reader lacks information about what will happen in the future.

- *Curiosity*. Curiosity can occur when the reader is presented with information about the present, also eliciting a desire for information about the past (Sternberg, 2003). For example, the reader is told that character B is found with several stab wounds, but is not told how they have gotten said wounds.

- *Surprise*. An event can be surprising if the readers' idea of the event being described is challenged through new information (Sternberg, 2003). For example, the reader knows that character A and character B are having a "normal" conversation, but suddenly, the reader is presented with the information that character A has stabbed character B. This could result in an "error" in the mental organization of the information previously acquired by the reader via the story, sparking a feeling of surprise.

Former research has used Sternberg's constructive approach to narrativity to construct computational models using some of the three universals. Doust and Piwek (2017) developed a computational model to detect suspense and found that, when compared with human judgements, their model predicted suspense rather well. However, their approach only used human judgements as a way to compare results, rather than attempting to use human judgements to train the model. A similar approach has also been used by Wilmot and Keller (2020).

There is a lack of research where all three universals are utilised to detect narrativity. While researchers have attempted to model one of the three universals by means of textual elements, they used human judgements as a way of evaluation, rather than as an approach to model suspense. Detection of narrativity by means of human judgements of suspense, curiosity and surprise can provide an insight into the relation between a story and its reader. Therefore, the question which will be tested is whether it is possible to detect narrativity utilising all three of Sternberg's universals. The approach taken will utilise human annotation to train a machine learning model and calculate narrativity scores based on readers' perception.

3 Data

The data used within this research was a corpus constructed and provided by Piper and Bagga (2022), consisting of 17,706 documents, ranging across 20 unique genres (Table 1). Examples of the genres within this corpus are historical non-fiction, fairy tales, documents from the Supreme Court of the United States, scientific abstract, and flash fiction. These documents contain short textual fragments of roughly 5 sentences, hereafter referred to as "passages". Out of the 17,706 passages, 334 have been manually annotated and used to build a model for detecting and predicting narrativity (Piper and Bagga, 2022). We reused the same annotated dataset for our own annotations and to build a new predictive model.

4 Methods

4.1 Annotation

The original dataset contains annotations referring to textual features identified on the basis of the following 3 statements (Piper et al., 2021):

- Agency: "This passage foregrounds the lived experience of particular agents."

Table 1: Finalised distribution of genres in the corpus and annotated dataset by Piper and Bagga (2022). Percentages within brackets refer to the ratio with respect to the total number of texts in the corpus and in the annotated dataset respectively.

Genre	Corpus	Annotated
ABSTRACT	993 (5.6%)	26 (7.8%)
APHORISM	486 (2.7%)	19 (5.7%)
BIO	990 (5.6%)	17 (5.1%)
BREVIEW	864 (4.9%)	-
FABLE	273 (1.5%)	10 (3%)
FAIRY	784 (4.4%)	20 (6%)
FLASH	889 (5%)	12 (3.6%)
HIST	1075 (6%)	25 (7.5%)
LEGAL	1115 (6.3%)	31 (9.3%)
LITSTUDY	544 (3.1%)	16 (4.8%)
MIXED NONFIC	1000 (5.6%)	-
NOVEL-CONT	974 (5.5%)	23 (6.9%)
NOVEL19C	1050 (5.9%)	25 (7.5%)
OPINION	1611 (9.1%)	-
PHIL	558 (3.1%)	20 (6%)
POETRY	1000 (5.6%)	-
REDDIT	1000 (5.6%)	20 (6%)
ROC	1000 (5.6%)	23 (6.9%)
SCOTUS	1000 (5.6%)	35 (10.5%)
SHORT	500 (2.8%)	12 (3.6%)
Total	17,706	334

- Event sequencing: "This passage is organized around sequences of events that occur over time."
- World-making: "This passage creates a world that I can see and feel."

Additionally, we annotated the data based on 3 statements regarding readers' perception (Sternberg, 2003):

- Suspense: "This passage presents information indicative of future events and postpones a feeling of resolution."
- Curiosity: "This passage presents information indicative of past events and leaves me wondering about missing information."
- Surprise: "This passage presents information, which I experience as unexpected, about an event."

The annotators expressed their agreement with the statements by means of a five-point Likert scale (Strongly disagree, Somewhat disagree, Unsure, Somewhat agree, Strongly agree). The choice to use a scalar rather than a categorical approach for annotation is in accordance with the theoretical framework adopted, namely that these cognitive aspects can be experienced as a spectrum. A passage can not only be defined as being suspenseful or not, some passages can be more or less suspenseful than others. Similarly, Piper et al. (2021)'s objectivist features can be experienced with different degrees of intensity in a text.

To test whether the selection of the dataset by Piper and Bagga (2022) was suitable for the annotation of the narrative universals defined by Sternberg (2003), one annotator annotated the 20 passages with the lowest and highest narrative probability, according to Piper and Bagga (2022), thus 40 passages in total. Since we are looking at *degrees* of narrativity, we used Kendall rank correlation coefficient (τ) to compare the ranking of the average annotated narrativity with the ranking of Piper's narrative probability scores. Kendall's τ for the annotations by Piper and Bagga and Piper's narrative probability scores was 0.385 ($p < .001$), while Kendall's τ for our initial annotations and Piper's narrative probability scores was 0.377 ($p < .001$). These values are close and indicate a strong rank correlation (> 0.3), hence this data set is suitable for annotation using Sternberg's universals.

Out of the initial experiment, 9 passages were extracted to exemplify each universal: 3 passages per universal, having low, medium, and high degree of each universal. We prepared an annotation guidebook with instructions and the commented examples, also including a brief background of the research goal, the theoretical framework, and an explanation of common annotation pitfalls, so that these can be avoided.[1]

We did a first round of annotation to check whether the constructed guidebook was clear and instructive enough. A total of 7 annotators (6 Dutch Information Science students and one Italian professor of computational humanities) annotated approximately 20 passages each, randomly assigned from the data set. Each passage was annotated by 3 annotators. Thus, this round yielded 47 annotated passages. We calculated Inter-rater reliability (IRR) using the average deviation index (ADI), as discussed by Burke et al. (1999). Since we used a 5-point scale, the ADI should not exceed the threshold value of 0.5. The final ADI score of the first round was 0.35, thus the guidelines did not need further improvements. Based on feedback from the annotators, we only added that the annotation should take into account the entirety of the passage, rather than just a part of it. However, we now acknowledge that this specification may be misleading in some cases, namely when the need for information related to curiosity or suspense is triggered and fulfilled in the same passage (see examples in Appendix).

In the second and final round 6 annotators annotated the remaining 278 passages, with approximately 138 passages per annotator. The ADI score of the second round was 0.37 and the ADI of both rounds combined was 0.36. Since both values are below 0.5, it can be concluded that there is a reasonable level of agreement between annotators.

Once we had annotated all passages, we compared them to Piper et al. (2021)'s annotations. We used Pearson's r and Kendall's τ to calculate the correlation between the results.

4.2 Models

Despite the theoretical framework adopted for the annotation, conceiving narrativity as a scalar property, Piper et al. (2021) eventually worked with computational models whose main goal is to classify texts into discrete categories (*Logistic Regression*, *Random Forest* and *Support Vector Machine*). To train a machine learning classifier, they used values ranging from 1 to 5 (average annotation on the Likert scale) but they also created an additional variable called "reader predicted label": if the average annotation value was higher than 2.5, it got the POS label, else, it got the NEG label. The resulting predicted narrativity for the whole corpus is thus the probability of either being a narrative or not. They also tested the performance of their classifiers using this 2-classes predictions.

Alternatively, we decided to implement a modelling approach consistent with our theoretical framework and predict the *degree* of narrativity of a text using linear regression models. Hence, we used both Piper and Bagga (2022)'s and our annotation to train several models (*Linear Regression*, *Lasso*, *Ridge*, *ElasticNet*, and *Theil-Sen*), predict narrativity scores ranging from 0 to 1, and test the models' performance on these continuous values. We did not try any neural approach because we wanted to be able to identify in a straightforward way the predictive power of various features.

For the selection of the textual features to supply to the model when training, we relied on Piper et al. (2021) but also tried a few other features that we thought could perform well. The features we used from Piper et al. (2021) are *unigrams*, *tense*, *mood*, *voice*. The latter three are composite features computed with the Python package *BookNLP*[2]. We also adapted the *concreteness* score (Brysbaert et al., 2014) by extending it with the lexicon developed by Muraki et al. (2022), which consists of 62 thousand English multiword expressions. The concreteness score of a document is the sum of all concreteness scores for all expressions in a document, divided by the total number of words. To explore the relation between semantics and narrativity, other features that we used are *Tf-idf* and Doc2Vec (Le and Mikolov, 2014). We tried different combinations of the selected features to train and test our models, focusing on predictions that correlate more strongly with the annotator scores. Due to limited size of our annotated data set, we used 5-fold cross-validation (train/test: 80/20). After having determined the best model, we trained it again twice using all the annotated data for each method (text-based and reader-based), and predicted narrativity scores for the complete corpus.

[1] https://github.com/maxsteg/Computationally-Narrativity-Detection

[2] https://github.com/booknlp/booknlp

5 Results and Discussion

The best predictive model for both types of narrativity (text-based and reader-based) is Theil-Sen Regressor (TSR) with two features: Tf-idf and concreteness (Table 2). However, given that the model using only Tf-idf explains almost the same amount of variance (.01 difference), for the sake of interpretability we decided to use this simpler model for the prediction of narrative probability. Interestingly, the words contributing the most to predicting narrativity are not all the same for the two theoretical frameworks. When detecting narrativity based on textual features, third person pronouns seem more relevant, but first person pronouns are better predictors of narrativity based on readers' perception (Table 3).

Table 2: Coefficient of determination (R^2) of the annotators' scores and various features when predicting the narrativity of texts using the Theil-Sen model.

Features	**R^2**	
	Piper	*Univ.*
unigrams	.50	.33
tfidf	**.68**	**.59**
doc2vec	-1.53	-1.99
concreteness	.34	.35
doc2vec concr	-1.48	-1.78
tfidf concr	**.69**	**.60**
doc2vec ttr concr	-1.52	-1.71
tense mood voice	.65	.50
tfidf doc2vec	.02	.07
tfidf doc2vec concr	.11	.13
tfidf doc2vec unigrams	.51	.38
tfidf unigrams concr	.51	.38
unigrams doc2vec concr	.51	.38
unigrams doc2vec tfidf concr	.51	.38

Before evaluating the predicted values, we looked at the annotations done using two different theoretical frameworks to define narrativity. In Table 4, it can be seen that there is a positive correlation for all statement pairs between Piper's framework and Sternberg's universals. However, two of these are only moderate: between "Event sequencing" and "Curiosity" (r = .63), and between "Event sequencing" and "Surprise" (r = .66). These results show that the textual and cognitive dimensions covered by the two theoretical frameworks do not completely overlap.

These findings are also supported by the total annotation averages: there is a strong positive correlation between the total annotation averages (r = .77), but there is some unexplained variance. Moreover, Kendall's τ shows a very weak correlation between the actual ranking of documents (τ = .03). This indicates that, even though there is a strong correlation between the predicted values, the way in which the documents are ranked by means of the predicted narrativity scores differ strongly between models. This does not imply that one of these theories is inherently correct, but that they are different ways of viewing narrativity. Notably, the distribution of annotations shows that text-based annotation led to a majority of passages with the highest narrativity score, whereas reader-based annotation led to the opposite result: the majority of passages has been assigned the lowest narrativity score (Figure 1).

Table 3: Top words positively and negatively associated with narrativity. Computed with the Python package ELI5. See Appendix for a longer list

Positive		**Negative**	
Piper	*Universals*	*Piper*	*Universals*
he	out	is	of
my	me	of	by
was	was	which	is
him	door	or	or
had	different	2d	for
derrick	woman	this	can
his	my	agreement	as
day	plane	even	may

Table 4: Correlations (Pearson's r) between the average annotators' scores for each statement based on Piper's framework and Sternberg's universals.

	Suspense	**Curiosity**	**Surprise**
Agency	.75	.72	.70
Event	.70	.63	.66
World	.76	.72	.73

If we look at values predicted for the whole corpus, we see that they have an even stronger correlation (r = .91) and span the whole narrativity spectrum in a more even way (although still skewed) than the annotated passages, confirming that high or low narrativity texts are not more frequent than those with a moderate degree of narrativity (Figure 2). Conversely, Piper and Bagga (2022)'s use of a binary classifier (Logistic Regression) pushed the predictions towards extreme values, biasing the interpretation.

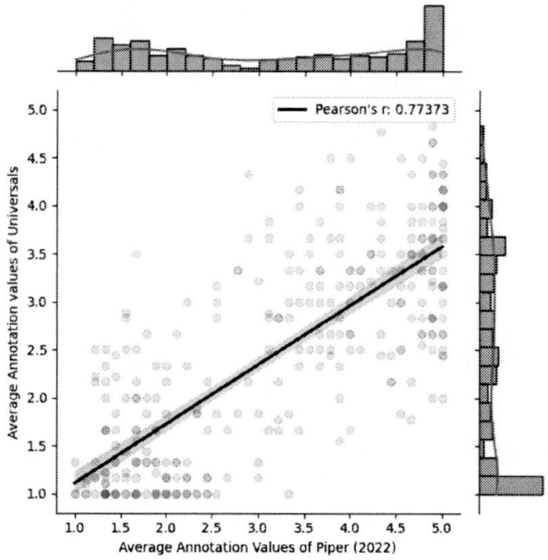

Figure 1: Scatterplot of Annotation Piper (2022) vs. Annotation Universals (n = 325)

We also looked at the average predicted probabilities for each genre (Table 5) and they are in line with what could be expected. For example, legal documents (LEGAL, SCOTUS) have low narrativity, between .06 and .3. This applies to academic texts (LITSTUDY, ABSTRACT), philosophy (PHIL), and book reviews (BREVIEWS) as well. All other genres have relatively high narrativity scores, with Reddit posts having the highest degree. Regardless of the theoretical framework employed, the variation in the degree of narrativity between genres is similar. However, the values are remarkably lower when narrativity is computed based on the narrative universals (mean = .39 vs. mean = .57). This result may be due to the different distribution of the annotated passages and the consequent unbalanced training sets, biased in different ways: towards high narrativity scores for text-based annotation and towards low narrativity scores for reader-based annotation. Follow-up research should aim for a larger and more balanced annotated dataset.

6 Conclusion

As narratology moved towards the idea that narrativity is a local, scalar, and multidimensional characteristic of texts, this research aimed to answer the questions *"To what extent can suspense, surprise and curiosity as a form of readers' perception be employed to detect narrativity?"* and *"Is there a*

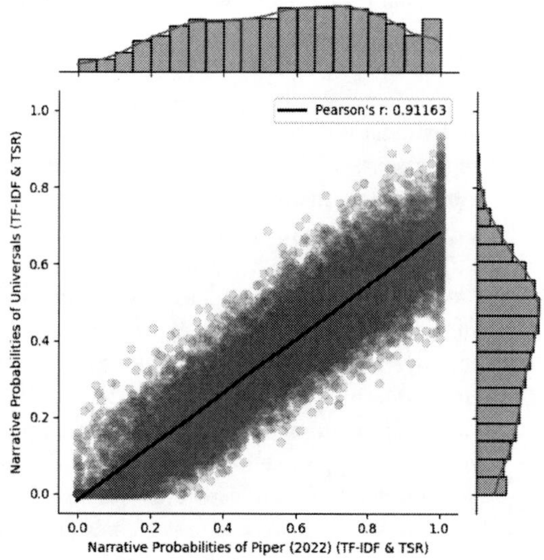

Figure 2: Scatterplot of narrativity scores predicted using a Theil-Sen regression model based on Piper and Bagga (2022) annotation vs. based on annotation related to Sternberg (2003) Universals (n = 17,372)

Table 5: Average predicted degree of narrativity per genre (TF-IDF & TSR model)

Genre	**Avg. narrativity**	
	Piper	*Universals*
ABSTRACT	.31	.13
APHORISM	.30	.27
BIO	.68	.43
BREVIEW	.45	.31
FABLE	.77	.51
FAIRY	.79	.54
FLASH	.75	.53
HIST	.60	.37
LEGAL	.17	.06
LITSTUDY	.37	.26
MIXED-NONFIC	.60	.40
NOVEL-CONT	.77	.56
NOVEL19C	.71	.50
OPINION	.53	.34
PHIL	.32	.24
POETRY	.61	.45
REDDIT	.82	.61
ROC	.81	.50
SCOTUS	.30	.15
SHORT	.78	.56

relation between textual features associated to narrativity and reader response identified by narrative universals?".

To accomplish this, we performed multiple rounds of annotation to quantify readers' perception by means of three cognitive effects of narrative (suspense, curiosity, surprise). We found that the annotators generally agree with each other and there are moderate to strong correlations between text-based and reader-based narrative dimensions.

As for the computational aspect, we trained a quite accurate regression model on a single highly predictive feature (*Tf-idf*). Comparing our results to the results by (Piper and Bagga, 2022), we found that there is a strong positive correlation between their and our approach to defining narrativity as a scalar property of texts. However, we also found that text-based and reader-based conceptions of narrativity do not completely overlap.

While this research has been able to capture narrativity by means of readers' perception as defined by Sternberg (2011), it is not able to capture narrativity as a whole. As mentioned before, narrativity can be defined in various ways and thus there are many plausible ways to detect it. Future research could combine both text-based and reader-based approaches to better grasp the complex, multidimensional nature of narrative. For instance, principal component analysis could help identify dimensions that could be conflated and dimensions that are irreducible to objective and textual properties.

Acknowledgments

The authors are grateful to Andrew Piper and Sunyam Bagga for sharing the data and code ahead of publication of their article.

References

Marc Brysbaert, Amy Beth Warriner, and Victor Kuperman. 2014. Concreteness ratings for 40 thousand generally known english word lemmas. *Behavior research methods*, 46(3):904–911.

Michael J Burke, Lisa M Finkelstein, and Michelle S Dusig. 1999. On average deviation indices for estimating interrater agreement. *Organizational Research Methods*, 2(1):49–68.

Richard Doust and Paul Piwek. 2017. A model of suspense for narrative generation. Association for Computational Linguistics.

Gérard Genette and Ann Levonas. 1976. Boundaries of narrative. *New Literary History*, 8(1):1–13.

David Herman. 2009. *Basic elements of narrative*. John Wiley & Sons.

Quoc Le and Tomas Mikolov. 2014. Distributed representations of sentences and documents. In *International conference on machine learning*, pages 1188–1196. PMLR.

Daniele Metilli, Valentina Bartalesi, and Carlo Meghini. 2019. Steps towards a system to extract formal narratives from text. In *Text2Story@ ECIR*, pages 53–61.

Emiko J Muraki, Summer Abdalla, Marc Brysbaert, and Penny M Pexman. 2022. Concreteness ratings for 62 thousand english multiword expressions.

Franco Passalacqua and Federico Pianzola. 2016. Epistemological problems in narrative theory: Objectivist vs. constructivist paradigm. *Narrative Sequence in Contemporary Narratology*, pages 195–217.

Andrew Piper and Sunyam Bagga. 2022. Towards a data-driven theory of narrativity. *New Literary History*, (forthcoming).

Andrew Piper, Sunyam Bagga, Laura Monteiro, Andrew Yang, Marie Labrosse, and Yu Lu Liu. 2021. Detecting narrativity across long time scales. *Proceedings http://ceur-ws. org ISSN*, 1613:0073.

Sara Rodrigues, Ana Figueiras, and Ilo Alexandre. 2019. Once upon a time in a land far away: guidelines for spatio-temporal narrative visualization. In *2019 23rd International Conference Information Visualisation (IV)*, pages 44–49. IEEE.

Meir Sternberg. 2001. How narrativity makes a difference. *Narrative*, 9(2):115–122.

Meir Sternberg. 2003. Universals of narrative and their cognitivist fortunes (ii). *Poetics today*, 24(3):517–638.

Meir Sternberg. 2011. Reconceptualizing narratology. arguments for a functionalist and constructivist approach to narrative. *Enthymema*, (4):35–50.

Ika Willis. 2021. Reception theory, reception history, reception studies. In *Oxford Research Encyclopedia of Literature*.

David Wilmot and Frank Keller. 2020. Modelling suspense in short stories as uncertainty reduction over neural representation. *arXiv preprint arXiv:2004.14905*.

Appendix

In this Appendix there is a list of the words contributing the most to predicting low narrativity (red) and high narrativity (green), and examples of passages for which the two models disagree the most about the degree of narrativity (Figures 4 to 8).

Weight?	Feature
+0.568	he
+0.483	<BIAS>
+0.426	my
+0.418	was
+0.411	him
+0.376	had
+0.362	derrick
+0.338	his
+0.337	day
+0.306	her
+0.281	out
+0.273	while
+0.250	they
+0.245	she
+0.243	down
+0.243	me
+0.242	them
+0.242	plane
+0.240	would
+0.236	house
+0.236	maddie
+0.234	said
+0.231	we
+0.215	again
+0.214	staring
+0.213	freezer
+0.205	do
+0.202	army
+0.202	children
+0.200	stood
+0.197	kittens
+0.193	honest
+0.191	recital
+0.190	back
+0.189	thinking
+0.185	night
+0.185	minutes
+0.182	called
+0.181	more
+0.179	really
+0.178	then
+0.178	sam
+0.175	middle
+0.175	benton
+0.175	clay
+0.174	make
+0.174	stopped
+0.172	road
+0.169	few
+0.169	red
+0.167	living
... 3352 more positive ...	
... 4549 more negative ...	
-0.152	forth
-0.152	meaning
-0.153	religion
-0.156	letter
-0.156	such
-0.156	anything
-0.158	who
-0.159	pleasure
-0.160	client
-0.161	case
-0.163	human
-0.164	states
-0.166	platform
-0.166	subsided
-0.166	grace
-0.166	delirium
-0.166	yarmouth
-0.166	civ
-0.166	leonora
-0.167	may
-0.167	activity
-0.176	set
-0.177	itz
-0.178	are
-0.179	term
-0.181	makes
-0.184	knowledge
-0.185	germany
-0.186	shall
-0.190	fees
-0.191	ice
-0.194	dog
-0.197	mother
-0.198	co
-0.201	be
-0.202	longer
-0.208	servant
-0.210	john
-0.215	by
-0.218	can
-0.223	everything
-0.229	in
-0.233	even
-0.262	agreement
-0.264	this
-0.274	2d
-0.336	or
-0.476	which
-0.623	of
-0.667	is

Weight?	Feature
+0.466	out
+0.405	me
+0.378	was
+0.318	door
+0.304	<BIAS>
+0.295	different
+0.294	woman
+0.288	my
+0.283	plane
+0.268	while
+0.264	too
+0.241	man
+0.234	back
+0.233	think
+0.232	his
+0.225	later
+0.225	said
+0.223	she
+0.216	us
+0.215	know
+0.214	him
+0.213	one
+0.201	honest
+0.199	did
+0.199	boat
+0.199	fairies
+0.196	night
+0.193	stood
+0.185	head
+0.184	second
+0.183	ali
+0.178	hallo
+0.178	traveller
+0.178	facing
+0.178	wider
+0.178	you
+0.177	would
+0.175	stand
+0.174	he
+0.173	dad
+0.169	clinton
+0.169	saw
+0.168	house
+0.168	sent
+0.167	down
+0.167	tree
+0.166	someone
+0.165	going
+0.164	fire
+0.163	them
+0.161	leonard
... 3249 more positive ...	
... 4582 more negative ...	
-0.115	ii
-0.115	public
-0.116	themselves
-0.116	novel
-0.116	work
-0.120	developer
-0.122	lad
-0.123	lucid
-0.124	less
-0.126	such
-0.127	caulaincourt
-0.127	community
-0.127	securities
-0.128	known
-0.128	thrombocytopenia
-0.128	caterpillar
-0.131	use
-0.133	itz
-0.134	than
-0.135	fee
-0.136	case
-0.136	farmer
-0.137	liability
-0.138	only
-0.141	maddie
-0.143	board
-0.143	were
-0.143	better
-0.144	agreement
-0.145	finally
-0.145	makes
-0.147	shall
-0.150	control
-0.151	john
-0.151	fees
-0.154	are
-0.155	2d
-0.155	sheriff
-0.155	wages
-0.155	law
-0.157	party
-0.157	state
-0.158	may
-0.180	as
-0.183	can
-0.190	for
-0.200	or
-0.253	is
-0.291	by
-0.359	of

Figure 3: Words positively and negatively associated with narrativity for the two models: text-based on the left (Piper) and reader-based on the right (Universals). Computed with the Python package ELI5

Piper | 1

tom had the day off from work . he wanted to just lounge around all day . he realized how messy his apartment was . tom decided to spend the day cleaning instead . he was a bit tired but felt accomplished .

Universals | .43

tom had the day off from work . he wanted to just lounge around all day . he realized how messy his apartment was . tom decided to spend the day cleaning instead . he was a bit tired but felt accomplished .

Figure 4: Passage id: f1979b1e-dd8f-4c91-b9f2-ade48d8b3596; genre: ROC

Piper | 1

the kids were at a petting zoo . they saw a very funny llama . they kept trying to pet it . but he would run away ! they spent all day trying to play with the llama . finally he let them pet his ear .

Universals | .43

the kids were at a petting zoo . they saw a very funny llama . they kept trying to pet it . but he would run away ! they spent all day trying to play with the llama . finally he let them pet his ear .

Figure 5: Passage id: 0f7c0e3f-3974-4271-af05-0d39cf3fba2e; genre: ROC

Piper | 1

barry was on his computer all day long . he worked writing a blog for a local newspaper . when barry would have breaks he would smoke cigarettes . barry tried to quit one day and struggled immensely . he was finally able to stop by substituting snacks for cigarettes .

Universals | .41

barry was on his computer all day long . he worked writing a blog for a local newspaper . when barry would have breaks he would smoke cigarettes . barry tried to quit one day and struggled immensely . he was finally able to stop by substituting snacks for cigarettes .

Figure 6: Passage id: ab7e5971-590b-4e59-8e47-ffd4f4c00e91; genre: ROC

Piper | .99

nick found $ 1000 . he had been poor all his life . he spent it all on lottery tickets . he lost all of it . he wished he had put it in the bank instead .

Universals | .42

nick found $ 1000 . he had been poor all his life . he spent it all on lottery tickets . he lost all of it . he wished he had put it in the bank instead .

Figure 7: Passage id: b49fdceb-29b8-4e83-9cf2-b3abd7b34aa5; genre: ROC

Piper |.92

he had been diagnosed with melanoma , and it had metastasized to his brain . he told her that he had only three months to live . she spent the rest of that fall flying back and forth from new haven to hilo , a journey of more than twelve hours . chunks of time spent at her father ' s bedside were interspersed with hours on the phone with cate . each day , cate would send her a new electron-density map by fax or email , and they would talk about ways to interpret it .

Universals | .34

he had been diagnosed with melanoma , and it had metastasized to his brain . he told her that he had only three months to live . she spent the rest of that fall flying back and forth from new haven to hilo , a journey of more than twelve hours . chunks of time spent at her father ' s bedside were interspersed with hours on the phone with cate . each day , cate would send her a new electron-density map by fax or email , and they would talk about ways to interpret it .

Figure 8: Passage id: Code-Breaker-The-Walter-Isaacson; genre: BIO

Towards a contextualised spatial-diachronic history of literature: mapping emotional representations of the city and the country in Polish fiction from 1864 to 1939

Agnieszka Karlińska
Institute of Literary Research of the Polish Academy of Sciences

Cezary Rosiński
Institute of Literary Research of the Polish Academy of Sciences

Jan Wieczorek
Wroclaw University of Science and Technology

Patryk Hubar
Institute of Literary Research of the Polish Academy of Sciences

Jan Kocoń
Wroclaw University of Science and Technology

Marek Kubis
Adam Mickiewicz University in Poznan

Stanisław Woźniak
Wroclaw University of Science and Technology

Arkadiusz Margraf
Institute of Bioorganic Chemistry of the Polish Academy of Sciences

Wiktor Walentynowicz
Wroclaw University of Science and Technology

Abstract

In this article, we discuss the conditions surrounding the building of historical and literary corpora. We describe the assumptions and method of making the original corpus of the Polish novel (1864-1939). Then we present the research procedure aimed at demonstrating the variability of the emotional value of the concept of 'the city' and 'the country' in the texts included in our corpus. The proposed method considers the complex socio-political nature of Central and Eastern Europe, especially the fact that there was no unified Polish state during this period. The method can be easily replicated in the studies of the literature of countries with similar specificities.

1 Introduction

The main objective of our paper is to introduce a comprehensive workflow employing NLP methods and Linguistic Linked Open Data (LLOD) that allows for conducting literary research in temporal and spatial dimensions while taking into account local specificities arising from historical, socio-cultural, and infrastructural factors. The proposal addresses, on the one hand, the current criticism towards Digital Humanities (DH), in particular distant reading, and on the other hand, the call for a new way of describing the complex relationship between fiction and imaginary geography put forward in non-digital literary studies.

Criticism of the distant reading approach revolves around the gap between the development of methods and tools and the use of their potential to address new research questions or discover new phenomena. It has been argued that applications of NLP in literary research, while spectacular, are often limited to confirming already known insights (Brennan, 2017), and that much of the research is aimed solely at the tools' validation (Hammond, 2017). Computational analysis of literary texts has also been criticised for reductionism, observation triviality, ahistoricism and the disregard of the socio-cultural determinants of the patterns detected (Bode, 2017).

Addressing the call arising from the above criticism, to embed computational analyses within broader disciplinary contexts and knowledge (Underwood, 2019), the workflow we developed was tailored to current debates and trends in humanities research. We draw on studies within the horizons of geography of literature and literary affect studies, trends highly influential in contemporary humanities that emerged from the topographical and affective turns (Peraldo, 2016; Rybicka, 2014; Ahern, 2019; Nycz et al., 2015). Our goal is to take into account local circumstances and to trace the impact of historical and spatial factors on the dynamics of literary processes. At the current stage, we focus on Central and Eastern Europe (CEEC). However, the workflow was designed for reusabil-

Proceedings of the 6th LaTeCH-CLfL Workshop, pages 115–125
October 16, 2022.

ity and should be adaptable to other local contexts, including non-European.

Studies referring to CEEC as a region undergoing extensive geopolitical changes, highly diverse in terms of nationality, language and culture, build more and more on linguistic resources and metadata for embedding literary texts in socio-cultural realities. Although some CEEC languages are on track to achieve a well-resourced status, there are still many gaps to bridge (Vetulani and Vetulani, 2020; Goldhahn et al., 2016), especially in terms of historical resources. This applies not only to language technology (LT), but also to DH in general. There are very few solutions suited to the processing and analysis of literary texts, e.g. Named Entity Recognition or stylometric analysis. Moreover, the metadata produced by CEEC institutions is incomplete and there is no single relevant and reliable metadata retrieving source. It leads to the necessity of combining various resources, mappings, and harmonisation of disparate data types (Király, 2019).

In the research presented in this paper, the workflow was applied to reconstruct the urban-rural dichotomy, i.e., the attribution of distinguishing values and emotions to urban and rural geo-entities, as a prominent example of reflection from the field of literary geography. This topic's long-standing presence in non-digital literary studies (e.g. (Rybicka, 2003; Williams, 1975)) resulted in the burden of cliché interpretations. Not only do we intendWe intend to verify these interpretations, but also to broaden the scope of investigation by taking into account both historical and geographical dimensions, crucial for CEEC-oriented research and neglected in literary studies. This will allow for a thorough evaluation of the workflow regarding its strengths and shortcomings.

We surveyed Polish novels from 1864 to 1939, representing three consecutive literary periods, Positivism, Young Poland, and the Interwar Period. At the end of the 18th century, Poland ceased to exist as a sovereign state. The Polish territories were divided into three partitions and remained under the control of the Habsburg Monarchy, the Kingdom of Prussia and the Russian Empire until 1918. The partitions differed substantially in terms of the pace of socio-economic development, the extent of urbanisation, and civil liberties (Kaczynska, 1970). These contrasts led to differences in the imaginary, including the dominant discourses of urbanity and rurality, which persisted even after Poland regained independence (Chwalba, 2009). To reconstruct the evolution of the Polish variant of the urban-rural dichotomy, we posed three research questions: (i) Did the level of discrepancy between urban and rural depictions change over time?; (ii) How have the emotional representations of the city and the country changed over time; and (iii) Did the form of the urban-rural dichotomy and the valuation of geo-entities vary according to the partition in which the unit was located?

Related works

The establishment of Spatial Humanities and the rapid growth of Digital Literary Cartography (Cooper et al., 2016; Gregory et al., 2015) on the one hand, and new developments in sentiment analysis for computational literary studies (Jacobs, 2019; Kim and Klinger, 2018), on the other, have not yet translated into systematic research on emotion in relation to fictional representations of space and place. While the recognition, disambiguation, and mapping of toponyms in literary works have been relatively well explored, methodological support for the literary geography of emotions is still lacking and no comprehensive framework has been developed to serve as a reference point (Morariu, 2020). Attempts in this direction have been made in two projects: 'The Emotions of London' (Heuser et al., 2016) and 'High Mountains Low Arousal? Distant Reading Topographies of Sentiment in German-Swiss Novels in the early 20th Century' (Herrmann et al., 2022). The former was a crowdsourcing experiment combining quantitative and qualitative methods of literary geography and focused specifically on the fictional representation of London. The latter (still ongoing) has a much broader scope. It aims to explore whether representations of the landscape can be regarded as a part of the construction of different national identities. The project is based on a comparative analysis of German-language novels from the early 20th century, employing methods well established in computational literary studies, i.e. sentiment analysis and Named-Entity Recognition (NER). The authors do not focus on creating new solutions and workflows; instead they mainly use and validate existing tools and resources. Although their approach may work well for regions that have not experienced significant geopolitical transitions or for well-resourced languages, it is overly simplistic to apply to CEEC.

In the absence of methodological support for the literary geography of emotions, it is necessary to develop our own solutions, combining several components, ranging from the creation of historical corpora through NER, Named-Entity Disambiguation (NED), and Named-Entity Linking (NEL) to sentiment analysis. To compile an optimal procedure, we reviewed the solutions and identified potential challenges.

The corpus linguistics literature points out that the fulfillment of the balanced source selection postulate (Biber, 1993) encounters many more obstacles in the case of historical corpora than in the case of contemporary text corpora (Gruszczyński et al., 2020). A fundamental and unfathomable problem is the limited knowledge of the writing of a particular era, which makes the decisions during corpora compilation arbitrary and often based on speculation with purely theoretical assumptions. The balance of the corpus is complicated by the disproportion between the number of extant texts from earlier eras and the number of texts from later ones (Górski, 2018). Projects aiming to build literary corpora that are as representative and balanced as possible (e.g., KOLIMO(Herrmann and Lauer, 2020) or dProse 1870-1920, (Gius et al., 2021)) have reduced speculativity by using data from bibliographic records on the production and reception of texts.

One of the most recent and most ambitious projects of this type is the European Literary Text Collection (ELTeC) composed of 11 national sub-corpora, each containing 100 novels published between 1840 and 1920. It was assumed that each sub-corpus should fulfill the same compositional criteria with some level of flexibility (Schöch et al., 2021). However, the construction of the corpus raises some concerns. Foremost, the arbitrary categorisation of the texts into four twenty-year time periods, which do not correspond to the caesuras marked by significant socio-political events, both on a pan-European and regional level, is questionable. In the case of the Polish-language sub-corpus (ELTeC, 2021), the incorporation of texts published after 1920 and the lack of a description of the procedure for obtaining metadata, crucial for assessing the quality of the corpus, can also be considered problematic.

In the case of Polish, we have several NER solutions. Liner2 (Marcinczuk et al., 2017) is a tool based on the Conditional Random Fields (CRF) method, which uses morphological information and sets of manually prepared features to identify named entities. The latest method dedicated to Polish is PolDeepNer2 (Marcinczuk and Radom, 2021). It is a neuronal model based on a RoBERTa-type language model. Another tool for the NER task with support for Polish is spaCy (Honnibal and Montani, 2017). While very fast and adapted to industrial language work, it is marginally less efficient than PolDeepNer2.

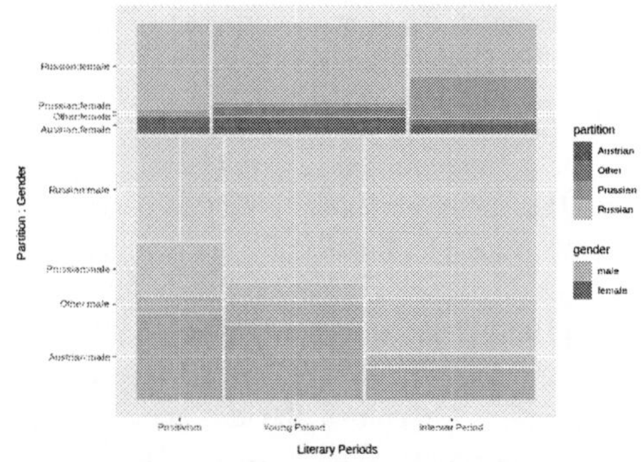

Figure 1: Mosaic diagram of the relationships between the characteristics of the novels in 19/20MetaPNC: the gender of the author, the partition in which the novel was published, and the literary period.

There are several sentiment analysis systems for Polish described in (Wawer, 2019), but none of them is available as an open service. One open system that can be used for sentiment analysis is the MultiEmo service[1] (Kocoń et al., 2021), available through the CLARIN-PL project. It is a new solution based on transformer-type models, available for more than 100 languages, thanks to the LaBSE (Language Agnostic BERT Sentence Embeddings) model (Feng et al., 2022).

Data

Currently, there is no representative and balanced historical corpus of novels in Polish that could function as a referential corpus for various research purposes. For Polish, there are literary corpora that do not meet the standard criteria for composition and have not been robustly described with metadata. An exception is the Polish-language ELTeC subcorpus, which can function as a benchmark for the development of historical literary corpora, despite the aforementioned drawbacks (see Related works). Sampled literary texts are also a

[1] `https://ws.clarin-pl.eu/multiemo`

component of the general corpora of Polish, such as NKJP (Przepiórkowski et al., 2012) and KPWr (Marcińczuk et al., 2016).

For the requirements of spatial-diachronic literary research, it was necessary to design a new corpus, reusable, historically and geographically balanced, precisely described with the possibly complete metadata, which would enable the selection of predefined subcorpora for comparative purposes. We named the designed collection "Metadata-enriched Polish Novel Corpus from the 19th and 20th centuries" (19/20MetaPNC). The specific nature of the geopolitical and socio-cultural context of the Polish territories in the second half of the 19th and first half of the 20th century determined the metadata structure and content as well as the criteria for balancing the corpus. Due to the impossibility of precisely defining the population of texts and the lack of data on literary production and reception of the period covered by the study, our efforts were focused on the aspect of proper balancing and precise description with regard to the metadata of the available textual resources. The basic criteria for the selection of texts, in addition to the time horizon adopted in the project, were the genre and language of the text — we decided to include in the corpus novels originally written in Polish and first published as books between 1864 and 1939. An additional criterion was the time of the plot, which could not be earlier than 1815. This was the year of the Congress of Vienna, which defined the national borders that remained in force with minor modifications for more than 100 years. We assumed that the corpus should be balanced with regard to the individual novel's belonging to one of the three literary eras distinguished in Polish literary studies — Positivism (1864-1890), Young Poland (1890-1918) and the Interwar Period (1918-1939) — determined by the date of first publication, the Partition in which the novel was first published, the gender of the author and the level of reception. Following the same approach as in ELTeC (Schöch et al., 2021), we decided that the corpus should include both: novels that can be considered part of the contemporary canon and works that have been mostly forgotten. As a measure of the level of reception, we took the number of reissues of a given publication.

The process of text selection for the corpus was conducted in three stages. In the first stage, we identified and sourced potential candidate texts. The collected texts come from several distinct sources. We started with 100 novels gathered in the ELTeC that are encoded in TEI format. Next, we included 193 texts from the Wolne Lektury library (Modern Poland Foundation, 2022), an online repository that is primarily focused on school readings and offers contemporised editions of novels that have fallen into the public domain. The data in Wolne Lektury is available in a custom XML format that preserves information about paragraph boundaries. Afterwards, the 225 novels from the Polish edition of the Wikisource project (Wikimedia Foundation, 2022) were added. These texts are transcriptions of printed books whose copyright has expired. They are encoded in the MediaWiki format and proof-read by Wikisource editors, but contrary to the Wolne Lektury volumes, the original spelling is preserved, hence orthographic forms that do not appear in modern Polish can be observed. The last and most demanding source of texts for our corpus is the Polona digital library maintained by the National Library of Poland (2022). Polona offers scans of printed books along with the OCR-derived textual layer. The raw texts from Polona are neither proof-read nor contemporised, but the volume of available data is an order of magnitude greater than in the other resources. We downloaded approx. 6,000 digitised volumes from Polona. After merging multi-volume editions of novels, we obtained 4,808 complete Polona texts. From the 5,326 pieces of literary fiction that formed our initial dataset we selected exactly one edition of every novel. For the purpose of further processing the texts from Wolne Lektury, Wikisource and Polona were converted into a uniform, tab-separated format inspired by CONLL-U Plus representation[2].

In the second phase of corpus construction, we focused on completing the metadata of the collected texts. The work was carried out in an automated and manual procedure. We linked metadata of digital copies of texts to metadata from library catalogues, using the services of the National Library of Poland, and then enriched the entities with permanent identifiers (PIDs) of widely used databases: VIAF, Wikidata, and Geonames. From the data available in the authority databases, we extracted information required for corpus balancing and relevant from the perspective of spatial-diachronic literary research. Simultaneously, the

[2]https://universaldependencies.org/ext-format.html

collection of texts was manually annotated, which covered the time of the novel's action (before or after 1815) and also verified for original language and genre (not always correctly described in the National Library). On this basis, we have again made a selection of texts, rejecting texts that are not novels, written before or after the period covered by the evaluation, and those set before 1815. We also identified and removed duplicates, thus obtaining a database of 1,707 unique novels. The texts were described with the following metadata: author, author's gender, author's Wikidata ID (if available), author's place of birth with coordinates (this information was available for 1,198 items), title, year of first publication, place of first publication, first publication place coordinates and geopolitical territories (Russian, Austrian, and Prussian Partition or foreign countries), number of reprints, number of tokens.

In the third stage, we balanced the corpus. Because it was impossible to keep equal proportions between the classes, we determined the minimum and maximum share of a particular text class in the corpus. We gave priority to balancing by date and place of publication. We assumed that each of the three partitions should be represented by at least 15% of the texts, while each of the three literary eras should be represented by at least 20% of the texts. Following the approach of the ELTeC authors, we determined that at least 10% and a maximum of 50% of the titles should have a female author, at least 30% of the titles should have a low (no more than 2 reprints) and at least 30% a high (2 reprints and more) reception. The proportion of titles for each balance criterion is presented in Fig. 1. 19/20MetaPNC will be published by the end of 2022 in the CLARIN-PL Repository.

Methods

Taking into consideration that the novels gathered in our corpus come from sources that vary in quality, the preliminary steps undertaken to process the collected texts depend on their origin. The proposed workflow for contextualised spatial-diachronic literary research is presented in Fig.2. In the case of ELTeC and Wolne Lektury data we simply split texts into paragraphs and sentences and perform tokenization. OCR-derived texts from Polona are additionally pre-processed by a normalisation script that determines proper word segmentation by looking up correct word forms in the

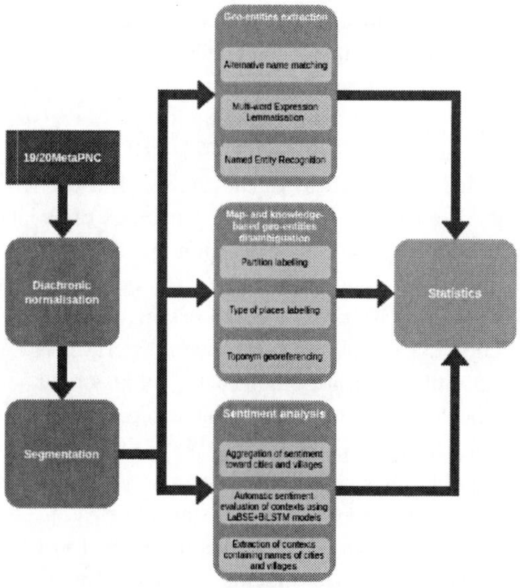

Figure 2: The workflow for retrieving statistics for literary research in temporal and spatial dimensions.

PoliMorf dictionary (Woliński et al., 2012) following the algorithm for OCR gap elimination outlined in (Kubis, 2021). The texts from Wikisource and Polona are contemporised with the use of a diachronic normalizer (Jassem et al., 2017) in order to improve the performance of NLP tools designed for modern Polish that are used in the following steps.

In order to retrieve named entities in the text, we used the PolDeepNer2 system[3] and its pretrained model, learned from the KPWr corpus (Marcinczuk, 2020). We decided to implement this model because it is the best available model for PolDeepNer2 in terms of general texts. After the process of recognising named entities, a pre-selection of the entities of interest was made based on their class. All classes related to the administrative names of locations and verb entities from the names of locations were included. The data extracted in this way was lemmatised with the Polem (Marcinczuk, 2017) tool[4]. The authors of the publication report the effectiveness of the PolDeepNer2 systems as 0.899 F1-Score measure on the PolEval 2018 set, and the Polem as 0.979 F1-Score measure (with a refinement of 0.846 F1-Score measure for NER) on KPWr corpus. Since the names of cities and villages in CEEC changed

[3]https://gitlab.clarin-pl.eu/information-extraction/poldeepner2

[4]https://github.com/CLARIN-PL/Polem

with geopolitical transformations, the final step in preparing the data for the standardisation stage was to include alternative names and varieties for the locations. We used geographic-historical registers, directories and dictionaries selected on the basis of the completeness of the sources and the territorial coverage of the Three Partitions of Poland as data sources. Data extraction involved an OCR process. To identify place names in the documents' page area, we developed an original solution using hierarchical agglomerative clustering (HCA) algorithm to identify the structure of historical documents (tables, indices, and appendices) regardless of their digital copy quality. We specified that the algorithm would analyse clusters in one dimension and applied the Euclidean distance measure. This approach allowed for visualising the performance of the algorithm and facilitated controlling the selection of other parameters.

To identify and standardise geographic entities (geo-entities), we applied an experimental three-stage toponym disambiguation workflow, based on leading approaches in Geographical Information Retrieval (GIR) (Buscaldi, 2011; Derungs and Purves, 2014). We used mainly the Geonames database supplemented with additional data sources (i.e., Wikidata and Wikipedia). The goal of the first stage was to unambiguously assign records from the Geonames database for the geo-entities identified in the text. We used a list of historical name variants prepared in the first stage to query the Geonames database and pre-filter the search results. We included only those geo-entities for which we found the corresponding names in the 'name' or 'alternateName' fields of a Geonames record. If we received only one record after initial filtering of the results, we retrieved its complete information and assigned it to geo-entity. If we obtained several Geonames records, we selected the geo-entity whose coordinates were closest to the area mapped using the coordinates of other locations identified in a given text.

In the second stage, we determined whether the name refers to a city or a village. For this purpose, we used the records from stage one, since they contained the dates of granting municipal rights, as well as contextual information extracted automatically from the text (the terms 'city' and 'village' and their synonyms occurring in the immediate vicinity of the named entity).

The third stage of the disambiguation process was to determine the partition in which a village or a city was located, using a map-based approach. For this purpose, we used historical maps of Polish territories under the post-1815 partitions. Given the raster form of the maps, we used the open source software QGIS that allows georeferencing of the maps in a form that allows automatic processing and the OpenStreetMap resources. Then, we plotted three polygons on the map corresponding to each partition, which allowed us to determine the precise coordinates of their borders. Once the coordinates of the partitions and geoentities were determined, it was possible to assign the geoentity's affiliation to a particular partition.

Next, we automatically determined the sentiment of contexts containing proper names representing cities and villages. For this purpose, we used the MultiEmo tool (Kocoń et al., 2021) trained on sentences annotated with sentiment within the PolEmo 2.0 corpus (Kocoń et al., 2019). This corpus contains more than 8k consumer reviews and more than 50k sentences. Both texts and sentences were annotated using four sentiment labels: positive, negative, neutral and ambivalent. The model achieves very good quality, i.e. an F1-score of about 85%. Next, we evaluated all sentences representing proper names pertaining to cities and the countries. We decided to use a sentence-level sentiment model because the model is more domain-independent and there were more training examples than for a model dedicated to analysing entire reviews.

Results

We identified 130,635 mentions of places in the corpus, for 86,568 (66.3%) mentions we found matches in the Geonames service, which provided information about the partition in which the place was located, and we included these mentions in further analysis. 51.2% of them referred to cities, 48.8% to villages.

This proportion varied over the years and between partitions. The share of mentions reffering to city (Fig. 3) was the lowest and most stable over the years in the Russian partition. In the case of the Austrian and Prussian partitions, there are substantial fluctuations over time, although it is difficult to determine trends. In the former case, a large increase in the share of city mentions was observed at the beginnig of the 20th century and immediately after World War I, while in the latter case, a large

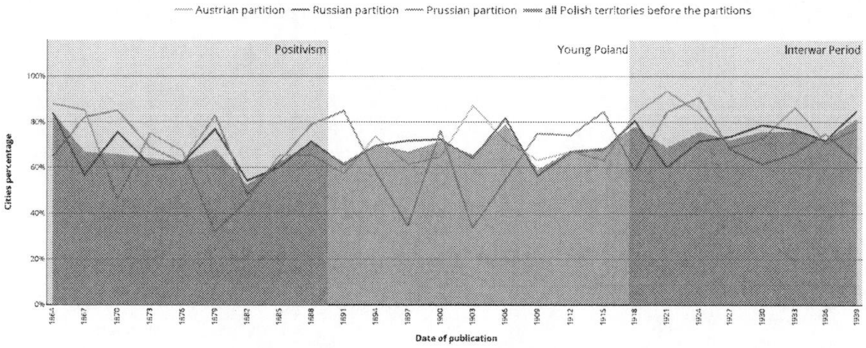

Figure 3: Percentage of city mentions in successive years.

	Estimate	Std. Error	z value	Pr(>|z|)	0.95 Conf. Interval	
					Lower	Upper
(Intercept)	11.4263	0.6777	16.86	0.0000	10.10	12.75
status: village	0.0593	0.0180	3.29	0.0010	0.02	0.09
partition: Austrian	-0.0403	0.0277	-1.46	0.1455	-0.09	0.01
partition: Prussian	0.0241	0.0338	0.71	0.4749	-0.04	0.09
partition: Russian	0.1024	0.0206	4.96	0.0000	0.06	0.14
year	-0.0065	0.0004	-18.19	0.0000	-0.01	-0.01
gender: male	0.0153	0.0174	0.88	0.3774	-0.02	0.05

Table 1: Regression coefficients of the negative sentiment prediction model.

increase was observed in the early 1880s, during World War I and in the mid-1920s. Overall, city mentions dominated over village mentions.

Most mentions (68%) had neutral sentiment, 31% were negative, 1.2% positive and 0.01% ambivalent. The results of the sentiment analysis confirm the urban-rural dichotomy. The difference in the proportion for each sentiment dimension (positive and negative) between cities and villages, decreases with time (Fig. 4). In the case of positive sentiment, the decrease is visible from the last decade of the 19th century (the beginning of Young Poland), in the case of negative sentiment the decrease is less evident, but it appears that from the beginning of the 20th century the dichotomy between cities and villages begins to decrease, although the disproportion is still greater than for positive sentiment.

Mentions with positive sentiment refer to cities and villages equally, with the majority of positive mentions beginning to refer to cities during the Interwar Period. In the case of negative sentiment, the dominance of the villages is clear and this does not change over the literary periods.

While in the case of negative mentions in which a given place was located, the urban-rural dichotomy decreased in subsequent years (with some fluctuations) in all partitions, in the case of positive mentions the dichotomy clearly decreased in the Russian partition, however in the Austrian and Prussian partitions a decrease occurred in Young Poland, and increased in the Interwar Period.

Among the negative mentions referring to places located in the Russian partition, mentions of villages definitely dominate. Among the positive ones, on the other hand, this pattern persists during Positivism but reverses in subsequent literary periods. The mentions relating to places in the Prussian and Austrian partitions demonstrate similar shifts: the positive mentions are dominated by cities, but there are years when the dominance of villages is very apparent. In the case of negative mentions relating to the Prussian partition, in Positivism mentions of villages prevail, and from the end of Positivism mentions of cities are more prevalent (not without exceptions). In the case of negative mentions relating to the Austrian partition mentions of villages tend to dominate until the end of Young Poland, while in the Interwar Period mentions of cities are predominant.

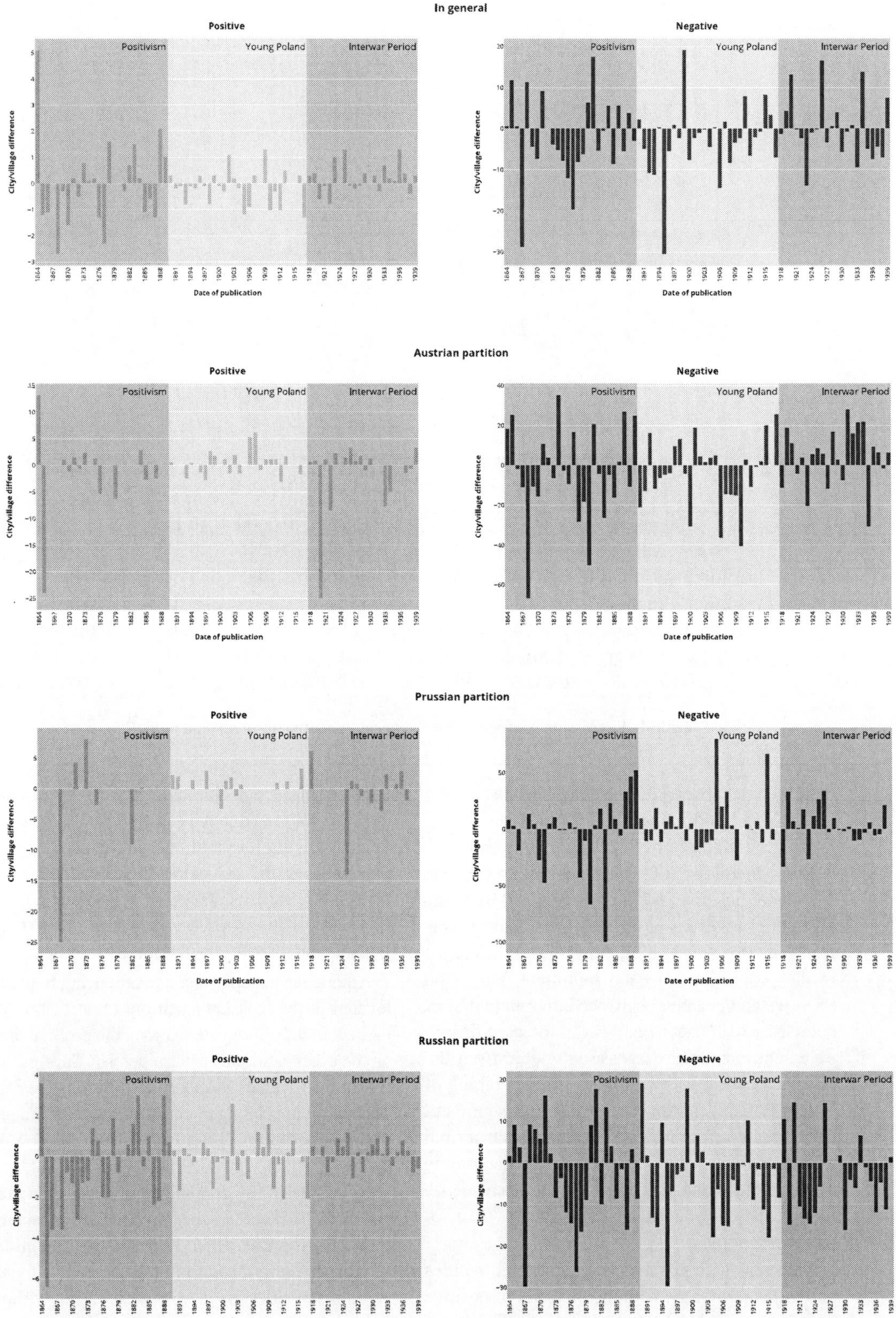

Figure 4: The difference in the proportion for each sentiment dimension (positive and negative) between cities and villages, both in total and by partition, in successive years. A score above zero means that a dimension dominates for the cities, and below zero for the villages.

Taking into account disproportion in the number of sentences belonging to particular sentiment categories we decided to further investigate the impact of location on the sentiment by constructing a model that discriminates between the negative sentiment and all the other categories considered jointly. For this purpose we fitted a binomial logistic regression model with the degree of negativity being the independent variable and location status (village or city), partition (Austrian, Prussian, Russian or abroad), publication year and author's gender being dependent variables. Table 1 presents the regression coefficients of the fitted model. The status of a village and belonging to the Russian partition contributes to the negative sentiment towards the location significantly. Furthermore, the sentiment tends to be less negative for more recent publications.

Conclusions and future work

The results of our study confirmed the urban/rural dichotomy manifested in the different valorisation of urban and rural geo-entities in literary texts. We also confirmed Rybicka's (Rybicka, 2003, 2014), statement that this dichotomy decreased over time, although the changes we observed occurred slightly later than the author assumed. We found that the negative sentiment of place mentions also decreased over time. However, we did not confirm the thesis of the dominance of the anti-urban myth (Rybicka, 2003) in depictions of the city and the country. On the contrary, we showed that villages were more negatively portrayed than cities. Nevertheless, this conclusion needs further research and stronger confirmation. What can be recognised as an important achievement is the group of conclusions concerning the differentiation between the partitions, which clearly indicates the need to include the spatial dimension apart from the temporal dimension.

The workflow component currently raising the most doubts is the sentiment analysis. An analysis with a tool trained on literary data, optimally historical data, would provide more precise results. It would be worthwhile to study the contexts of the occurrence of proper names representing cities and villages using neuro-symbolic models for sentiment (Kocoń et al., 2022), which may yield better results for texts from domains other than those used to train the sentiment model. However, as this postulate requires extensive efforts, in the nearer term it is more effective to refine other aspects of the proposed scheme. Firstly, following (Herrmann et al., 2022) it is worth preparing a dictionary of the names of the objects related to city and village (e.g. 'sawmill', 'manor', 'tenement', 'town hall') and use it to specify the geo-entity status. Secondly, due to the focus on determining the coordinates of recognised geo-entities, we excluded imaginary places from the analysis. They will be covered in subsequent project stages. Thirdly, in the paper we did not consider the phenomena of anaphora and coreference. Efforts are underway to adapt the tools for anaphora and coreference resolution to the specificities of literary texts. Fourthly, in order to address the bias associated with the potential overrepresentation of particularly long novels, we will balance the corpus by length of texts. Fifthly, we will take into account authors' biobibliographical data (e.g. place of birth, work and education) and address the question of mobility in the analysis.

Acknowledgements

The work was co-financed by the European Regional Development Fund as a part of the 2014–2020 Smart Growth Operational Programme, Digital research infrastructure for the humanities and arts sciences DARIAH-PL, agreement no. POIR.04.02.00-D0006/18-00 dated 28/12/2020.

The work was co-financed by the European Regional Development Fund as a part of the 2014–2020 Smart Growth Operational Programme, CLARIN – Common Language Resources and Technology Infrastructure, project no. POIR.04.02.00-00C002/19.

The work was co-financed as part of the investment: "CLARIN ERIC – European Research Infrastructure Consortium: Common Language Resources and Technology Infrastructure (period: 2022-2023) funded by the Polish Ministry of Education and Science (Programme: "Support for the participation of Polish scientific teams in international research infrastructure projects"), Agreement number 2022/WK/09.

References

Stephen Ahern. 2019. *Affect theory and literary critical practice: a feel for the text.* Palgrave Macmillan, Cham.

Douglas Biber. 1993. Representativeness in Corpus Design. *Literary and Linguistic Computing*, 8(4):243–257.

Katherine Bode. 2017. The equivalence of "close" and "distant" reading; or, toward a new object for data-rich literary history. *Modern Language Quarterly*, 78:77–106.

Timothy Brennan. 2017. The Digital-Humanities Bust. *The Chronicle of Higher Education*, 64(8).

Davide Buscaldi. 2011. Approaches to disambiguating toponyms. *SIGSPATIAL Special*, 3(2):16–19.

Andrzej Chwalba. 2009. Dziedzictwo zaborów. In *Polski wiek XX*, volume 1, pages 7–24. Bellona i Muzeum Historii Polski, Warszawa.

David Cooper, Christopher Donaldson, and Patricia Murrieta-Flores. 2016. *Literary Mapping in the Digital Age*. Routledge, Warszawa.

Curdin Derungs and Ross S. Purves. 2014. From text to landscape: locating, identifying and mapping the use of landscape features in a Swiss Alpine corpus. *International Journal of Geographical Information Science*, 28(6):1272–1293.

ELTeC. 2021. Polish novel collection (ELTeC-pol). Ed. by Joanna Byszuk. COST Action Distant Reading for European Literary History.

Fangxiaoyu Feng, Yinfei Yang, Daniel Cer, Naveen Arivazhagan, and Wei Wang. 2022. Language-agnostic BERT sentence embedding. In *Proceedings of the 60th Annual Meeting of the Association for Computational Linguistics (Volume 1: Long Papers)*, pages 878–891.

Evelyn Gius, Svenja Guhr, and Inna Uglanova. 2021. "d-Prose 1870–1920" a Collection of German Prose Texts from 1870 to 1920. *Journal of Open Humanities Data*, 7(0):11.

Dirk Goldhahn, Maciej Janicki, and Uwe Quasthoff. 2016. Corpus collection for under-resourced languages with more than one million speakers. Workshop on Collaboration and Computing for Under-Resourced Languages (CCURL), LREC.

Ian N. Gregory, Christopher Donaldson, Patricia Murrieta-Flores, and Paul Rayson. 2015. Geoparsing, GIS, and Textual Analysis: Current developments in spatial humanities research. *Int. J. Humanit. Arts Comput.*, 9:1–14.

Włodzimierz Gruszczyński, Dorota Adamiec, Renata Bronikowska, and Aleksandra Wieczorek. 2020. Elektroniczny korpus tekstów polskich z XVII i XVIII w.– problemy teoretyczne i warsztatowe. *Poradnik Językowy*, (0):32–51.

Rafał L. Górski. 2018. Metody korpusowe i kwantytatywne w językoznawstwie historycznym. In *Metodologie językoznawstwa. Od diachronii do panchronii*, pages 65–81. Wydawnictwo Uniwersytetu Łódzkiego, Łódź.

Adam Hammond. 2017. The double bind of validation: distant reading and the digital humanities' "trough of disillusionment". *Literature Compass*, 14(8):e12402.

Berenike Herrmann, Giulia Grisot, and Simone Rebora. 2022. High mountains low arousal? Distant reading topographies of sentiment in German-Swiss novels in the early 20th century. `https://mountain-sentiment.github.io/`. Accessed: 2022-07-10.

Berenike Herrmann and Gerhard Lauer. 2020. Kolimo. a corpus of literary modernism for comparative analysis. `https://kolimo.uni-goettingen.de/about`. Accessed: 2022-07-10.

Ryan Heuser, Mark Andrew Algee-Hewitt, and Anna Lockhart. 2016. Mapping the Emotions of London in Fiction, 1700–1900: A Crowdsourcing Experiment. In *Literary Mapping in the Digital Age*, pages 43–64. Routledge.

Matthew Honnibal and Ines Montani. 2017. spaCy 2: Natural language understanding with Bloom embeddings, convolutional neural networks and incremental parsing.

Arthur M. Jacobs. 2019. Sentiment Analysis for Words and Fiction Characters From the Perspective of Computational (Neuro-)Poetics. *Frontiers in Robotics and AI*, 6.

Krzysztof Jassem, Filip Graliński, and Tomasz Obrębski. 2017. Pros and Cons of Normalizing Text with Thrax. In *Proceedings of 8th Language & Technology Conference*, pages 230–235.

Elżbieta Kaczynska. 1970. *Dzieje robotników przemysłowych w Polsce pod zaborami*. Warszawa.

Evgeny Kim and Roman Klinger. 2018. A survey on sentiment and emotion analysis for computational literary studies. *ArXiv*, abs/1808.03137.

Péter Király. 2019. *Measuring Metadata Quality*. [Doctoral's thesis, Faculty of Humanities of the Georg-August-Universität Göttingen].

Jan Kocoń, Joanna Baran, Marcin Gruza, Arkadiusz Janz, Michał Kajstura, Przemysław Kazienko, Wojciech Korczyński, Piotr Miłkowski, Maciej Piasecki, and Joanna Szołomicka. 2022. Neuro-symbolic models for sentiment analysis. In *International Conference on Computational Science*, pages 667–681. Springer.

Jan Kocoń, Piotr Miłkowski, and Kamil Kanclerz. 2021. Multiemo: Multilingual, multilevel, multidomain sentiment analysis corpus of consumer reviews. In *International Conference on Computational Science*, pages 297–312. Springer.

Jan Kocoń, Piotr Miłkowski, and Monika Zaśko-Zielińska. 2019. Multi-level sentiment analysis of

Polemo 2.0: Extended corpus of multi-domain consumer reviews. In *Proceedings of the 23rd Conference on Computational Natural Language Learning (CoNLL)*, pages 980–991.

Marek Kubis. 2021. Quantitative analysis of character networks in Polish 19th- and 20th-century novels. *Digital Scholarship in the Humanities*, 36(Supplement_2):ii175–ii181.

Michal Marcinczuk. 2017. Lemmatization of multi-word common noun phrases and named entities in polish. In *Proceedings of the International Conference Recent Advances in Natural Language Processing, RANLP 2017, Varna, Bulgaria, September 2 - 8, 2017*, pages 483–491. INCOMA Ltd.

Michal Marcinczuk. 2020. KPWr n82 NER model (on polish RoBERTa base).

Michal Marcinczuk, Jan Kocoń, and Marcin Oleksy. 2017. Liner2 — a Generic Framework for Named Entity Recognition. In *BSNLP@EACL*.

Michał Marcińczuk, Marcin Oleksy, Marek Maziarz, Jan Wieczorek, Dominika Fikus, Agnieszka Turek, Michał Wolski, Tomasz Bernaś, Jan Kocoń, and Paweł Kędzia. 2016. Polish Corpus of Wrocław University of Technology 1.2. CLARIN-PL digital repository.

Michal Marcinczuk and Jarema Radom. 2021. A single-run Recognition of Nested Named Entities with Transformers. In *KES*.

Modern Poland Foundation. 2022. About the Project. `https://wolnelektury.pl/info/o-projekcie/`. Accessed: 2022-07-10.

David Morariu. 2020. The affective geography of paris in the 19th century romanian novel: Between admiration and aversion. *Metacritic Journal for Comparative Studies and Theory*, 6:129–147.

National Library of Poland. 2022. About Polona Website. `https://polona.pl/page/about-polona/`. Accessed: 2022-07-10.

Ryszard Nycz, Anna Łebkowska, and Agnieszka Dauksza, editors. 2015. *Kultura afektu - afekty w kulturze : humanistyka po zwrocie afektywnym*. Nowa Humanistyka, t. 19. Wydawnictwo Instytutu Badań Literackich PAN, Warszawa.

Emmanuelle Peraldo. 2016. *Literature and geography: the writing of space throughout history*. Cambridge Scholars Publishing, Newcastle upon Tyne.

Adam Przepiórkowski, Mirosław Bańko, Rafał L. Górski, and Barbara Lewandowska-Tomaszczyk, editors. 2012. *Narodowy korpus języka polskiego: praca zbiorowa*. Wydawnictwo Naukowe PWN, Warszawa.

Elżbieta Rybicka. 2003. *Modernizowanie miasta: zarys problematyki urbanistycznej w nowoczesnej literaturze polskiej*. Universitas, Kraków.

Elżbieta Rybicka. 2014. *Geopoetyka: przestrzeń i miejsce we współczesnych teoriach i praktykach literackich*. Towarzystwo Autorów i Wydawców Prac Naukowych "Universitas", Kraków.

Christof Schöch, Roxana Patras, Tomaž Erjavec, and Diana Santos. 2021. Creating the European Literary Text Collection (ELTeC): Challenges and Perspectives. *Modern Languages Open*, (1):25. Number: 1 Publisher: Liverpool University Press.

Ted Underwood. 2019. *Distant Horizons: Digital Evidence and Literary Change*. University of Chicago Press, Chicago, IL.

Zygmunt Vetulani and Grazyna Vetulani. 2020. The case of Polish on its Way to Become a Well-Resourced-Language. In *Proceedings of LT4All*, Paris. European Language Resources Association.

Aleksander Wawer. 2019. Sentiment analysis for polish. *Poznan Studies in Contemporary Linguistics*, 55(2):445–468.

Wikimedia Foundation. 2022. About Wikisource. `https://wikisource.org/wiki/Wikisource:About_Wikisource`. Accessed: 2022-07-10.

Raymond Williams. 1975. *The country and the city*. Oxford University Press, New York.

Marcin Woliński, Marcin Miłkowski, Maciej Ogrodniczuk, and Adam Przepiórkowski. 2012. PoliMorf: a (not so) new open morphological dictionary for Polish. In *Proceedings of the Eighth International Conference on Language Resources and Evaluation (LREC'12)*, pages 860–864, Istanbul, Turkey. European Language Resources Association (ELRA).

Measuring Presence of Women and Men as Information Sources in News

Muitze Zulaika and **Xabier Saralegi** and **Iñaki San Vicente**
Orai NLP technologies
Zelai Haundi 3, 20170 Usurbil, Spain
{m.zulaika, x.saralegi,i.sanvicente}@orai.eus}

Abstract

In the news, statements from information sources are often quoted, made by individuals who interact in the news. Detecting those quotes and the gender of their sources is a key task when it comes to media analysis from a gender perspective. It is a challenging task: the structure of the quotes is variable, gender marks are not present in many languages, and quote authors are often omitted due to frequent use of coreferences. This paper proposes a strategy to measure the presence of women and men as information sources in news. We approach the problem of detecting sentences including quotes and the gender of the speaker as a joint task, by means of a supervised multiclass classifier of sentences. We have created the first datasets for Spanish and Basque by manually annotating quotes and the gender of the associated sources in news items. The results obtained show that BERT based approaches are significantly better than bag-of-words based classical ones, achieving accuracies close to 90%. We also analyse a bilingual learning strategy and generating additional training examples synthetically; both provide improvements up to 3.4% and 5.6%, respectively.

1 Introduction

Text mining in general, and Natural Language Understanding (NLU) in particular, are being successfully used as support tools on various areas of the humanities. In many studies, evidence is encoded in natural language, either in text or audio collections, and NLU techniques help significantly in the task of finding such evidence.

Within the humanities, one of the fields that has gained momentum in recent years is gender studies, which has come to cover a wide range of topics. This paper focuses on gender studies aimed at analysing the presence of women in the narratives constructed by the press. The objective of this kind of research is to quantify the presence of women compared to men in the news according to various indicators. The Global Media Monitoring Project (GMMP) is a long running international project carrying out such studies. It has a consolidated methodology that evaluates a wide number of indicators (Macharia, 2020), such as:

- Sex of presenters, reporters and news subjects & sources in newspaper, television and radio news.
- Subject and source selection by sex and by sex of reporters in print, television and radio stories.
- Function of subjects & sources in newspaper, television and radio news.
- Subjects & sources quoted directly in newspapers.

All of those indicators are analysed manually, which implies a great effort that limits the frequency and the size of the sample on which the studies are carried out. It is therefore appropriate to research whether such indicators can be measured using artificial intelligence. This paper focuses on those that require language comprehension. Specifically, we tackle the indicator dealing with the presence of women and men as information sources in the news, by means of NLU techniques. We approach the task using a binary gender identification schema, due to technical reasons. This decision should not be interpreted as a denial of a more complex reality.

This paper presents an attempt to measure the presence of women as sources of information for news stories, in the line of work started by (Asr et al., 2021). We approach the problem by using a simple strategy whose core is a multiclass supervised classifier. The main task consists on identifying sentences including quotes and detecting the gender of the sources of those quotes. This is no trivial task. The structure of the quotes is variable, in some languages there is no gender marking, and,

Proceedings of the 6th LaTeCH-CLfL Workshop, pages 126–134
October 16, 2022. ©2022 International Conference on Computational Linguistics

moreover coreferences are often used and thus the source of the quote is not explicit.

Example 1

[EU] Sagarduik[1] ohartarazi du «kostatuko» dela kutsatze-tasa 60 puntura jaistea.

[ES] Sagardui advierte de que «va a costar» reducir la tasa de contagio a 60 puntos.

[EN] *Sagardui warns that 'it'll be hard' to reduce the contagion rate to 60 points.*

A manual analysis of a sample of news items (see Section 3.1) showed that it is not necessary to solve all cases of coreference in order to measure the presence of women and men as sources of information. This fact allows us to tackle the task with a relatively simple pipeline. The pipeline consists of two steps; first lexical substitutions involving surnames (See Example 1) are resolved, and afterwards a multiclass classifier detects the sentences in the news that correspond to utterances as well as their corresponding gender. To address the multiclass classification task, different strategies based on fine-tuning neural language models have been compared to Bag-of-Word paradigm based approaches.

The contributions of this work are the following:

- This is the first work addressing the task measuring the presence of women as sources of information for news stories using a supervised approach.
- We provide the first datasets for Basque and Spanish, including a bilingual benchmark for the task[2].
- Study of approaches based on pretrained language models to address the task.
- Study of cross-lingual learning and data-augmentation strategies to cope with the scarcity of training data for this task.

From here on, the paper is organized as follows: the next section reviews the state of the art. In section 3 we present an analysis about the measurement of the presence of women and men as information sources, how datasets were prepared and what criteria we followed in the annotation. Section 4 presents the approaches analysed to tackle the task as well as the results obtained. Finally, some conclusions are drawn.

[1] *Sagardui* is the surname of the source, the full name is *Gotzone Sagardui*.

[2] Datasets are publicly available under CC-BY license at `https://github.com/orai-nlp/news-src-gender`.

2 State of the Art

When developing policies to address social challenges, evidence-based diagnostics are necessary, and the digital press is a source of such evidence, or more specifically, the narratives of reality that they offer. This type of analysis based on NLP techniques has already been carried out for several social challenges. (Lee, 2019) applies several text mining techniques such as collocations, word co-occurrences and topic-modeling (LDA) for extracting information about immigrant workers in Korea. (Chouliaraki and Zaborowski, 2017) study the narratives in the press about the refugees during the 2015 refugee crisis across eight European countries. (Lansdall-Welfare et al., 2017) focus on gender equality, using an approach based on counting n-gram frequencies and extracting Named Entities on a large British news corpus. (de Oliveira et al., 2021) present a comprehensive survey of the challenges fake news detection in social media pose, including NLP approaches. In the same field, (Khaldarova and Pantti, 2016) analyse fake news narratives generated about the Ukrainian conflict and Twitter users' reactions to those stories.

Regarding gender related research, we can find numerous works that make use of NLP. (Hu et al., 2021) apply sentiment analysis techniques to identify sexist attitudes in Chinese social media. (Kozlowski et al., 2020) study gender stereotypes in male-oriented magazines and female-oriented magazines. They use Topic Modelling techniques to analyse the topics associated with each gender and their evolution over time. (Nagaraj and Kejriwal, 2022) present a large scale analysis of the gender disparity in literature published in the pre-modern period by means of NERC and NED techniques. (Underwood et al., 2018) use similar techniques, namely the BookNLP pipeline (Bamman et al., 2014), to research the evolution of the meaning of gender in works of fiction published between the 18th and 21st century. (Sims and Bamman, 2020) deals with the task of modelling the propagation of information in literature by paying attention to gender dynamics and their relationship to the representation of men and women in novels. To do so, they use, among others, coreference resolution and speaker attribution techniques. Other authors (Garnerin et al., 2019; Lebourdais et al., 2022; Doukhan et al., 2018) study the presence of gender on audio content in order to analyse the presence of men and women in audiovisual media.

(Asr et al., 2021) present a system for the analysis of gender bias in the news. This is the work in the literature closest to ours. The system allows measuring indicators of the presence of men and women who are mentioned in the news and as sources of quotes included in the news. The following pipeline is used to measure the presence of men and women as authors of quotes: 1) extraction of quotes, 2) identification of their sources, and 3) prediction of their gender. For quote extraction, a strategy combining a symbolic approach based on syntactic dependencies and regular expressions is used. For source identification, they apply a NERC model to detect person names and a coreference model to link names with quotes. The gender of the person's name is determined by searching a name database.

Quote extraction and speaker attribution are tasks that have been addressed in the literature. Three types of quotes are distinguished in the literature: direct quotes, indirect quotes, and mixed quotes. Early approaches to citation extraction focused on direct quotes and made use of symbolic strategies (Pouliquen et al., 2007; Glass and Bangay, 2007). (Elson and McKeown, 2010) also focus on direct quotes and propose a more complex strategy combining a NERC process, linguistic rules based on syntactic information and a supervised classifier. (Pareti et al., 2013) presents the first large-scale experiments on direct quotes, indirect quotes, and mixed quotes extraction. They deal with the task with a supervised approach based on Conditional Random Field (CRF) models and maximum entropy classifiers.

The work closest to ours is (Asr et al., 2021). As we have already mentioned, they deal with the measurement of women as source of information as well, but unlike ours, it is based on a symbolic approach that also requires a more complex pipeline than the one we propose. On the other hand, there have also been published works (Pareti et al., 2013; Elson and McKeown, 2010; Pouliquen et al., 2007) on quote extraction, which are somehow related to the measurement of this indicator. These approaches, supervised in some cases, also present pipelines with a complexity that exceeds what is necessary to address the task we propose.

3 Presence of women as source information in news

The measurement of the indicator of presence of women and men as sources of information in the news can be approached as an aggregation of the measurement of that indicator on the sentences that make up a news article. Therefore, the NLU tasks to be addressed would be to identify the sentences that correspond to quotes and then classify the gender of the authors of these quotes. We can define the whole challenge as follows:

Given a document $D = \{s_1, ..s_i, ..s_n\}$ detect the sentences $\{s_i\}$ that correspond to quotes and assign the corresponding gender to the source of the quote $gen(s_i) = \{m, f\}$.

Unfortunately, the presence of coreferences, as well as the lack of explicit gender information in some languages, makes this task very difficult to solve. However, since the ultimate goal is the measurement of a macro indicator, it may not be necessary to resolve all quotes. In order to clarify these two points, we present a study carried out on a manually annotated sample in section 3.1. On the one hand, we analyse the complexity of the task in Spanish and Basque, Basque being a language without gender marks, and on the other hand, whether resolving all quotes is necessary to measure the presence of women and men as sources of information.

Once the analysis was done, we further annotated a large number of examples in order to construct the datasets for training and evaluating the supervised approaches proposed in this work. Details about annotation guidelines and datasets preparation are given in section. 3.2.

3.1 Analysis of the task

In order to analyse the difficulty of the task of measuring the presence of women and men as sources in the news, an annotated sample was created from a collection of news items. In total, the sample contained 400 news in Basque and 400 news in Spanish, randomly selected from a collection of news articles crawled from various digital press websites in the Basque Country[3]. All sentences of each news item were manually analysed, marking those corresponding to quotes as well as the

[3]News were collected between February 2021 and March 2022. Spanish news were crawled from El Diario Vasco, El Correo and Noticias de Alava, and Basque news from Argia and Berria.

	ES		
	F	**M**	**%**
All quotes	401	401	100%
No coreference	97	91	22.69%
Coreference	304	310	77.56%
Ellipsis	154	174	43.39%
Surname lex. sub.	77	63	15.71%
Other lex. sub.	73	73	18.20%
Gender mark	170	164	40.90%
No gender mark	231	237	59.10%

Table 1: Statistics of the Spanish sample.

	EU		
	F	**M**	**%**
All quotes	302	302	100%
No coreference	38	50	12.58%
Coreference	264	252	87.42%
Ellipsis	145	151	48.01%
Surname lex. sub.	91	70	30.13%
Other lex. sub.	28	31	9.27%
Gender mark	42	51	13.91%
No gender mark	260	251	86.09%

Table 2: Statistics of the Basque sample.

source's name and gender in the quote. Coreferences were also solved manually.

To annotate the examples we follow the criteria used in the GMMP methodology guide (GMMP, 2020). We have annotated the gender of each person in the story who is quoted, either directly[4] or indirectly[5]. Only quotes by individual people are annotated, quotes from sources such as groups, organizations or collectives are not considered.

The final samples are composed of an equal number of quotes by women and men, specifically, 401 quotes per gender for Spanish and 302 per gender for Basque. In order to reach this equality, we had to collect news that explicitly contained quotes by women, since the initial random sample yielded an imbalanced number of quotes toward male sources (74.63% and 67.59% for Basque and Spanish, respectively). The manual effort required for this annotation is high: on average, a quote is found in the 9% of the Spanish sentences analysed (up to 14% in Basque). A total of 5274 sentences were annotated in Spanish, and 2667 in Basque. The number of annotated examples is lower in Basque due to time constraints and limited resources.

Tables 1 and 2 present the statistics of the samples. Regarding sentences containing quotes, in most cases the sentence does not contain information regarding the gender of the source (**No gender mark** row), especially in Basque (86.09%). Coreferences are also abundant in both languages. Most of those coreferences are ellipsis (**Ellipsis** row), 43.4% in Spanish and 48% in Basque, a type of coreference that is very difficult to resolve (Soraluze et al., 2017). The rest of the coreferences detected in the quotes correspond to lexical substitutions, including a significant number of substitutions of the full name for the surname (**Surname lex. sub.** row) which is a type of coreference very easy to resolve. The rest of lexical substitutions (**Other lex. sub.** row) correspond to pronoun and job position related substitutions.

Being the objective of this work the measurement of the indicator of presence of women as sources in large-scale news, we have analysed whether to obtain an estimate of this indicator is necessary the resolution of all types of coreference.

As a formula for calculating the presence indicator in a collection of *n* news items, we have established the following ratios for each gender:

$$FQ = \frac{\sum_{i=1}^{n} \frac{\#F\_quotes_i}{\#F\_quotes_i + \#M\_quotes_i}}{n} \quad (1)$$

$\#F\_quotes_i$ is the number of quotes in news item *i* whose authors are women, and $\#M\_quotes_i$ is the number of quotes in news item *i* whose authors are men.

We analysed whether the ratios (at news article level) calculated taking into account only the quotes that include gender information and/or easily treatable surname type coreferences (**Quotes with gender marks** in Table 3) correlate with the ratios that take into account all quotes (**All_Quotes** in Table 3). The Pearson correlation values obtained are 0.940 and 0.938 for Basque and Spanish news of the sample respectively, meaning that to measure the indicator it is sufficient to consider only citations that include gender or surname coreference information. It remains for future work to

[4]A person is quoted directly if their own words are printed in the story - e.g. 'I am disappointed and angry about the continued use of drugs in sport' said the President of the Olympic Committee.

[5]A person is quoted indirectly if their words are paraphrased or summarised in the story - e.g. The President of the Olympic Committee today expressed anger at the incidence of drug use.

check whether this correlation also holds for subsets of news items with different attributes such as time period, subject area or news source. These specifications significantly simplify the pipeline required to estimate the indicator and the classification task to be solved by the multiclass classifier.

	FQes	FQeu
All_Quotes	0.33	0.26
Quotes with gender marks	0.35	0.30

Table 3: Presence of women as source in news sample estimated by taking into account all quotes (**All_Quotes**) and taking into account only quotes including gender information and/or surname type coreferences (**Quotes with gender marks**).

3.2 Dataset

The sample annotated in the previous section is limited and created with the objective of analysing the task. A dataset to train and test supervised classifiers for our use case must fulfill certain requirements: it has to be large enough, maintain a balance between female and male categories, and have no gender bias. In addition, we set to make development and test sets as similar as possible between languages. Thus, datasets presented in section 3.1 were increased. Examples were further annotated in Basque and Spanish, meeting the aforementioned conditions. In order to make the Basque and Spanish datasets equal, examples were translated from one language to the other and added to the respective dataset. Thus, Basque and Spanish datasets will have the same content in all sentences. However, it should be kept in mind that the Basque language is a language without brand gender, so some Spanish female and male sentences, in Basque will be tagged as 'Other' (see section 4 for details about annotation scheme). Therefore, although the datasets of the two languages are made up of the same sentences, the evaluations are not comparable between languages, since a number of sentences have different labels in each language.

To correct the gender bias, an equivalent example was generated for each example quote but with the opposite gender of the source. Let's take the example "*Partidaren atarian, **Axier Arteagak** onartu zuen norgehiagoka «zaila» izango zuela.*[6]". The equivalent example is generated by selecting the name of a real person from the same domain (Basque pelota in the example) but with the opposite gender: "*Partidaren atarian, **Ane Mendiburuk** onartu zuen norgehiagoka «zaila» izango zuela.*[7]".

In addition, we added more F, M and Other (see section 4) sentences to increase the training dataset. To do this, we process news sentences with a quote classifier. This classifier detects whether sentences contain quotes or not. Gender detection of sources (F and M labels) was performed manually. The classifier detected quotes in 2,000 randomly selected news for each language. In total, we added 792 female expressions, 792 male ones and 2,922 corresponding to the 'Other' category in Spanish. The respective numbers for Basque were 666, 666 and 3,770.

The statistics of the final datasets constructed are shown in Tables 4 (Spanish) and 5 (Basque), including all the aforementioned improvements. In this task, positive examples are quotes with gender marks (F and M), and the rest of the sentences (Other) are negative. That is, the 'Other' category includes quotes without gender marks and sentences without quotes. For the sake of the experiments, we assume that substitution type coreferences can be solved automatically, hence, we've added their manual resolutions and classified them as positive.

	F	M	Other	All
Train	884	884	5,323	7,091
Dev	184	184	1,022	1,390
Test	125	125	1,049	1,299
All	1,193	1,193	7,394	9,780

Table 4: Statistics of Spanish monolingual datasets, number of sentences per class.

	F	M	Other	All
Train	695	695	3,690	5,080
Dev	184	184	1,022	1,390
Test	89	89	1,121	1,299
All	968	968	5,833	7,769

Table 5: Statistics of Basque monolingual datasets, number of sentences per class.

[6]Before the match, **Axier Arteaga** accepted that it would be a "difficult" competition.

[7]Before the match, **Ane Mendiburu** accepted that it would be a "difficult" competition.

4 Identification of quote and source's gender

We propose to measure the indicator of presence of women as a source in news by dealing with the task at sentence level. Once solved at the sentence level, we can aggregate sentence results to compute the indicator at news article level, and subsequently at the collection level. We have shown in section 3.1 that the task at the sentence level can be simplified and not all types of coreference need to be taken into account. It is enough to consider only those citations that include gender marks and/or surname-type coreferences. The proposed approach to address the task has two steps: (i) lexical substitutions (surnames) are resolved at the news item level, and (ii) sentences from the news item are processed by a multiclass classifier that determines whether the sentence contains a quote and the gender of the source of the quote.

We approach the problem of identifying quotes and the gender of their sources as a single sentence classification task. Each sentence of the news article is classified based on three categories:

- **F**: Quote made by a woman including gender marks.
- **M**: Quote made by a man including gender marks.
- **Other**: Non-quote or quotes without gender marks.

To implement the multiclass classifier, two approaches have been compared: a) bag-of-words representation and SVM (Support Vector Machine) and LR (Logistic Regression) classifiers, and b) dense fine-tuned representation approach using a pretrained BERT neural models.

To implement the first approach we used the vocabulary with minimum absolute document frequency of 4 and maximum relative document frequency of 0.6. We used the TFIDF statistic as the weight in the vector representation.

To implement the neural approach, we adopted the fine-tuning strategy proposed by (Devlin et al., 2019), using various BERT models and fine-tuning them over the datasets presented in sections 3.1 and 3.2. We have analysed the following BERT models:

- **BERTeus** (Agerri et al., 2020) is a BERT-base-cased language model for Basque pretrained on a corpus containing 224.6M words, including news articles from online newspapers and the Basque Wikipedia.
- **IXAmBERT** (Otegi et al., 2020) is a multilingual language model pretrained with English, Spanish and Basque texts. The model was trained on a corpus composed of Wikipedia dumps of the three languages, and Basque news articles from online newspapers.
- **BETO** (Cañete et al., 2020) is a Spanish language model pretrained on a 3B token corpus from various sources. It is similar to BERT-base-cased, although its vocabulary contains 31k BPE subword tokens and the model was trained for 2M steps.

All the fine-tuning experiments were carried out using an Nvidia Titan RTX3090 GPU card. Initial learning rate was set to 3e-5 and the best model was chosen over the results obtained in the development set, after fine-tuning up to ten 10 epochs. We report the best result out of 5 random initializations. The Transformers library (Wolf et al., 2020) was used.

	Precision		**Recall**		**F-score**		
	F	M	F	M	F	M	AVG
LR	0.33	0.27	0.44	0.35	0.38	0.31	0.35
SVM	0.35	0.30	0.35	0.34	0.35	0.32	0.34
BETO	0.86	0.83	0.85	0.90	0.85	0.87	0.86

Table 6: Monolingual results for Spanish quote and gender detection.

	Precision		**Recall**		**F-score**		
	F	M	F	M	F	M	AVG
LR	0.21	0.21	0.46	0.38	0.29	0.27	0.28
SVM	0.28	0.23	0.43	0.35	0.34	0.27	0.30
BERTeus	0.87	0.84	0.92	0.89	0.90	0.86	0.88

Table 7: Monolingual results for Basque quote and gender detection.

Tables 6 and 7 present the results of the monolingual experiments. For each system, we report precision, recall and F-score results over F and M categories. We leave the category "other" out, since F and M are the relevant ones for measuring the indicator of the gender presence as information source. As a general metric of the systems' performance, we report the average of the F and M categories' F-score values (see the last column of the tables 6 and 7). Analysing the results, we arrive at two conclusions that hold for both languages: (i) neural language models perform significantly better than bag-of-words based classical algorithms, up to 51 points F-score for Spanish and 58 points for Basque; and (ii) using neural language models, the classifier detects with a high F-score the quotes of the news and the gender of its sources.

Regarding the classical algorithms, results obtained with the two algorithms are very similar, both for LR and SVM the recall is higher than the precision, achieving a F-score of 0.35 and 0.30 for Spanish and Basque, respectively. On the other hand, neural language models classify the gender of sources with a high F-score average value, 0.86 and 0.88 for Spanish and Basque, respectively.

As for gender, it is observed that female and male sources are not detected with the same F-score, however, the difference is small and the classifiers perform similarly for both genders.

4.1 Multilingual training

One of the strategies proposed in the literature to cope with the shortage of training examples is to combine the examples available for different languages and use a multilingual model as a base pretrained model. The logic behind this approach is that multilingual models are able to generalize across languages, and thus they will benefit from training examples in different languages. We performed experiments combining the Basque and Spanish training datasets and optimizing the number of epochs with the development dataset of the evaluation language. We constructed a combined dataset maintaining language balance, which includes 5,080 sentences per language[8]. The full bilingual training dataset consists of 1,390 female quotes, 1,390 male quotes and 7,380 other quotes.

	Multilingual (IXAmBERT)						
	Precision		**Recall**		**F-score**		
	F	M	F	M	F	M	AVG
ES	0.90	0.85	0.90	0.89	0.90	0.87	0.89
EU	0.88	0.89	0.99	0.88	0.93	0.88	0.91

Table 8: Multilingual training results for quote and gender detection.

The results of this experiment are shown in Table 8. With the multilingual model we have managed to improve monolingual results, we have achieved a 3 point improvement in both languages.

[8]Basque language training dataset is used as reference, since it is the smaller one. Spanish examples are selected randomly.

4.2 Synthetic examples

Error analysis of both monolingual and multilingual experiments surfaced a few cases where the classifier predicts the opposite gender, although the source name is written directly in the sentence. Our hypothesis is that this error may be related to the number of names of sources that the model has seen in training, because the training examples contain only a limited number of names. This implies that the model may not know the gender of the nouns present in the test, because they are missing in the train dataset. In order to tackle the problem of Out-Of-Vocabulary (OOV) names, we include synthetically generated examples in the training. Specifically, we generate new examples from examples that exist in training, replacing name occurrences with other names included in a list.

The aim of this experiment is to test whether adding examples including OOV names to the training set directly influences the detection of the gender of information sources. Hence, we performed the experiment under ideal settings.

The name list includes names that appear in the test but not in the training data. Our error analysis shows that sentences with source's names that appear once or not at all in the training dataset, are correctly classified with a 17.91% accuracy, while names that appear two or more times achieve an0 89%. Therefore, taking into account these statistics, we've created two synthetic examples for each OOV name. For example, using the OOV name Denisa and random training quotes we have generated two examples:

Example 2

[EU_1] «Ahal den bezain azkarren eutsiko diogu berriro horri», adierazi du Denisa Urtiagak.
[$Translation_1$] *"We will get back to it as soon as possible," says Denisa Urtiaga.*

[EU_2] Joera aldaketa horren atzean kontzientziazio lan handia dagoela uste du Denisa Molinak.
[$Translation_2$] *Denisa Molina believes that there is a great awareness-raising work behind this change of trend.*

Tables 9 and 10 present the results of the synthetic examples experiment. If we compare this results with the previous experiment, we observe that both for monolingual and multilingual models,

	Synthetic Monolingual						
	Precision		**Recall**		**F-score**		
	F	M	F	M	F	M	AVG
BETO	0.95	0.92	0.83	0.88	0.89	0.90	0.89
BERTeus	0.90	0.90	0.90	0.90	0.90	0.90	0.90

Table 9: Synthetic training results, monolingual model.

	Synthetic Multilingual (IXAmBERT)						
	Precision		**Recall**		**F-score**		
	F	M	F	M	F	M	AVG
ES	0.97	0.94	0.91	0.94	0.94	0.94	0.94
EU	0.87	1.00	1.00	0.85	0.93	0.92	0.92

Table 10: Synthetic training results, multilingual model.

the use of synthetic examples has a beneficial effect on gender detection.

Both monolingual and multilingual models benefit from using synthetic examples. For Spanish, the monolingual model performs three points higher (first row in Table 9) and the multilingual model performs five points higher (first row in Table 10). Regarding Basque, the same behavior is observed, the use of synthetic examples brings up the performance of the monolingual model two points (2nd row in Table 9) and one point with the performance of the multilingual model (2nd row in Table 10).

5 Conclusion

This work addresses the task of automatically measuring the presence of women and men as sources of information in the news. This is a standard indicator in media monitoring processes for gender balance.

We have shown that the large-scale measurement of this indicator can be automated using NLU techniques. To the best of our knowledge, this is the first work proposing a supervised approach to tackle this problem. The experimentation has been validated on two languages with different characteristics, Spanish and Basque.

According to the analysis of our datasets, in order to estimate the presence indicator at the collection level it is not necessary to solve all the cases of coreference associated with the quotes, which simplifies the pipeline required for the measurement of the indicator.

Experiments show that the tasks of citation detection and author gender classification can be tackled jointly by means of a supervised multiclass classifier based on neural language models. Fine-tuning a pretrained neural model provides significantly better results than supervised approaches based on bag-of-words paradigm.

The supervised approach based on neural language models can achieve better results if they are trained with examples from both languages and a multilingual pretrained model is used. Further improvement can also be achieved by adding synthetic examples to the training set, generated for person names not included in the training.

6 Acknowledgements

This work has been supported by Emakunde, the Basque Institute for Women. Muitze Zulaika is also funded by the Investigo programme included in the framework of the European Union's NextGenerationEU plan.

References

Rodrigo Agerri, Iñaki San Vicente, Jon Ander Campos, Ander Barrena, Xabier Saralegi, Aitor Soroa, and Eneko Agirre. 2020. Give your text representation models some love: the case for basque. In *Proceedings of the 12th International Conference on Language Resources and Evaluation.*

Fatemeh Torabi Asr, Mohammad Mazraeh, Alexandre Lopes, Vasundhara Gautam, Junette Gonzales, Prashanth Rao, and Maite Taboada. 2021. The gender gap tracker: Using natural language processing to measure gender bias in media. *PloS one*, 16(1):e0245533.

David Bamman, Ted Underwood, and Noah A Smith. 2014. A bayesian mixed effects model of literary character. In *Proceedings of the 52nd Annual Meeting of the Association for Computational Linguistics (Volume 1: Long Papers)*, pages 370–379.

José Cañete, Gabriel Chaperon, Rodrigo Fuentes, Jou-Hui Ho, Hojin Kang, and Jorge Pérez. 2020. Spanish pre-trained bert model and evaluation data. In *PML4DC at ICLR 2020.*

Lilie Chouliaraki and Rafal Zaborowski. 2017. Voice and community in the 2015 refugee crisis: A content analysis of news coverage in eight european countries. *International Communication Gazette*, 79(6-7):613–635.

Nicollas R de Oliveira, Pedro S Pisa, Martin Andreoni Lopez, Dianne Scherly V de Medeiros, and Diogo MF Mattos. 2021. Identifying fake news on social networks based on natural language processing: trends and challenges. *Information*, 12(1):38.

Jacob Devlin, Ming-Wei Chang, Kenton Lee, and Kristina Toutanova. 2019. BERT: Pre-training of

Deep Bidirectional Transformers for Language Understanding. In *Proceedings of the 2019 Conference of the North American Chapter of the Association for Computational Linguistics: Human Language Technologies, Volume 1 (Long and Short Papers)*, pages 4171–4186.

David Doukhan, Jean Carrive, Félicien Vallet, Anthony Larcher, and Sylvain Meignier. 2018. An open-source speaker gender detection framework for monitoring gender equality. In *2018 IEEE international conference on acoustics, speech and signal processing (ICASSP)*, pages 5214–5218. IEEE.

David K Elson and Kathleen R McKeown. 2010. Automatic attribution of quoted speech in literary narrative. In *Twenty-fourth AAAI conference on artificial intelligence*.

Mahault Garnerin, Solange Rossato, and Laurent Besacier. 2019. Gender representation in french broadcast corpora and its impact on asr performance. In *Proceedings of the 1st International Workshop on AI for Smart TV Content Production, Access and Delivery*, pages 3–9.

Kevin Glass and Shaun Bangay. 2007. A naive salience-based method for speaker identification in fiction books. In *Proceedings of the 18th Annual Symposium of the Pattern Recognition Association of South Africa (PRASA'07)*, pages 1–6.

GMMP. 2020. *Global Media Monitoring Project (GMMP) Methodology Guide*, pages 8–32.

Bing Hu, Fang-Ling Luo, Zeng-Wen Peng, and Shi-Qi Lin. 2021. Sexism and male self-cognitive crisis: Sentiment and discourse analysis of an internet event. *Journal of Broadcasting & Electronic Media*, 65(5):679–698.

Irina Khaldarova and Mervi Pantti. 2016. Fake news: The narrative battle over the ukrainian conflict. *Journalism practice*, 10(7):891–901.

Diego Kozlowski, Gabriela Lozano, Carla M Felcher, Fernando Gonzalez, and Edgar Altszyler. 2020. Gender bias in magazines oriented to men and women: a computational approach. *arXiv preprint arXiv:2011.12096*.

Thomas Lansdall-Welfare, Saatviga Sudhahar, James Thompson, Justin Lewis, FindMyPast Newspaper Team, and Nello Cristianini. 2017. Content analysis of 150 years of british periodicals. *Proceedings of the National Academy of Sciences*, 114(4):E457–E465.

Martin Lebourdais, Marie Tahon, Antoine Laurent, Sylvain Meignier, and Anthony Larcher. 2022. Overlaps and gender analysis in the context of broadcast media. In *LREC 2022*.

Changsoo Lee. 2019. How are 'immigrant workers' represented in korean news reporting?—a text mining approach to critical discourse analysis. *Digital Scholarship in the Humanities*, 34(1):82–99.

Sarah Macharia. 2020. *Global Media Monitoring Project (GMMP) 2020-2021 final report*, pages 1–6.

Akarsh Nagaraj and Mayank Kejriwal. 2022. Robust quantification of gender disparity in pre-modern english literature using natural language processing. *arXiv e-prints*, pages arXiv–2204.

Arantxa Otegi, Aitor Agirre, Jon Ander Campos, Aitor Soroa, and Eneko Agirre. 2020. Conversational question answering in low resource scenarios: A dataset and case study for basque. In *Proceedings of The 12th Language Resources and Evaluation Conference*, pages 436–442.

Silvia Pareti, Tim O'keefe, Ioannis Konstas, James R Curran, and Irena Koprinska. 2013. Automatically detecting and attributing indirect quotations. In *Proceedings of the 2013 Conference on Empirical Methods in Natural Language Processing*, pages 989–999.

Bruno Pouliquen, Ralf Steinberger, and Clive Best. 2007. Automatic detection of quotations in multilingual news. In *Proceedings of Recent Advances in Natural Language Processing*, pages 487–492.

Matthew Sims and David Bamman. 2020. Measuring information propagation in literary social networks. In *Proceedings of the 2020 Conference on Empirical Methods in Natural Language Processing (EMNLP)*.

Ander Soraluze, Olatz Arregi, Xabier Arregi, and Arantza Díaz de Ilarraza. 2017. Enriching basque coreference resolution system using semantic knowledge sources. In *Proceedings of the 2nd Workshop on Coreference Resolution Beyond OntoNotes (CORBON 2017)*, pages 8–16.

Ted Underwood, David Bamman, and Sabrina Lee. 2018. The transformation of gender in english-language fiction. *Journal of Cultural Analytics*, 3(2):11035.

Thomas Wolf, Lysandre Debut, Victor Sanh, Julien Chaumond, Clement Delangue, Anthony Moi, Pierric Cistac, Tim Rault, Rémi Louf, Morgan Funtowicz, Joe Davison, Sam Shleifer, Patrick von Platen, Clara Ma, Yacine Jernite, Julien Plu, Canwen Xu, Teven Le Scao, Sylvain Gugger, Mariama Drame, Quentin Lhoest, and Alexander M. Rush. 2020. Transformers: State-of-the-art natural language processing. In *Proceedings of the 2020 Conference on Empirical Methods in Natural Language Processing: System Demonstrations*, pages 38–45, Online. Association for Computational Linguistics.

Author Index

Association for Computational Linguistics
209 N. Eighth Street
Stroudsburg, Pennsylvania 18360

ISBN 978-1-7138-6152-2

CURRAN ASSOCIATES INC.
proceedings.com